LINCOLN CHRISTIAN COLLEGE

P9-CRH-908

Helping Your Teenager
Deal with Stress

Also by Bettie B. Youngs:

Stress in Children: How to Recognize, Avoid and
Overcome It

Helping Your Teenager Deal with Stress

Bettie B. Youngs, Ph.D.

Author of *Stress in Children*

JEREMY P. TARCHER, INC.
Los Angeles
Distributed by St. Martin's Press
New York

Library of Congress Cataloging in Publication Data

Youngs, Bettie B.
  Helping your teenager deal with stress.

  Bibliography.
  Includes index.
  1. Adolescence.   2. Adolescent psychology — United States.
3. Parenting — United States.   4. Stress (Psychology)   I. Title.
HQ796.Y5824   1986   305.2'35   86-14370
ISBN 0-87477-399-7
ISBN 0-87477-462-4 (pbk)

Copyright © 1986 by Bettie Youngs-Bilicki, Ph.D.

All rights reserved. No part of this work may be reproduced or transmitted in
any form by any means, electronic or mechanical, including photocopying and
recording, or by any information storage or retrieval system, except as may be
expressly permitted by the 1976 Copyright Act or in writing by the publisher.
Requests for such permissions should be addressed to:

Jeremy P. Tarcher, Inc.
5858 Wilshire Blvd., Ste. 200
Los Angeles, CA 90036

Manufactured in the United States of America
10 9 8 7 6 5 4 3 2

To Parents Everywhere

115881

1863 n

To My Teen-ager

It's hard sometimes, when people
are changing their lives, to
understand each other, or even
to talk. You are struggling right
now for independence and the
right to live your own way . . .
and I sometimes struggle for
the strength to let you do it.
I wish now and then for the days
when a kiss or a hug could make
your world bright again; but
your world is more difficult now,
and you want to make your own
way in it—which is as it should be.
I only want you to know . . .
that when you get hurt, I will
hurt for you; and that deep
down, I always have confidence
in your ability to find your place
in your world. If you ever need a
caring heart, or someone to listen
to your deepest dreams or concerns,
I will be there for you;
and remember, above all else . . .
that I love and care for you.
                                    —M. Joye

Copyright © Blue Mountain Arts, Inc. 1984. All rights reserved. Reprinted by permission of Blue Mountain Arts.

CONTENTS

"MANUAL LABOR": THE PLAN OF THIS BOOK

Wouldn't it be great if your child came with a parts-and-maintenance manual so that you could troubleshoot what was wrong and take steps to remedy it?

Consider this book your manual. It is full of information and suggestions to help you do your best in coping with your teenager and, more importantly, in teaching him to cope with his own stresses.

Helping Your Teenager Deal with Stress is designed so that you can turn to any chapter that fits your current needs to learn how to identify problems and to choose from among several suggested solutions. Stories and tests help you learn to recognize what's going on; skills and techniques help you to cope.

The following is a brief overview of what each chapter covers.

Chapter 1: *Recognizing Teenage Stress.* This chapter introduces you to the concept of teenage stress by pointing out common signs and symptoms. It includes a stress test for teenagers and also helps you determine whether you are contributing to or alleviating your child's stress. Consider it a basic course on stress itself.

Chapter 2: *Great Expectations: The Stress of Parenting.* Here, you learn what your teenager expects of you, as well as what you can realistically expect of yourself. Discover what being a parent entails, how it changes your life forever, and how you can accept and learn to love those changes. You will learn to recognize the stages your child is going through, and you'll learn, too, how those stages often conflict with your own, resulting in both personal and marital stress. Suggestions are presented on lowering stress levels and giving your child guidance and firm support at the same time that he is demanding (in a voice that cracks!) self-rule.

Chapter 3: *Do You Remember Adolescence?* This chapter takes you through the development of a child's self-concept—that is, how he begins to see himself as an individual rather than simply as your child. It discusses how both internal (physical) and external (societal) influences create stress that can inhibit or alter this self-conceptualization. A teen of today experiences a greater variety and intensity of demands than you and I did as teenagers, and these demands create stresses we never had to face. Skills are given for helping your adolescent—and you—to survive these years. This chapter also includes a brief discussion of music and other "noise."

Chapter 4: *War and Peace: Family Stress.* Here, I detail the ways in which today's families are vastly different from those of just a decade or two ago and how these different family styles create stress and anxiety for an adolescent. While exploring the stresses and strains the family is heir to, chapter 4 emphasizes the importance of family and realistically assesses the damage that weak familial relationships can have on a child. It explains how some family situations can harm rather than help a teenager, as well as how you can identify and eradicate such situations.

Chapter 5: *Sex and the Single Teenager.* If you were to give this book to your teenager, he or she would probably turn to this chapter first! Recognizing the importance of a teenager's budding sexuality, this chapter talks about how society's morals and values, so different today from when you and I were teens, place additional stresses and demands on a child. Rejection, first-time sex, responsible sex, teenage pregnancy, sexually transmitted diseases, homosexuality, and molestation are discussed. Even if you feel that your child is too young to be sexually active, take the time to go through this chapter. Remember: The parent is always the last one to know!

Chapter 6: *School: The Toll of a Thirteen-Year Career.* School is the teenager's "job." Like any other job, it places incredible demands on the worker and causes stresses that seem insurmountable, especially to a child who has no backlog of experiences to use as an aid in handling them. This chapter discusses the teenager's view of school, the problems that are unique to the hours spent in class and in school-related activities, and the ways in which you can recognize and lessen the resulting stresses.

Chapter 7: *Alienation: Feeling Lonely, Being Alone.* Nothing is more stressful than feeling unwanted. In this chapter I discuss how a teenager who seeks only to be accepted often has to come to terms with feeling rejected. Many children have parents who are physically or emotionally absent, and the effect can be devastating to a child during his hypersensitive teenage years. One result has been an upswing in the rate of teen suicide. Too few parents are aware of the very real danger of suicide. The greatest danger for any parent with regard to suicide is the belief that "my child would never do that." Every 83 minutes, a U.S. youth commits suicide. This chapter explains the many subtle ways in which teenagers can be made to feel unloved and unwanted, what causes a teenager to want to commit suicide, how to recognize suicidal tendencies in your child, and how to get help before matters go any further. In the skills portion, you will learn to examine your pattern of interaction with your teen to see whether you are providing him with the support he needs or whether you are leaving him with the impression that he is unwanted and rejected.

Chapter 8: *Substance Abuse: A "Capsule" History.* Drug and alcohol use may often be symptoms of stress, indications that a teenager can't cope with his life. This chapter alerts you to the allure of substance abuse for teens, helps you to identify whether your child has a substance-abuse problem and, if so, what you can do to diagnose the underlying causes and thus help stop the abuse. You will be given the skills you need to help your child find alternative ways of dealing with stress.

Chapter 9: *Lasting the Distance: Intervention and Prevention.* Chapter 9 emphasizes the role of diet, nutrition, exercise, and relaxation in alleviating stress. It discusses why a growing teen is especially vulnerable to stress and how proper techniques can prevent stress from becoming an overwhelming problem. Since this chapter focuses on helping you keep your adolescent well and on helping him take responsibility for his own health and wellness, you can consider it to be the "good-news" chapter.

If you are ready to learn more about your teenager's life and times, more about what he is feeling and how he is reacting to it, more about how you can show your love and support, you're ready for this book. Now all you need is enough time away from your teenager to read it.

Onward!

ACKNOWLEDGMENTS

Over the past eighteen years I have conducted numerous courses and workshops throughout the world for parents and children, professional educators, psychologists, and pediatricians; I have listened to and learned from many parents, watched and learned from their children, taught both adolescents and adults for many years, and have the privilege of being a parent myself. As I shared with others, they shared with me. They helped reaffirm in me that it all begins in the home, with the quality of the parent/child relationship. To all parents and their teenagers, then, this book is a giving back. I thank you.

The special ability of teenagers to be astute social critics never ceases to amaze me. For that I thank the many teenagers who actively participated in formulating the thesis for this book; in particular, I thank my own daughter, Jennifer, who continues to expand my life every day.

I wish to acknowledge my agent, Bill Gladstone, who was instrumental in my writing this book, for his belief and support in this work; my publisher, Jeremy P. Tarcher, who specializes in converting dreams to reality; and the members of his able staff, for their kindness and professional efficiency. A special thanks to the legendary Janice Gallagher for her superb editorial wisdom and her sense of humor throughout this project. Her lighthearted memos and prose shall forever remain plastered to the walls of my office!

I have been awed and warmed by the outpouring of encouragement and support from the many wonderful friends and colleagues who so generously gave of their time and expertise. For their counsel, the strength of their commitment to excellence in educating young people, and the warmth of their endearing friendship, Chris Christiansen, Diane Peyton, and Ruth Glick were invaluable. Special recognition goes to researchers Janet Patti, Anu Sjaardema, and Donna Grenoble and to my secretary, Lucy Melano, for their tireless effort and devotion to the project.

I lovingly thank the many friends who called often to see when I "could come out to play" for not losing faith that at some point I *could!*

To my family: my parents, for their years parenting, and Fran and Peter Bilicki, for their abundant packages of unconditional parental love and care and concern for my well-being.

Again to my teenage daughter, Jennifer, who worried about my sleep, fiercely protected our time together, and stepped up her own crusade of helping by being extraordinarily responsible for her share of home and family responsibilities as well as for her schoolwork.

And to my husband, Pete Bilicki, who shares the adventure of life and love and purpose, for his constant nurturing and gifts of endless patience, early-morning cappuccinos, and for his many walks on the beach in the role of listener. In addition to his own career demands, he lent more than a generous hand to help with my share of home and family responsibilities, and he remained positive and encouraging. In spite of the considerable energy and attention I devoted to writing this book, he managed to find all the right ways to playfully distract me and keep me whole.

CHAPTER ONE

Recognizing Teenage Stress

Like you, I am a parent. I wrote this book because I believe with my whole heart that we parents want to nurture, not just "raise," our teenage children. We want to show our adolescents our love and to be loved and respected by them in turn.

I also believe that because the physical, emotional, and social needs of adolescent children are so different from those of younger children, these needs are often misunderstood. Unprepared for the marked changes that suddenly occur in the stages of adolescent growth and development, and sometimes unsure of how to decipher the emotional upheavals of teens in a time of dynamic social change, we parents sometimes lose confidence in ourselves and in our abilities to parent teenagers. It's difficult to be sure we are the steadfast anchors our adolescents need as they come to grips with their new and changing selves.

Parenting children of any age isn't easy. I remember hearing my eight-month-old daughter cry years ago when I was a new parent. I had been told by a pediatrician that if an infant cries for no apparent reason, the parent should not always run to her child's side. Doing so would teach the infant that "needless" crying could elicit attention. So there I was, sitting on the floor outside my daughter's room, crying in frustration because I wanted so much to hold and caress her, yet I feared that I might thwart her emotional growth if I did so. Luckily, after a time, my instinct overshadowed my fears, and I responded to my needs and those of my infant's by going to her and holding her. I realized eventually that holding and hugging my daughter, rather than establishing an overdependence on me as I had feared, gave her a feeling of security that allowed her to grow and become independent.

In the same vein, parents of teenage children can find themselves "outside the room," listening to their children crying out —and, much like an infant, in a language parents don't always understand—for affection, human warmth, and attention. In short, adolescence is a period when parents and their teenagers can become estranged, at a time when they both want and need each other very much.

Apparently, we parents have been sitting outside for too long. The number of adolescents who do not understand their intense feelings or how to cope with them continues to increase. It is very saddening to read statistics indicating that our adolescent children are experiencing a great deal of stress, that they have many fears and anxieties, that they worry more than we might suspect, and that they wish they were happier. It is very depressing to find out that in their desire to escape from pain, teenagers take routes such as alcohol and drug abuse, truancy, delinquency, sexual promiscuity, aggression and violence, and running away from home—routes that lead them into problems more overwhelming than those they were trying to escape. Although the taking of such escape routes by our children can make us feel that forces outside ourselves exert a stronger influence on our children than we do, we must recognize such actions as cues to cope: they are cries for help.

This book, then, is written for you, the parent of that irritating, demanding, confusing . . . precious, cherished, and well-loved person in your life: your teenage child.

The first premise of this book is that stress has always been a part of our lives but that today's stressors are quite different from those that we experienced even just a decade ago. Changing mores, shifting values, and contemporary markers—divorce, stepfamilies, teen pregnancy and abortion, suicide—are all difficult experiences for both parents and children and require adaptive coping skills.

Until recently, the society we were preparing our youngsters to enter as adults was relatively stable and predictable. As a consequence, we could concentrate on a precisely defined and constant course for our lives. Today, things are different; we are living in the middle of a profound revolution. Because of this, we have no blueprint for helping adolescents in the 1980s and beyond. There is no longer one "right" way to handle teenagers.

Don't despair. Although the contextual aspect of society differs over time with each passing generation, life's milestones remain quite similar. Regardless of age, sex, or generation, the basic goals appear to be the same: successful adaptation and the maintenance of personal well-being. Much of this book is directed toward meeting this challenge, helping you to help your teenager acquire the necessary insights and skills to meet life's milestones.

In order to help our adolescents, we need to be aware of our own feelings about the child-as-adolescent and about our perceptions of our abilities to help our teenagers deal with the stressors that are a part of their lives. We parents experience the same emotions that our children do: negative ones such as anxiety, stress, loneliness, fear, alienation, and anger, and positive ones such as hope, love, joy, compassion, and belonging. To be true to our emotions, to understand and manage them well, will help us better understand and manage emotions in our children.

Loving our adolescent child is not enough in and of itself. To ensure success in personal development, a child will need a positive spirit, a firm commitment to growing and going forward, and the skills necessary to do so. Parents need to shoulder the responsibility for guiding and supporting this learning encounter.

To prepare our children to manage their lives both now and in the future, we need to help them develop self-awareness, self-understanding, and self-acceptance. In addition, we have to be able to teach them the skills of stress management, skills that we ourselves may still be seeking to master. We must help our adolescents gain the inner wisdom, strength of character, and determination to accomplish worthwhile goals. We must also teach them to recognize and maintain their distinctness from others without fear, shame, anxiety, or regret. They must come to consistently see themselves as successful copers, adept at finding and using their own resources. This is no easy task in contemporary society.

A final premise of this book is that while the parenthood role is associated with stress, it is certainly not without reward. Parenting can be one of the most memorable and meaningful experiences in a person's life. We parents and our adolescents need not be estranged: the wear and tear experienced, the physical and psychological damage wrought, and the sheer loss in personal power is too high a price to pay.

Harmonious living with a sense of personal fulfillment is possible between parent and adolescent. High-intensity parenting makes possible the highest level of joy and well-being in the parent-child relationship.

You are the expert in helping your child. Through listening to him or her, you know your child better than anyone else. Although counselors and school personnel can be of great help to our children, they are not in as strong a position as you are to turn your child's world around.

As parents, we're all in this together. I hope, through this book, to provide you with information you can use to help your teenager deal with stress. In doing so, I hope you can reach these goals: to better understand what stress is and how it translates into human suffering; to learn and put into practice ways of helping your adolescent develop the inner resources needed for coping successfully with life; to know that you can help your teenager strengthen these resources by helping him develop the skills he needs for managing and reducing stress; and to realize that each of these goals works with the others to help our children come closer to the true meaning of personhood.

By increasing our practical understanding of the issues involved in teenage stress and beginning the helping process, we parents will aid both our teenagers and ourselves.

STRESS SIGNS

Virtually no one feels free from stress these days, and each person defines stress somewhat differently. The businesswoman may think of it as frustration or emotional tension, the air-traffic controller as a problem in concentration, the biochemist as a purely chemical event, the athlete as muscular tension, the parent as an overwhelming and demanding schedule, the small child as a stomachache.

How would your teenager define stress? You may feel that a teenager has little to be worried or anxious about. After all, she doesn't need to provide shelter, food, clothing, or security for herself; you and your spouse do all that. Probably all she has to do is go to school. But have you looked at what going to school entails today? The following is a schedule that a typical "carefree" teen might follow during the week.

6:00–6:15	Prepare for school
6:15–6:30	Walk to school
6:30–7:30	Marching-band practice, school football field
7:30–7:45	Return to school building
7:45–8:00	Homeroom
8:00–8:55	Science
9:00–9:55	Foreign language
10:00–10:55	Algebra
11:00–11:55	Creative writing
12:00–12:20	Lunch
12:20–12:55	Student council
1:00–1:55	English
2:00–2:55	Physical education
3:00–3:15	Study skills
3:15–4:00	Cheerleading practice
4:00–4:15	Return home
5:00–5:45	Clarinet practice
6:00	Dinner with family—help prepare, clear table
7:00–9:00	Football game, cheerlead
9:00–9:30	Return home

9:30–11:30   Tonight's homework: forty-five algebra
equations; six-page paper analyzing Hemingway's use of
stream of consciousness; study for a 100-word French
test; study for a quiz on the parts of speech; science fair
proposal, minimum of six to eight pages.

You also undoubtedly had your share of anxiety and stress
when you were a teenager. Mother Nature had her fun with you,
as she had with countless others before you. Yet, apart from the
trauma of pimples, sweaty palms, and overactive hormones, you
probably enjoyed your teen years and didn't experience a great
deal of outside stress. Things have changed since then. Let's take
a few minutes to examine just how different things are for today's
teens.

A TIME OF TRANSITION

When you were young, your parents and society in general
recognized that you were undergoing change, that you were in a
period of transition from childhood to adulthood. You heard the
expression "growing pains" applied to explain your moodiness,
and you thus were relieved of some of the guilt you might have
felt for being so grouchy and impossible to live with. "After all,"
you might have reasoned, "I'm a teenager. I'm supposed to make
my parents' life miserable." Today's teens have no such luxury.
The period of transition has been significantly altered by the pace
of contemporary society, and it seems as though our children
emerge from childhood as small versions of adults. Why? Because we give them less time to experiment with their new
minds and bodies, less time to ponder on the changes they are
experiencing.

AN UNDEFINED ROLE

A few years ago, teenagers had a role in society. They had a
clearly defined position in the social structure as "the next generation," as future leaders. You and I knew that we had time to grow

and develop, and we knew what we were going to grow and develop into. We felt needed, appreciated, wanted. Do today's children feel the same? Probably not. Too often a teenager today is made to feel that he or she is a burden on society, a freeloader who should be going out and making a living NOW. A teenager who is not a straight-A student, who is not going to go to college, may actually feel guilty for staying in school and getting a high-school diploma. While we were encouraged to graduate from school, teenagers today feel ever-increasing pressure to go out and get a job as soon as possible.

A LACK OF PARENTAL SUPPORT

Our parents had time for us. Many of us had mothers who made full-time careers of child rearing, who were revered by society for staying home and taking care of us. Motherhood was a full-time job; today it is a part-time position. Many women cannot or choose not to stay at home and rear their children full-time. They work and have to juggle careers and families. There aren't enough hours in the day; something has to give. Too often, what gives is the time and support a parent can give her child. During the most vulnerable time of life, a teenager is left alone to cope with physical, mental, and emotional changes.

FOR EVERY ACTION, THERE IS AN EQUAL AND OPPOSITE REACTION

Obviously, all this societal rush and parental laissez-faire takes its toll on a teenager. Being forced to become an adult before working through the normal teen crises has effects on an adolescent. One such effect is stress, something to which adolescents are particularly vulnerable. They spend great portions of energy quickly and become prime targets for fatigue, moodiness, psychosomatic illness, migraine, and other diseases of maladaptation, including burnout. What a laundry list of illnesses, woes, and problems! If stress can cause all of these disorders, it's worth your attention.

BODY LANGUAGE: THE BIOLOGY OF STRESS

As discussed earlier, the concept of *stress* means something different to each of us. A first step toward understanding exactly what stress is, how it translates into human suffering, how it can be reduced, and the methods through which we can effectively and productively manage it is to look at it as a biological occurrence. The notion that stress is just in the mind is simply not true.

To some extent, however, stress is individualistic: while two individuals may experience the same stressor, their responses may vary. For example, suppose two teenage girls lose their backpacks. Cara gets to school, sees her backpack is missing, and simply calls her mother. She doesn't become upset, just annoyed that she will have to wait for her mother to bring it to her and worried that she might get a lecture from her mother on carelessness. When Kristin sees that her backpack is missing, she has a totally different reaction. She rushes around school, hoping against hope that she has left it in her locker, under her desk, with a friend. She asks everyone for help in finding it. She is afraid to call her mother and decides just to do without the pack during the day. Knowing she will not be able to turn in her homework, she gets knots in her stomach and becomes unable to concentrate. She is close to tears; her whole day is shot.

Each girl had the same cause for stress, but it is Kristin's reaction to a stressful event or chronically stressful condition that produces both a physiological and emotional response. Every system of the body is affected at some point in the stress response by nervous stimulation of an organ or of the endocrine glands.

Most people think of stress in terms of the daily demands of life. Technically, these demands are called "stressors," with "stress" being the actual wear and tear on the body. Hans Selye, M.D., an international authority on the subject of stress, has repeatedly demonstrated that irrespective of whether the stressor is a biochemical insult (for example, a dose of drugs or alcohol), a physical injury, or emotional arousal (fear, anger, love), the mind/body responds in the same manner. The response, called the General

Adaptation Syndrome, has three stages: (1) alarm reaction, (2) resistance, and (3) exhaustion.

ALARM REACTION

From your own experience, you may recognize some of the alarm-reaction responses set up by the autonomic nervous system.

1. Have you ever had "butterflies (or eagles!) in your stomach? Because it is more important to be alert and strong than to digest food in the face of danger, digestion slows so that blood can be directed to the muscles and the brain.
2. Can you remember trying to catch your breath after being frightened? Breathing becomes more rapid so that more oxygen can be supplied to the needed muscles.
3. Do you remember how your heart pounded when that speeding car wheeled around the corner and just missed you? The heart speeds up, and blood pressure soars, forcing blood to parts of the body that need it.
4. Have you noticed that you use extra deodorant when you know you are going to be under stress? Perspiration increases to cool the body, thus allowing the body to burn more energy.
5. Have you ever complained of a stiff neck or of chest pain after a stressful day? Muscles tense in preparation for important action.
6. Have you noticed how quickly some wounds stop bleeding? Chemicals are released to make the blood clot more rapidly. When you are injured, this clotting can reduce blood loss.
7. Have you ever gotten a "second wind" or been surprised by your strength and endurance during an emergency? Sugars and fats pour into the bloodstream to provide fuel for quick energy.

RESISTANCE STAGE

Almost immediately, and in direct relationship to the diminishing of an exterior threat, the organism attempts to return biochemically to its normal balance (homeostasis). This resistance stage essentially reverses the biochemical processes of the alarm stage, and the body attempts to adapt itself to a state of calm and tranquility by a relowering of blood pressure, heart rate, respiration, and core body temperature.

EXHAUSTION STAGE

When a period of stress is prolonged beyond six to eight weeks, the adaptive mechanisms are eventually depleted and the body enters the exhaustion stage. Sometimes this biochemical exhaustion is referred to as *burnout.* The supply of life energy and the ability to withstand stress are gone, and the alarm stage reactions disappear; however, tension produces physical wear and tear on the body, and the longer the tension continues, the greater the bodily damage may be.

Stress becomes pathological when the person's body reacts as though it is threatened long after the actual threat has passed. Elevated blood pressure under stress is perfectly normal, but when it persists it becomes hypertension; heart-rate acceleration, if prolonged, is diagnosed as tachycardia; and a normal blood shift away from the stomach, if it continues beyond the period of stress, becomes a loss of appetite. When normal stress reactions are prolonged and unabated, then a psychosomatic illness is also likely to develop.

SCIENCE OF MIND: THE PSYCHOLOGY OF STRESS

When an individual is forced to adapt or readjust to an event, reaction occurs in both the mind and the body. Why some individuals become ill and others do not under the same stressful conditions is determined to a great extent by the individual's interpretation of the stressor. While for some individuals stress is experienced as no more than anxiety or physical nervousness, for others it can lead to emotional despair, psychosomatic illness, and even mental illness.

In discussing the psychological response to stress, we must first look at its effects in psychosomatic terms. The word *psychosomatic* refers to bodily and mental symptoms stemming from mental conflict. The basis of the psychosomatic concept is that the mind plays an important role in many diseases. Psychosomatic illnesses fall into two basic categories: psychogenic and somatogenic.

Psychogenic disorders are physical diseases caused by emotional stress. In vaudeville, a favorite sight gag was a tombstone reading, "It's all in my mind!" While positive thinking may work in some cases, it isn't enough in many others. When emotional stress is present, actual structural and functional organ damage may occur—yet none of the usual underlying physical causes of organic disease are present. Backaches, headaches, and stomachaches are common conditions that may fall into this category and can lead to such conditions as ulcers, high blood pressure, and migraine. Emotional turmoil is translated into physical symptoms.

Somatogenic disorders are organic diseases and infections caused by emotional disturbances. A healthy body fights off many invading organisms through its natural defense mechanisms, but distress impedes the body's natural defensive role. The result is a breakdown of physical health and an increase in susceptibility. Intense or prolonged stress may accelerate the rate at which disease spreads throughout the body by hampering the body's natural immune system. Indeed, the onset or dissipation of severe stress in an individual's life may be the deciding factor in bringing on or warding off disease.

How many times when under stress have you awakened with an aggravation of an old injury, such as a trick knee, or gone to bed sniffling, certain you would have a cold by the morning? At the time, you probably thought, "Oh, great, just what I need—to be sick as well as stressed." You probably never made the connection that you were becoming ill *because* you were stressed.

EARLY WARNING SIGNS

At this point you should be wondering how you can tell just how stressed your child is. As his parent, you know your child better than anyone else. Even you, however, can't always read his moods, can't always tell whether the latest slammed door or bellowed, "Mo-THER!" is a natural reaction to a bad day or a symptom of more serious stress. The next section contains a stress test for teens. If your teenager is not very compliant about test-taking, consider the following warning signs and learn to recognize these symptoms early. While many children do show some of these symptoms every now and then, the time to worry is when your teenager shows prolonged or very strong symptoms.

Physical	*Emotional*	*Behavioral*
sleep difficulties (i.e., insomnia)	nightmares	impulsive behavior
	panic	fighting
loss of appetite (or excessive appetite)	dramatic mood changes	stealing
	feelings of being unworthy	deliberately doing subpar work
chronic fatigue	suspiciousness	skipping school
vague stomach distress, indigestion	feelings of failure	loss of interest in appearance
	apathy	alcohol or drug use
diarrhea	feelings of unreality	poor attitude toward others
weakness, dizziness	excessive worrying	attention-getting antics
increased perspiration	negative feelings	accident proneness
low-grade infections	nervous or inappropriate laughter	yelling
rashes		arson
frequent colds or flus		
headaches		
lower-back pain		

STRESS TEST FOR TEENS

The adolescent years have traditionally been considered a turbulent period because of rapid emotional and bodily changes, but the capacities of teenagers to resist and cope with unwanted stress can vary greatly. Some become overwhelmed easily by outside pressures, while others endure such pressures with no ill effects or are even stimulated by the challenge. Still others develop healthy frustration tolerance, learning to remain flexible and to take daily irritants in stride. Transient stresses usually pose no threat to physical or mental health. The problem arises when troubling situations linger or occur simultaneously. This quiz will enable you and your teenager to determine both the level of stress in his life right now and how well he handles it.

Your youngster should keep his answers as honest and accurate as possible. If he is afraid to take the test or belligerently refuses to do so, encourage him in terms that he can understand and appreciate. Words like "I SAID, take the damn test!" aren't going to do much good. Instead, your teenager needs you to point out that taking this test will put him more in touch with his own feelings and will help him understand why he sometimes seems "out of it." Perhaps you could take the test with him, or have him take it with a sibling or a friend. One suggestion: Never use the word *test*, especially if you give this on a weekend; *inventory* or *profile* is a good substitute.

When your teen has finished the test, score it and go through an explanation of the score with him. Then let him go back to his records and tapes and review the test once more yourself. Would you have predicted your child's answers accurately? Do you know him as well as you thought? Don't be surprised if your answers to both of these questions are no. This book is designed to help you understand more about your child, the stress that he is going through, and how you can help lessen it.

TEEN SCENE: STRESS TEST

OFTEN SOMETIMES SELDOM NEVER

(a)(b)(c)(d)

1. During the past three months, have you been under considerable strain, stress, or pressure? _ _ _ _
2. Have you experienced any of the following symptoms: palpitations or a racing heart, dizziness, blushing, painfully cold hands or feet, shallow or fast breathing, nail biting, restless body or legs, butterflies in stomach, insomnia, chronic fatigue? _ _ _ _
3. In general, do you have headaches or digestive upsets? _ _ _ _
4. Do you have any crying spells or feel like crying? _ _ _ _
5. Do you have any recurring nightmares? _ _ _ _
6. Do you have pain in your neck, back, or arms? _ _ _ _
7. Do you feel depressed or unhappy? _ _ _ _
8. Do you worry excessively? _ _ _ _
9. Do you ever feel anxious even though you don't know why? _ _ _ _
10. Are you ever edgy or impatient with your parents or other family members? _ _ _ _
11. Are you ever overwhelmed by hopelessness? _ _ _ _
12. Do you dwell on things you should have done but didn't? _ _ _ _
13. Do you dwell on things you did but shouldn't have? _ _ _ _
14. Do you have any problems focusing on your schoolwork? _ _ _ _
15. When you're criticized, do you brood about it? _ _ _ _
16. Do you worry about what others think? _ _ _ _
17. Are you bored? _ _ _ _

18. Do you feel envy or resentment that someone has something you don't? ＿＿＿＿
19. Do you quarrel with your boyfriend/girlfriend? ＿＿＿＿
20. Are there serious conflicts between your parents? ＿＿＿＿

	YES	NO
21. Lately, do you find yourself more irritable and argumentative than usual?	—	—
22. Are you as popular with friends as you'd wish?	—	—
23. Are you doing as well in school as you'd like?	—	—
24. Do you feel you can live up to your parents' expectations?	—	—
25. Do you feel that your parents understand your problems and are supportive?	—	—
26. On the whole, are you satisfied with the way you look?	—	—
27. Do you have trouble with any of your teachers?	—	—
28. Do you sometimes worry that your friends might be turning against you?	—	—
29. Do you have enough spending money to cover your needs?	—	—
30. Have you noticed lately that you eat, drink, or smoke more than you really should?	—	—
31. Do you make strong demands on yourself?	—	—
32. Do you feel the limits imposed by your parents regarding what you may or may not do are justified?	—	—
33. Do your parents always criticize you?	—	—
34. Do you have any serious worries concerning your love relationships with the opposite sex?	—	—
35. Are any of your brothers or sisters overly competitive with you?	—	—

	YES	NO
36. Do you feel left out in social gatherings?	—	—
37. Do you habitually fall behind in your schoolwork?	—	—
38. Do you feel tense and defensive when you're around someone your age of the opposite sex?	—	—
39. Have you, or has anyone in your family, suffered a severe illness or injury in the last year?	—	—
40. Do you experience any conflict between your own standards and peer pressure to engage in certain activities?	—	—
41. Have you recently moved to a new home, school, or community?	—	—
42. Have you been rejected by a boyfriend/ girlfriend within the last three months?	—	—
43. Is it very difficult for you to say "no" to requests?	—	—
44. Have your grades taken a sudden drop lately?	—	—
45. Do you often become ill after an emotional upset?	—	—

Scoring: Add up your points based on this answer key.

	(a)	(b)	(c)	(d)		(a)	(b)	(c)	(d)
1.	7	4	1	0	11.	7	3	1	0
2.	7	4	1	0	12.	4	2	0	0
3.	6	3	1	0	13.	4	2	0	0
4.	5	2	1	0	14.	4	2	0	0
5.	6	3	1	0	15.	4	2	0	0
6.	4	2	0	0	16.	4	2	0	0
7.	7	3	1	0	17.	4	2	0	0
8.	6	3	1	0	18.	4	2	0	0
9.	6	3	1	0	19.	5	3	1	0
10.	5	2	0	0	20.	5	3	1	0

	Yes	No		Yes	No
21.	4	0	34.	5	0
22	0	3	35.	3	0
23.	0	4	36.	4	0
24.	0	5	37.	3	0
25.	0	5	38.	3	0
26.	0	4	39.	6	0
27.	3	0	40.	5	0
28.	4	0	41.	3	0
29.	0	3	42.	4	0
30.	5	0	43.	3	0
31.	4	0	44.	4	0
32.	0	3	45.	5	0
33.	4	0			

WHAT YOUR SCORE MEANS

116–203. A score in this range indicates that your troubles outnumber your satisfactions and that you are currently subjected to a high level of stress. No doubt, you are already aware of your problems and are rightfully concerned.

You should do everything possible to avoid as many tense situations as you can until you feel more in control of your life. Review the quiz to pinpoint the major sources of your stress. Try to develop more effective ways of dealing with difficult human relationships and circumstances. Perhaps you are overreacting to problems or are not as willing to cope as you could be. Think about getting some kind of professional help. Sometimes even a few hours of counseling can be beneficial.

62–115. A score spanning this range signifies that the level of stress in your life is moderate, or that you are handling your frustrations quite well. However, because you have occasional difficulty managing the effects of stress, consider some new methods of overcoming disappointments. Remember, we all have to face and live with frustrations and anxieties.

0–61. A score in this range points to a relatively low stress level. In spite of minor worries and concerns, you are not in any serious trouble. You have good adaptive powers and are able to deal successfully with situations that make you temporarily uptight.

ARE YOU A HELP OR A HINDRANCE?

How parents react to their child's problem often initially determines whether the symptoms continue, as in the case of sixteen-
year-old Mike. Mike had not been to school in two years. His
father insisted on one medical test after another, but he always
stormed out of the doctors' offices when they recommended he
take Mike to a psychologist. To this day, Mike is home, doing as
he wants.

You wouldn't overreact that way, you say? You can't picture
yourself giving in to your child's whims and caprices? What about
going overboard in the other direction? Have you ever ignored a
valid complaint of your child's on the grounds that it was insignificant?

Suppose that you and your child are at the dentist, and your
child feels sick and wants to go home. If your child doesn't seem
particularly ill, you might say, "You're nervous about seeing the
dentist, so it's not unusual for your stomach to get upset. But it's
important for you to see the dentist, so we're not going home." At
this stage, you feel you have been a good parent, firm in your
resolve to help your child help himself even if both of you perish
in the process. But what if your child's upset condition was more
severe than you recognized? Could you be hurting him by unwit-
tingly forcing him to do something that is truly terrifying to him?
This is a lesson I learned the hard way myself.

A few years ago I took my daughter, then eleven, to the doctor.
A blood test from a lab was recommended. My daughter cried,
pleaded with me, and kicked the walls on the way to the lab. At
the lab door, she screamed and refused to enter. She then fainted.
After I had cared for her immediate needs and removed her from
the environment, I sat with her on the lawn outside the medical
complex. Nearly thirty minutes later I learned the source of her
fear. It seems that she had seen cartoons in which shots were
given out of spite, with very long needles. My daughter proceeded
to describe a foot-long needle, which she imagined would start at
the base of her wrist and extend to her elbow. Under no circumstance was she about to be a victim to that! After debunking the

myth, explaining the correct procedure, and agreeing that she first be allowed to watch blood being drawn, I got her consent. She was then able to go through with the relatively painless (though scary) procedure in a relaxed manner. Although both she and I remember the details of the incident to this day, what is most poignant is that through that incident we came to understand just how important trust is between parent and child. I had to trust that her fear was real and that it was painful, and she had to trust that my control over ensuing matters would take into account her sensitivity to fear and pain. She had to believe that the decisions I made valued her sensitivities as much as my own insistence that the lab procedure occur ("No, we can't come back tomorrow; this must be taken care of as soon as possible") or the convenience of the doctor (who had said he would be leaving town the next day for three weeks).

Children are no more immune to stress-related illness than adults are. In fact, they may be even more vulnerable, because they have little control over their own lives and may either be unable to articulate their problems or afraid to say what's troubling them. Three months after fourteen-year-old Miya began having severe headaches for no apparent reason, her parents remembered that her best friend of five years had moved 1300 miles away. Her parents had restricted long-distance phone calls, and in spite of the barrage of letters the girls sent back and forth, the miles between them seemed like an insurmountable obstacle. Certainly no one had asked for Miya's opinion about the move, nor had they noticed how she pined for her best friend. In fact, no one had prepared her for the trauma she was about to experience.

Miya's illness was a cue—a signal—that she wasn't adjusting well (she described the move as a "loss"). She sorely needed more effective ways to alleviate her immediate stress, with counseling to help her come to terms with the reality of what had happened and guidance in generating effective ways of preserving the cherished friendship. Fortunately, Miya's parents recognized that their daughter's illness was caused by stress. They were able to sit down with her, listen to her fears about losing her friend, and give her a shoulder to cry on. They explained to her that separation doesn't necessarily mean the end of friendship, suggested ways in which she could preserve the friendship, and told her that she would have new friends soon. Through her parents' love and guidance, Miya learned to accept the changed situation. Her friendship did not end, but her headaches did.

If parents can't tune in to an adolescent's way of thinking and encourage her to express herself, they may miss the cues that indicate that their child's illness is related to stress. Also, they forfeit the chance to help their child learn healthy ways to handle such feelings as loss, powerlessness, fear, anger, and hurt.

Parents of children with psychosomatic symptoms are likely to offer their children reassurance without helping them to actually deal with the underlying anxieties. If a child is having trouble at school, a parent may not say, "I can sure understand why you're sad about what happened at school today. Would you like to tell me about it?" Instead, the parent might say, "Oh, don't worry about that," or "Everything will be okay." The result is that children will be filled with conflict and confusion. Over the years I have found asking the very simple question "If you could make three wishes, what would you wish for?" to be very revealing of what is behind children's psychosomatic illnesses. The answers are sometimes painfully touching, and they are always illuminating.

You cannot protect your child completely from stress, nor should you. I like the idea of what is known as "psychological immunization," which means that children become more psychologically capable of dealing with the larger stressors in life by first learning how to deal effectively with the smaller, manageable ones (such as thwarted desires, the death of a pet, the move of a friend, or a failed test). The most successful parents are those who are protective but are willing to explain things to their children. They set rules, but they talk, too. Being able to talk honestly and respectfully with your child is perhaps the best protection against psychosomatic ills.

How can you tell whether your child seriously has a problem or is just going through a phase? To do so, you need to pick up on the child's long-term stress responses.

PROLONGED STRESS = BURNOUT = DROPOUT

Think for a moment about yourself, your friends, and working associates. How many of you could be described as being burned out? As adults, we recognize that burnout exists, and we accept it as a fact of our fast-lane lifestyles. We more often pity than scorn someone who has gone through burnout.

Yet there's a double standard here. If a child burns out, we consider that child a failure. We say that he or she can't cut it or is giving up. A teenager intuitively senses this double standard and thus rarely admits to burnout.

But teens *do* burn out. Prolonged stress can lead to burnout and eventually to a child's dropping out. When a child drops out of school, do we think, "This teenager became overwhelmed by the stress and couldn't handle it?" No. We think, "The lazy kid isn't giving it his best." This is usually untrue and unfair. Some children give it their absolute best, and still can't do the job. The reactions that children demonstrate to stress should be viewed as their best attempt at a solution to what is being experienced.

Jena is a sad example of a teenager suffering from burnout. After two years in high school, Jena became a runaway. "Mom wanted me to have all the advantages, good grades, clarinet practice, foreign languages, ballet, tennis lessons, and pets to care for. What's more, I was to be good, really good, at all of it. At first it was fun—I just ran by the schedule. But one day I forgot my 'to-do' list at home, and I couldn't even function! After two semesters the days blurred into weeks, the weeks into months. I don't even remember the past four months. I just got so tired. Soon it became more work than fun. I felt I just couldn't go on. I no longer wanted to be a National Merit Scholar finalist, first-chair clarinet, and an editor of the school paper. I tried all the remedies my friends suggested—from diet pills and No-Doz to just coffee—to help tackle the agenda. I even found myself stealing diet pills from the grocery store when my allowance wouldn't cover them. After a while, even those didn't work. I would be really wound up for the first few hours and then experience this incredible tiredness by noon. I resigned from student government, began skipping a class here and there, and started to copy homework assignments from friends. I felt so ashamed and so down on myself. I felt like I had really let everyone down, especially my parents."

Jena is back home now. With the help of her parents, family counseling, and the family physician, she is regaining her health and is slowly rebuilding her confidence to cope with daily life. Jena's case may seem overly exaggerated, almost melodramatic to you, but it is not uncommon. Your child may have had some of the same feelings, on a lesser scale, that Jena had. Do you try to live through your child, seeking for him or her the popularity you never had? Do you insist that your child take piano lessons because your friends' kids all play? How do you suppose your child feels about these things? Quite possibly, he feels trapped. Because he loves you, he wants to please you; because he needs to be his own person, he wants to have more control over his own life.

Jena ran away rather than face her problems. Is your child running away emotionally, withdrawing further and further from you? Does your child have so much stress that he is using all his energy just to stay in one place?

We must find helpful ways of breaking through this cycle of conflict, ways of diverting our children's energy away from the anxious feelings that accompany stressful events and that lead to more problems; ways that help children to develop self-control, to experience interpersonal success, to master their environments, and to establish lifelong foundations for personal worth and dignity.

CHAPTER TWO

Great Expectations:
The Stress of Parenting

One day I was watching a tennis match on television. As the camera scanned the court, I admired the lithe and trim bodies of the athletes. Suddenly the camera focused on the sidelines, showing a man who seemed to be totally out of place. Instead of being an Adonis with muscles everywhere, he was just an average-looking guy with a beer belly and knock knees. I commented on this to my teenager who was watching with me, and was told, "Oh, he's the coach. A brilliant guy, a real winner. He doesn't have to play."

My teenager recognized a truth that you and I as parents should know: You don't have to be able to play the game yourself in order to help others. We're not teenagers anymore; we don't act like teenagers, can't do the things they do, and might not want to if we could. But why should we let these limitations blind us to what we can do?

Our children know, only too well, that we are not perfect. They know that we have stresses and anxieties of our own, that we too have problems. But because our teenagers don't have the backlog of experiences we do, they don't always know the nature of those problems. Such inexperience can make a child do one of two things: He may transform our problems into something terrible, or he may do just the opposite, feeling that since grown-ups don't have to deal with homework, dates, peer pressure, or allowances, they have nothing to worried about.

What every teenager should know about his parents is that we are real people too. Don't be afraid to tell your child of your fears, worries, and anxieties. Obviously, you will have to use good sense; you don't want to scare a child with a story of your financial woes when she has trouble comprehending a $10 debt, let alone one of $10,000. But teenagers are astute and clever. They can handle the truth if you give it to them in terms they understand. "Our margin calls are worrying me" means nothing to a sixteen-year-old, but "I don't know whether or not I will have enough money this month to get my car fixed" is real. Letting your child know what you're worried about does double duty. It calms his fears (you're not upset because of something he's done—it's just the money issue that's making you cranky) and lets him know that he's not alone. A child who is aware of his parent's worries can feel, "Hey, I'm not the only one who has worries. I guess it's normal to have problems; after all, even Mom and Dad have them."

I will be talking about how to help your adolescent better communicate openly with you later on in this chapter. Just as important is *your* communicating openly about your feelings and ideas in such a way that the child learns to listen to and accept you, gaining perspective on your views even though they may be different from his own. Revising, regrouping, adjusting, and acknowledging our mistakes verbally to our children sets us up as human, not divine. Teenagers who have experienced their parents as open are more likely to feel that their parents are fair. They are therefore more likely to trust their parents and seek their advice. Adolescents who know their parents well are also more apt to care about how their parents feel, about their viewpoint on decisions the teenager makes.

Sharing yourself is a relationship-building strategy, not a panacea for avoiding or solving conflicts in a parent-child relationship. One way to do this is by using "sharing-yourself" statements.

Sentences that start with *I* and don't include *you* tell about the feelings, ideas, values and expectations of the parent. When your sentences start with *I* you are, in a way, saying, "I want you to know me, to be close to me. You are somebody special."

Listen to yourself talk the next time you are with your teenager. How many times do you hear *I?* How many times do you hear *you,* in other than an admonishing tone ("Did you finish your chores, Leroy?'')? Monitor your own conversation for a while so that you can hear what your teenager is hearing. If you find you are not sharing yourself as much as you would like, practice doing so. The following examples may help.

NOT SHARING YOURSELF:

> "Michael, you never seem to be able to solve your problems. Go work it out and stop complaining. Listening to your whining gets old. Can't you see I'm trying to concentrate?"

> "John, you're making too much noise. Stop it."

> "Glenda, you're so selfish. You know I didn't bake that cake just for you."

> "Michelle, you made it on time!"

SHARING YOURSELF:

> "Michael, I'm very busy with income taxes now, so I can't talk to you. Give me a little time, and I'll be happy to help you puzzle that dilemma through. Would that be helpful, son?"

> "John, I'm balancing my checkbook. I need it quiet so I won't make a mistake."

> "Glenda, I made that cake for the whole family to enjoy. If it's not shared, I will be disappointed."

> "Michelle, I really appreciate it when you keep your word. It's such a special feeling to know that I can count on you."

STRESSFUL AGES, STRESSFUL STAGES

Do you remember those good old days when you tucked your baby into bed, leaned over the crib, and made the age-old comment that "he looks just like an angel when he sleeps"? Of course you do. That's just one of the many cherished memories you have, memories that are your reward for being a parent. Parenting can be one of the most memorable and meaningful experiences in your life. It can also be one of the most stressful ones. Children are constantly adapting to the tasks and demands of each new stage of growth and development. We adults have to adapt at the same time to our new parenting roles. The problem that arises is that while we are doing this, we are passing through our own stages, each of which brings its own tension and stress. Typical issues in adult stages are:

- personal growth
- career development
- care and feeding of a marriage
- pursuit of fitness or the maintenance of health and well-being
- social activities

Have you ever been to the theater and watched, almost mesmerized, as the scenery inched its way downward until it suddenly crashed completely? Usually, everyone but those onstage was aware of the impending disaster.

So it is in our lives when the stages our children and ourselves go through collide. There will inevitably be times when the nature of the parents' and children's developmental stages will conflict. We may not see the scenery coming down until it is on top of us in the form of arguments, recriminations, and tears. Understanding the complexity of each of the various cycles and acquiring the skills necessary to adapt successfully at each of the stages is a part of the overload that causes stress and tension in parenting. By recognizing each stage that our children go through and matching it with our own developmental stage, we can be prepared for conflict. Knowing what might happen will allow us to think about the best way to eliminate some problems and to lessen the impact of others, thus reducing stress.

Whenever change occurs, whether in a child or a parent, there will be a period of stress for both parent and child as the parties adjust. For example, a child entering the adolescent stage must focus on establishing autonomy and an independent identity. He tries to separate himself from his parents while still depending on them for care and support as well as for guidance with values. In particular, he needs his parents to help him control his aggressive and sexual impulses and to show him appropriate socializing. At some subconscious level, the adolescent recognizes and perhaps resents this dependency, which can make him surly and difficult to live with. Parents are left to adjust to this stranger as best they can.

During a child's adolescence, parenting issues hinge on an ability to allow the adolescent independence while still setting limits. A parent has the difficult task of providing experiences that keep the parent-child relationship healthy at a time when the adolescent is screaming for autonomy but still needs guidance. Add to this already difficult situation the fact that the parent is going through his or her own stages and changes, and you will understand the tensions that build up. How can parents deal with the budding sexuality and sexual curiosity of their teenagers while simultaneously facing the end of their childbearing years? It is difficult to provide counsel about birth control when you are aware that you will never have another child of your own, or to discuss love and intimacy when you may be reassessing your own relationship. How can you feel comfortable telling your crying daughter, "No guy is worth crying this much about or being this miserable over, honey" if you yourself are emotionally estranged from your spouse and crying all the time? How much stock will your son put in your telling him that a relationship demands commitment, that you have to work at it to make it strong, if you have just received your final divorce papers? These and other situations (remarriage, for example) traumatize you and drain you emotionally at the same time that your child needs your help, needs you to be emotionally strong for him.

Your marriage undergoes radical changes during each of the stages of your child's development. In fact, stress in parenting of adolescents is said to be a major cause of marital discord during the marriage life cycle. Issues for the couple at that time include reassessing the marriage and marital roles. At stake is the interpersonal relationship of parents.

In *Creative Marriage*, Mel Krantzler identifies and examines six natural passages of "marriages within a marriage" and delineates the many special demands made upon the marriage by children throughout their developmental stages. I strongly recommend this book. Couples aware of the demands on and the ensuing dynamics in their marriage are better equipped to fortify themselves and the marriage relationship and thereby are more likely to be of help to their children.

The strength of a couple's marriage is an integral part of a happy family and an important asset to each member of the family. Couples who enjoy a happy marriage are more likely to like and value themselves as individuals and as a couple. Each can respect and credit the other's differences in facets of parenting and can feel that what the other has to offer is important. The parents stand together in the buffeting the adolescent is giving them and are better able to provide solace to each other as the adolescent begins the process of gaining autonomy. One picks up when the other is incapacitated.

Your marriage serves as a model for your teenager. He will emulate similar styles and patterns of interaction in his intimate relationships with others. If you have a happy marriage, you are able to anticipate crises and needs because you work together in helping your child. You are able to hold firm when such a stance is appropriate and to move back, to let go, when such action is helpful. As you see your adolescent gain greater decision-making ability, you give him greater latitude. Because you are trusting and secure, you give your child greater responsibility as he is able to take it.

Because you and your partner enjoy being with each other, because you enjoy your lives separately from your child, he learns to enjoy his own life, to become a separate person without going through outbursts of guilt and self-recrimination. You make it relatively easy for your child to move toward adulthood.

Sometimes, however, you need to overcome the anxieties you have for your child. When you were a young parent, getting up for yet another 3:00 A.M. feeding, didn't you long for the days when your child would be independent? And now that you are an experienced parent sitting home at 12:00 A.M. waiting for your teenager to get back from a date, don't you sometimes long for the past, when you knew where your child was and that he or she was safe?

Raising a teenager doesn't really involve physiological demands, as raising an infant or preteen does. Part of the emotional stress of parenting children in the adolescent cycle arises from the parent's concern for the physical and emotional safety and well-being of the child. As noted, we become anxious and frustrated when we don't know the whereabouts of our teenager. Parents often fear that their child may be in an unsafe situation (perhaps with friends who feel that they drive better after "just a few beers") or will be treated unfairly by others (for example, ridiculed for being the tallest girl or shortest boy in the class).

Our experiences give us the vantage point of knowing the quality of choices we made or wish we had made. We grieve over the choices and actions of our teenagers that are likely to result in unhappiness and pain. We want to protect them from the hurt and misery we experienced as teens as well as from the deleterious impacts of contemporary social ills. In our anxiety, we sometimes set guidelines that are too permissive or too restrictive for our teenagers. Because we do not want our children to suffer from frustration and failure, we may not provide them with adequate opportunities to learn from the natural consequences of behavior. Adolescents learn by exploring and experiencing (in our day, it was called *trial and error*). During the adolescent years, when a child is pushing the boundaries of parental guidance and seeking as much autonomy as possible, it is especially important to give him or her the freedom to fail. Failure may be painful but valuable: A child who has tried and failed on his own has learned an important cause-and-effect relationship.

THE FOUR-STEP PROBLEM-SOLVING APPROACH

In groping for a solution to a problem he doesn't completely understand, your adolescent may act impulsively or make rash decisions. Although you may be tempted to jump in and solve the problem for him, your teen must learn to solve problems on his own. You can, however, help him learn to do so.

Effective problem solving is learned by confronting events, defining problems, experimenting, searching for sound solutions and trying them out, and then evaluating the consequences. There are a number of ways in which you can help your child learn the process of problem solving. A simple (but very effective) four-step process is shown below.

1. What is the problem?
2. How can I solve it? What are my alternatives?
3. What is my plan?
4. How did I do?

Re-create a scenario your child has recently encountered and go through this problem solving step by step. Following is a scenario for practice.

Fifteen-year-old Sonja has invited Jennifer to her house for an overnight stay. Jennifer, also fifteen, has told her parents of the plans and has asked for permission to stay out overnight. Upon learning that the plans include dinner and an at-home evening (and assured that Sonja's mother will be there), Jennifer's parents grant permission. When Jennifer arrives at Sonja's house after school on Friday, however, Sonja informs Jennifer that her mother will not be home and that her eighteen-year-old brother and his friend have volunteered to drive them to the movies. Jennifer and her parents have an agreement. She does not want to break the trust with her parents, but she wants Sonja to accept her, and she also wants to go to the movies. Jennifer's parents have made plans to visit a friend, so she cannot call and check with them about the new plans until much later in the evening.

Let's analyze Jennifer's problem using the four-step process.

1. WHAT IS THE PROBLEM?

Jennifer has accepted an invitation to an overnight stay based on certain criteria and has assured her parents of her plans; Sonja has changed plans without notifying Jennifer or her parents. Jennifer's parents are out, and she cannot contact them at this time to get permission regarding the changes.

2. HOW CAN SHE SOLVE IT? WHAT ARE THE CONSEQUENCES?

Action: She could go along with Sonja's new plans without telling her parents. Consequence: She will break the trust she and her parents have established.

Action: She could wait until her parents are home to contact them about getting permission to accept the new plans. Consequence: It will be too late to go, and everyone will be weary of waiting for her decision.

Action: She could tell Sonja that the new plans sound interesting but that she cannot accept them, since she has accepted the overnight invitation based on a set of criteria and is certain her parents would not approve of the new plans. Consequence: She will take the responsibility for her decision and run the risk that her friends will mock her.

Action: She could tell Sonja that she is a liar and a poor friend to put her in this predicament. Consequence: Sonja will feel offended, and it will put a strain on the friendship.

Action: She could leave a message on her parents' answering machine, telling them of the change in plans, and go off to the movies. Consequence: Jennifer's parents will most certainly feel taken advantage of and may not allow her overnights in the future.

3. WHAT IS THE PLAN?

Jennifer will tell Sonja that the new plans sound interesting but that she won't be able to accept them without first checking with her parents. She will tell Sonja now so that Sonja can make other plans if she wants to.

4. HOW DID SHE DO?

Great! Sonja was relieved to not have to follow through with her own revised plans. She had felt that her mother, too, would be upset when she learned of the incident.

You can help your adolescent examine the likely outcome of proposed actions by asking a question such as "If you do that, what do you think would happen?" This question is often followed by "And then what would happen?" If the adolescent proposes solutions that are not very realistic, guide her back to reality by asking, "What is the problem?" Encourage your adolescent to generate more alternatives to the problem and then to assess realistically the potential impact of each of these options. The goal is to help your teenager learn that there is more than one way of handling a problem, that not all solutions work equally well, and that thinking before you act can lead to a better outcome. Be realistic—don't expect that your teenager will always select the choice you would. Your teenager learns by the decisions she makes. Mistakes are important, too, since they show us what does not work, what is not appropriate. Be patient. When your teen does make an obvious mistake, avoid the "I told you so" routine. Point out that a different alternative might have led to a different outcome. Your overall role is to help guide, not direct, your adolescent.

Another way to help your teenager is through role playing, which allows you the opportunity to help your teen work out the variations of consequences. For example, Jennifer may *want* to tell Sonja that she won't be able to go to the movies. However, she may be intimidated by Sonja's older brother, who is standing there waiting for an answer, or she may lose her courage because she fears that Sonja will be angry with her decision.

Role playing is a technique used to evaluate the pros and cons of each proposed solution and to rehearse strategies and behaviors. It allows your teenager to seek the most acceptable and feasible (and probable solution) and to determine a course of action. You can really help your adolescent anticipate stressful interactions by exchanging roles. You can take the role of Sonja, and have your teenager, as Jennifer, confront you with her decision. Now respond as Sonja to Jennifer's decision. Go through each alternative.

By exchanging roles you help your teenager build confidence in her ability to assert her decision. Such preplanning reduces the stress in the situation by lowering the risk that your child will be overwhelmed at the time of confrontation. It also provides you with an opportunity to assess both your adolescent's understanding of the situation and her capacity to implement it under stress. *A Young Person's Guide to Managing Stress* listed in the resource section of this book is an excellent resource in helping your adolescent become more familiar with this and other skills in managing stress.

HIGH FINANCES, OR WHY DOES SHE NEED BRACES AND PIANO LESSONS, TOO?

Bringing up children is expensive. In 1986, the direct cost of raising a child to the age of eighteen was estimated to be about $162,000. By any method of calculation, the financial costs of raising children are considerable. How money is managed is a primary source of parental and family stress. A majority of families rely on earned income as the chief financial resource, and they therefore use budgets to manage family financial resources. Assigning priorities to competing financial needs and distributing the money may create strain. Stress builds up rapidly when income doesn't seem to be adequate to meet both current and future needs.

During a child's adolescence, additional strains on the family budget may be created by such needs as braces and related medical expenses, along with more discretionary cash outlays for sports, hobbies, and interests. Your teenager can be counted on to develop distinct interests that require greater financial commitments from you than were necessary during your child's earlier stages of development. For example, a teenager is keenly aware of fashion and desperately eager to be in style. Rapidly changing styles, along with rapidly growing children, mean frequent wardrobe replacement. Adolescents also "need" cars and sound systems. And, of course, as a parent you are acutely aware that funds will soon be needed for college or continuing education.

Sometimes the money just isn't there. The decline in family purchasing power and the consequent decline in family living standards require psychological, social, and behavioral adjustment. Teenagers must understand your financial limitations and accept their share of sacrifices. Not all of these sacrifices are as simple as buying one new sweater rather than two; some involve active participation. For example, many families today need dual incomes. When both parents work outside the home, their children must be prepared to assume more responsibilities and to make adjustments.

Not all the burden of adjustment is on the children; we must adapt as well. When adolescents work part-time in paid employment, parents must consider the ways in which their child's paycheck changes the dynamics of the parent-child relationship. Perhaps the child, with his new financial "independence," becomes less dependent in other ways as well. Adjusting to this new maturity in your child can be difficult, especially if you have enjoyed a benevolent paternalism (or maternalism), getting a glow from giving to your child. An additional complication arises when your child decides that since he earned his money, it is wholly his to spend as he likes. When that money is spent on something of which you disapprove, stress results.

How can you lessen or eliminate the stresses that money causes? A good first step is to take an honest look at the situation and determine whether money problems cause the stress, or whether stress from money problems is just a symptom of another, greater problem. Naturally, there will be times when money itself is the culprit. If your child absolutely, positively has to have money for a concert and you absolutely, positively cannot afford to give it to him, both of you recognize that money is the catalyst of your argument. However, while you cannot avoid all financial stress, you can control it. How each family does so is unique to that family.

There are as many different ways to handle family money matters as there are families. You probably have a prescribed course of action that you have been following for years. Take a moment now to evaluate it. Is it fair to all parties? Does it still work now that your child is a teenager, able to understand financial commitments, limitations, and problems? Does it involve your teenager in decisions, or does it ignore him entirely, making him feel he is not a part of the family when it comes to money? Do you and your teenager see your money-management system in the same way? That is, do you both understand the priorities? If you are unhappy with your current financial system, you may wish to consult a parenting-education center for information about money-management courses. You may also wish to review *CHOICES* (see resource section), which is perhaps the best guide for parents and their adolescents in addressing and personalizing issues pertaining to money management and family financial responsibilities. Having a solid, working system will not eliminate all financial stress, but it will help significantly.

THE ART OF PARENTING: HOW DO YOU MEASURE UP?

I still remember the look of pride on my husband's face when we overheard our teenage daughter boasting to her friend that her dad was the strongest and the most handsome man in the whole world. Every parent loves to hear how wonderful he or she is, that he or she is the best parent ever. Unfortunately, adolescents do not show their positive feelings as easily as they did when they were younger; we too rarely hear praise from them. When was the last time your teenager took a moment to tell you that you are a good parent? If you are lucky and have a good, solid relationship with your child, you may hear "I love you" occasionally, but you probably will not hear "You're a good parent" at all. Teenagers just don't think to tell us how we're doing at parenting.

There are measures of effective parenting. To a large extent, our role is to help our child unfold into productive adulthood. Our teenager's actions are the most visible reflection of our success or failure at this task. We take pride in our children's growth and accomplishments, and we are occasionally hurt or devastated by their misdoings. In short, we worry about how we are doing as parents. We love our children so much: Are we really doing our very best for them? Are we sometimes hurting them more than helping them? How can we tell?

Wayne Dyer recently asked hundreds of parents what they wanted most for their children. He included the results in his book *What Do You Really Want for Your Children?* Here's what they said:

1. I want my children to value themselves.
2. I want my children to be risk takers.
3. I want my children to be self-reliant.

4. I want my children to be free from stress and anxiety.
5. I want my children to have peaceful lives.
6. I want my children to live in the present moment.
7. I want my children to experience a lifetime of wellness.
8. I want my children to be creative.
9. I want my children to fulfill their higher needs and to feel a sense of purpose.

To these nine wants, I would add a tenth: Parents want their children to want these things for themselves, too, and they feel enormous tensions when teenagers do not.

If we examine this list closely we can see how we as parents need and desire to be protectors, friends, teachers, and care givers for our children. This nurturing response is our legacy to our children.

No matter what they say or how they act, teenage children wish to have close, loving relationships with their parents, and parents want always to be effective in guiding their adolescents. Parents who feel confident and competent about their ability to parent are more likely to empower their children. Empowered children— those who trust their parents and feel sure of their parents' love —are more likely to value their parents and embrace their teachings.

Child psychologists and others who work with children often report that they have never met a parent who purposely reared a child to be unhappy, maladjusted, and ineffective, yet millions of those children exist today. In the course of clinical interactions with families, what emerges is that the parents of these children are unaware of their own values and assumptions and of the many different means of managing and developing desirable and effective behavior in their children.

Teenagers, perhaps more than children of any other age, are constantly changing. You may not recognize your own child from one day to the next, and you may live in mortal terror of or (if you're lucky or brave) bemusement over his changing moods and personalities. For this reason, there is no one right or wrong way to interact with your child. Parents learn quickly whether or not an approach works; the important point to consider is *why* it has succeeded or failed. Learning to discern this is not easy. Let's look at two examples of ways to handle a problem in managing children.

MY MOM, THE OGRE

Twelve-year-old Peter and his older brother Michael are wrestling in the family room. Their mother is trying to watch the news on television, but she is distracted and annoyed by the ever-increasing volume of noise the boys are making. After gritting her teeth for several minutes, the mother explodes into the family room and tells the boys to quiet down or they will have to go to their rooms. Giving her sons a final withering glare, the mother leaves the room and returns to the news. All is quiet in the family room for a few minutes . . . and then the noise begins again, even louder than before.

Poor Mom didn't get much satisfaction from her approach, did she? Her results were all negative. She lost her temper, shouted at her sons, and gained only a brief respite from the noise. Perhaps a different approach is needed.

MY MOM, THE PARENT

The scenario is the same. This time, the mother walks slowly into the family room, smiles, and asks the boys what they are doing. They reply that they are just play-wrestling, and with another smile, Mom says, "That sounds like fun, but you know, I am watching the news and I can't hear because it is too noisy in here." On their own, her sons acknowledge the validity of the problem and propose a solution. Peter suggests that he and Michael put the mat down in the garage—"Our noise there won't bother you. Sorry, Mom."

What a world of difference in both the action and the reaction. It is obvious which is the "good" example and which is the "bad." What is not so obvious, but is critical, is the *why:* Why was the second approach so much more efficacious and satisfying than the first? The answer lies in force.

Whenever one person wants another person to do something, a certain amount of force comes into play. The secret is to maximize the effectiveness of the force, to have a good "force quotient."

Some parents believe that you must be forceful and firm in order to make children behave. However, effectiveness is more important than the logical merits of any one strategy.

Effectiveness means that there is no right or wrong way to interact with children in every circumstance, but rather a number of effective and ineffective ways of interacting. Related to the notion of effectiveness is the idea that the effectiveness of any technique will depend upon the parent-child relationship. Look at the force quotients in the two scenarios given above. The first approach used high force as a punishment and was not effective, while the second approach used low force as a strategy, as a means to an end. Whether to use force and, if so, how much force to use is dependent upon the parent-child relationship.

For example, Lynda and her mother, Judy, get along together wonderfully. They enjoy each other's company and respect each other's feelings. One day, Judy was planning to have some of her office staff over. She was running a little behind schedule and said to Lynda, "I'm afraid I'm not going to be ready when my staff comes." On her own, Lynda volunteered, "I'll do the vacuuming, Mom. Will that help?"

In contrast, Lana and her daughter, Mara, don't get along very well together. One afternoon Lana asked, "Mara, would you help me with the vacuuming so I can get the house cleaned up before my friends come over?" Mara answered, "I'll be right there." Twenty minutes later, Mara still had not come to help with the vacuuming.

Both mothers tried to get their daughters to help them. Each mother used low-force techniques, but only Lynda's mother achieved satisfaction; both women made the same reasonable request. The difference is that Lynda and Judy had a good relationship, Lana and Mara a poor one. Low-force methods work only when there is love and respect in the parent-child relationship.

The greater the amount of force used, the greater the cost to your relationship with your child. How good your relationship is right now should be a determinant in helping to decide how much force it can withstand, how much force you can be justified in using. The key, then, is to identify the quality and status of your parent-child relationship.

Are you concerned that you may have used up all the goodwill and respect that once existed between you and your child? You can tell with a simple checklist. Your relationship with your child is in danger of being bankrupt when

- You receive no messages of caring and affection from your child
- You frequently experience negative emotions concerning your child's behavior and allow yourself to get angry with the child
- Minor problems become catastrophes
- You use destructive patterns of communication, such as name calling, lecturing, sarcasm, shaming, blaming, and threatening, which undermine the child's self-confidence and sense of worth
- You frequently use high-force methods to obtain desired behavior from your child

There are also signs that indicate that your relationship with your child is a healthy, loving one. Positive signs are

- Frequent verbal and nonverbal (such as touching) messages of caring and affection
- Open expression of feelings (both positive and negative) between parent and child
- An atmosphere in which both parent and child feel free to express themselves
- Timely and orderly resolution of problems, along with a sincere desire for such a resolution

If your child cares for you and cares about your feelings, you have a very powerful, effective low-force method of dealing with his behavior. Simply because your adolescent wants to maintain his good relationship with you, his actions will be influenced by his knowing how you will respond to what he is doing. Within limits, he will strive to continue doing things that please you and will avoid doing things that he knows will irritate or anger you. When your parent-child relationship is strong, the child provides much of his own force, thus allowing you to use methods that are much lower in force than would otherwise be possible.

You are probably nodding your head in agreement with the concept that a child who monitors himself is much easier for a parent to deal with. What you probably want to know now is how to get such a "perfect" child. It is *not* that the child is perfect but that the relationship is "new and improved." Every parent can build a better relationship with his or her child. Love not only binds parents and children together but also provides essential emotional sustenance, buffering them against stress and preserving physical and emotional health. The following sections will help you to understand what your child wants and needs and will show you how you can strengthen your relationship by supplying simple things, allowing yourself to use low-force methods to change your child's behavior, ultimately reducing stress for all concerned.

A recent experiment demonstrated that growth and development may be thwarted in the absence of love. Researchers were studying cholesterol deposits in rabbits. As a control, all rabbits were fed the same diet, yet it was soon discovered that several of the rabbits had markedly reduced cholesterol deposits. Initially the researchers had no explanation for this occurrence. Questioning the staff, they learned that a night lab worker had grown fond of particular rabbits and had been playing with them. Every night as he cleaned out their cages, the assistant would give those rabbits his attention and affection. It was the "pet" rabbits that demonstrated lower cholesterol deposits. The researchers tested their theory that the affection had a direct effect on the cholesterol levels by repeating the study, this time deliberately giving certain rabbits more attention and affection. Once again, the rabbits that had received tender loving care were those with lower cholesterol deposits.

If rabbits in a lab responded physically to just a little extra attention, imagine how important that same attention is to a child. We as parents may feel that we are expressing our love by giving our children material things, objects we think will make them happy. Do we stop to ask ourselves what kind of a substitute a new outfit is for a hug and kiss or for a few minutes of our time?

Put yourself in this position: Which would mean more to you if you were stressed or sad, a present from your spouse or a big hug and kiss and a heartfelt, "I love you; you're everything to me"? Love is exchanged between people, not between people and things. Some children have a lot of material things but have very little human interaction with adults whom they love and want to be loved by.

PARENT AS ARTIST: MOLDING YOUR TEEN'S SELF-CONCEPT

A self-concept is the perception that a person holds about himself: what he is, what he stands for, what he does or does not do —in short, all those things that make him the individual that he is. A child is not born with a self-concept; he learns it through interacting with other people over long periods of time. Through the approval or disapproval of others, he develops an opinion about his self-worth and value as a human being. Who are these "others" who play such a vital role in forming self-concept? Some of them are your child's peers, his friends and companions. Others are aunts and uncles and sometimes even admired singers or movie stars. As a parent, however, you are the most significant individual with whom your child interacts and are thus the greatest factor in helping him form his self-concept. Your opinion matters, whether or not your teenager is willing to acknowledge it at this stage in his development.

Given that our love and acceptance are vital to helping a teenager develop a positive self-concept, how can we demonstrate to our child that we do indeed love and accept her as she is? We cannot simply assume that our child knows we love her; we must show our love over and over, especially during the teenage years, when that love is often tested. A teenager doesn't want to hear, "Of course I love you; I'm your mother, aren't I?" She wants to know that you love her because she's worth loving, not because parents are "supposed to" love their children. She wants to feel special. There are many different ways in which you can express this love.

VERBAL EXPRESSION

Tell your child you love him, then tell him again. Say the words directly—don't simply hint at them. There's no need to be coy or cute or to worry that you'll embarrass your child (as long as you don't "get mushy" in front of his friends). Say "I love you; you mean everything to me" as often as you feel it.

NONVERBAL EXPRESSION

Teenagers have long antennae. They can tell when there is sincerity or hypocrisy in the air. If you tell a teenager you love him while your fists are clenched and your jaw is set, he's not going to place a lot of stock in your words. Your facial expression and body language communicate your love to a child almost as directly as your words.

ACTIVE LISTENING

Active listening means attending fully to the words your child is speaking and to the feelings he is expressing. A parent who is a good listener builds a relationship with his or her child and sets the foundation for the sharing of personal feelings and problems. When we listen to a child, we are telling him that he is valuable, worthy of our time and attention. We show empathy and respond to what the child is saying. It's not always necessary to have a solution. Sometimes, just a few minutes of your undivided attention to his problem can tell a child all he wants to know about your acceptance. I will deal more fully with active listening later in this chapter.

TOUCHING

Touching is a very powerful way of showing our feelings, especially our love and acceptance of others. Taking a child's hand, patting him on the back, putting your arm around his shoulders, or simply touching his arm all express your love and pride in your child.

PROVISION

As parents, we provide for our children. We give them food, shelter, a safe environment. We supply both the essentials and the nonessentials. Every now and then, take a minute to let your child know that you give so much not because of parental duty but because you love him so much. A teenager should know that sometimes you want to give him a gift just because you love him, not because it's his birthday or because he did something right.

It's not very hard to express love when everything is going well, when your child is well-behaved and loving. But what about those times when he has just done something that angers or annoys you, those times when he needs discipline? You can use those times to mix in a little love with the discipline.

A child can't always separate a parent's anger or annoyance with something he has done from anger or annoyance with the child as a person. Children have difficulty in understanding that while we may not approve of what they have done, we still love them. Many adolescents, when faced with an angry parent, will think that something is wrong with them personally; they can't understand how parents can be upset with them yet still love them. It is important to show the child that your anger is directed toward what he has done, not toward who he is.

Consider the following example: You are washing your car and being "helped" by your child. After the tenth spilled bucket or watered-down backseat, you turn and screech, "Just get out of here. I'll do it myself. You never do anything right!" How do you suppose the child feels at this sudden attack? After all, he was only trying to help you wash a car, and suddenly he's a person who never does anything right! You have attacked the child himself, not his action. Try doing just the opposite. Show the child you are unhappy with his action but that you still love him for the good he is trying to do: "Eric, I know you like washing the car. I appreciate it when you do, but if you can follow the procedure we talked about and be more thorough, you'll do a better job. That way, I won't have to ask you to redo it, and we'll both feel better."

Think for a moment about the last few sentences. You began by empathizing with the child. You showed him that you know his feelings and understand them. Then you went on to a positive statement, saying that you appreciated his help. Next came constructive criticism, an analysis of what the child should be doing. The final part was the all-important justification, with your telling the child why he should do things your way. Instead of creating unnecessary stress by attacking the child, you have managed to express empathy, acceptance, guidance, and respect for his feelings. Not bad for a few sentences!

It is important that you understand a child's self-concept, because it is that self-concept that influences behavior. Two other influences on behavior are a child's beliefs about her competence and her sense of responsibility. As a child masters developmental tasks and sees the reactions of others to her mastery, she learns that she is competent. Responsibility follows when the child experiences the consequences of her actions. When a child sees a direct cause-and-effect relationship between her actions and their consequences (both positive and negative, acceptable and unacceptable), she realizes that she has obligations both to herself and to those around her. She learns to take credit as well as blame for the results of her actions and to alter her actions if she wants a different consequence.

Sixteen-year-old Diane learned responsibility through consequences when she arrived home from school two hours later than usual. A classmate had invited Diane to come to her home at the last minute. Diane had accepted, even though she knew she had daily chores at home as well as a special school project to do. Diane had originally planned on doing her chores and project and then attending a special movie with her older sister. When she arrived home, her mother said, "Diane, you won't be able to go out with your sister tonight. Your science fair project is due tomorrow, and your chores haven't been done."

Notice that Diane's mother pointed out the *consequences* of Diane's behavior, and thus her responsibility. She didn't say, "Diane, you are the most irresponsible child!" (thus attacking the child instead of the behavior). By wording her comments carefully, Diane's mother avoided an argument or an attempt by her daughter at self-justification. (Diane could probably have denied being irresponsible as a person, but she certainly could not have said that she had acted responsibly in this instance.)

Children should also learn that good behavior can bring about positive results. A caring parent can use praise to teach responsibility for actions. Take the case of thirteen-year-old Rachel, who came home from school and excitedly shared with her mother the news that she had received a high score on a history exam. "That's terrific, Rachel!" said her mother. "You studied very hard for that test and you earned that grade. You should be very proud of yourself."

The mother has thus pointed out to Rachel the consequences of her behavior: she has worked very hard, she has produced the good grade, and she therefore deserves to be very proud of herself. Her pride should lie in having done good work, not in having made her mother proud.

FORGING THE CHAIN OF COMMUNICATION

Communication is the linking element throughout parenting. I have talked briefly about how to communicate love and acceptance during good times and bad. I have also talked about teaching responsibility through communication. But how is communication achieved? The first step is to recognize that listening is critical.

Listening is one of the most-ignored aspects of communication and interpersonal relationships. We spend endless hours during our formative years learning to talk, read, and write, but we are given no instruction on how to listen. How do you know whether or not you are a good listener? How can you be certain you are hearing what the speaker is really saying, not just what you want to hear? Are there any criteria you can use to judge your listening skills?

Think about people who listen to you with only "half an ear." Don't you know someone who continually interrupts you or shows indifference or boredom with what you are saying? You probably feel rejected, stressed, inferior, and generally insignificant after speaking with such a person. After all, this person has made it pretty clear that you had nothing to say that held his or her interest. Your reaction is standard, as was demonstrated by an experiment on listening.

In a university classroom, an experienced professor was conducting a presentation. Her lecture was interrupted by a request that she go to the business office to get additional information on class enrollment. While she was gone, a researcher instructed the class in how to be an obnoxious audience. Upon the professor's return, some students were to drop their heads down on the table as though they were asleep, others were to gaze out the window, and still others were to scowl and shake their heads in disagreement.

When the professor returned and started to lecture, the students went into their "awful listener" modes. After only a few minutes of speaking, the professor stopped and inquired, "What is going on? What are you trying to do to me?"

Sometimes I imagine that very little listening would be done at all if we weren't waiting for our turn to talk next, and that's a problem. As parents, we must *want* to listen to our children. Listening is an attitude. This is made obvious by the case of a school in which public speaking was offered as an evening course. The course became so popular that it was expanded into three different classes. A listening course was offered at the same time (for four years). It was never once given, because no one enrolled.

ACTIVE LISTENING

Brian walked into the family study, where his brother Chad was working on the computer. Brian turned to leave, muttering, "Man, I can never get my homework done around here!" "You sound angry," said Chad. "Are you just angry, or are you angry at me?" Replied Brian, "I'm angry because I have a big homework assignment tomorrow that I don't want to do, and I need to use the computer. I'm not angry at you. I'm sorry for yelling. What time do you think you will be finished working on the computer?"

Active listening is a most effective tool for reducing stress. First of all, it is a defusing device: it defuses anger simply because of the acknowledgment given to one person by another. In this case, it became clear that yes, Brian is frustrated and angry. Second, listening clarifies the direction of the anger. Is it a personal, vindictive anger? Or is the angry person upset about an event, not with another person? Brian is frustrated with the amount of homework he has to do in the time in which he must do it. Third —and probably most important when we are talking about stress reduction—active listening allows you to decide whether and how you want to participate in someone else's anger. In contrast to responding by questioning, judging, defending, or rationalizing, active listening entails feedback that is objective and nonjudgmental. Chad has an opportunity to show empathy toward Brian and thus alleviate some of Brian's frustrations. For example, Chad could suggest that Brian use the computer immediately if his own work is not quite as urgent, or the two boys could generate other alternatives. Thus, the brothers have an opportunity to preserve their relationship.

In any given situation, whether the situation is stressful or not, there are three parts to the communication process. There is always (1) a sender of the message, (2) a receiver of the message, and (3) the manner in which the message is relayed. The message can be either verbal or nonverbal. When all three parts of the communication process are functioning smoothly, effective communication takes place, and there is little room for misunderstanding. However, if one or more of the three parts are not functioning correctly, the results may be an increase in stress levels and misunderstanding. Suppose a sender of a message has had a bad day and is feeling thoroughly frustrated, as is the case with Brian. Upon finding Chad using the computer, he says, "I can never get any work done around here!" The receiver of the message (Chad), who feels taken aback by the outburst, could take the exclamation personally and think, "My gosh, what did I do?" Active listening is an excellent method of checking out those assumptions; it is a legitimate way of breaking the emotional chain that could have evolved if Chad had replied, "I can't get my work done around here, either, and it's because of your frustration and outbursts!"

The following five steps can help you to listen actively:

1. *Clarify the content of the communication.* The first step in communication is to understand what is being said.
2. *Verify nonverbal messages.* The receiver needs to check out the consistency of body language and the tone of voice of the sender. An active-listening response can help you verify what is not being said as well as what is being said.

3. *Gather additional information.* Clarifying verbal and non-verbal messages and verifying the feelings of the speaker allows the receiver an opportunity to learn more and to better interpret the interaction before developing his personal view.
4. *Provide a genuine personal response.* Active listening promotes understanding and acceptance, clarifying both thoughts and emotions.
5. *Promote getting-in-charge behavior.* Once the sender's feelings have been identified, the interaction can be directed toward allowing him to reassess his message and reshape it in a more appropriate manner.

In responding to a highly charged, emotional statement, the receiver should *avoid* rationalizing, questioning, supportive pampering, defending, judging, or parroting. Let's return to Brian and Chad to see the effects of these various responses.

RATIONALIZING
Rationalizing is explaining away why the other person is feeling the way he does.

Brian (Sender): "I hate school. I always have so much homework to do I can never find time to have any fun!"

Chad (Receiver): "Oh, come on, it's just hot outside and you're just in a bad mood."

This response does not encourage clarification of the original message, nor does it acknowledge the emotion of the message. If anything, it may exacerbate the situation by irritating Brian even more.

QUESTIONING
Questioning is asking about the motive or reasoning of the sender in giving his original message.

Brian (Sender): "Everyone around here only looks after themselves, never caring about anyone else!" (muttered under his breath as he leaves the study).

Chad (Receiver): "Oh, really, who are you talking about? Me, huh?"

This response baits the sender, causing emotions to continue to flare, with no resolution to the issue.

SUPPORTIVE PAMPERING

Here, the sender verbalizes the message, and the receiver tries to solve the sender's problem for him before deciding whether it is appropriate to become involved at all.

Brian (Sender): "I hate school. I can never get all this work done!"

Chad (Receiver): "Now, now. It's going to be all right. I can help you" (without knowing what is involved).

This response does not acknowledge the content or emotion of the original statement and may get the receiver involved in a situation he might later wish he had avoided.

DEFENDING

Defending occurs when the receiver either backs up the apparent purpose of the message without further information or is defensive in response to the sender.

Brian (Sender): "I had been planning to get this work done tonight, and now you're using the computer. I can never get my work done."

Chad (Sender): "My work is just as important as your work is. Get out of here and stop disturbing me."

This response leads to escalation of stress and undermines the relationship between Brian and Chad.

JUDGING

Judging consists of making a judgment about the motive, personality, or reasoning of the sender regarding his message.

Brian (Sender): "Now my assignment won't be done for tomorrow and all the kids will laugh and my teacher will be mad."

Chad (Receiver): "You shouldn't feel that way."

This response tells the sender that the receiver isn't really interested and that he knows how the sender should feel.

PARROTING

Parroting is obnoxiously restating exactly what the sender has said.

> Brian (Sender): "I hate school, and I wish I could quit."
>
> Chad (Receiver): "It sounds like you hate school and wish you could quit."

This response provides virtually no acknowledgment of the intent of or reasoning behind the message and signals the sender that the receiver is not sensitive to what has been said.

Like all skills, active listening requires practice and should be a deliberate and intentional style of communication between you and your teenager. Two parents were told by the teacher of their ninth-grade boy that the child was becoming a distracting problem in school; mischievous attention-getting antics were an ever-increasing pattern of the child's behavior. The teacher had used all the customary ways of handling the situation, with little success. The parents scolded, punished, and even worked out a system of conduct rewards for their teenager, but the poor behavior persisted. The couple then decided to get some help and were exposed to the benefits of active listening. It dawned on them that they had not been providing the boy with much casual day-to-day listening time. They would come home from work and immediately become preoccupied with opening the mail, returning phone messages, preparing the evening meal, and talking about the day's happenings. These parents had looked upon their son almost as an intrusion into their time together. Practicing effective listening changed all that.

They started focusing more on the boy, talking with him about his day's activities, his friends, and so on. Within a short time the serious behavior difficulties at school melted into the ordinary restless energies of any fourteen-year-old. It is, of course, unreasonable to suppose that listening is the solution to every adolescent's problem, but this example points out that good listening can certainly have positive results.

You must sincerely want to hear what the other person has to say. If your supervisor wanted fifteen minutes of your time, you would no doubt feel flattered. But if your adolescent wanted fifteen minutes of your time, would you also feel flattered? Yet who is more important to you?

GETTING AND GIVING NEGATIVE FEEDBACK

When you were in high school, how many notes did you write, but never deliver, to The Object of Your Desire? How many dozens of sheets of paper did you cover with your thoughts, and how many hours did you spend in front of a mirror practicing speeches that you never gave? What is important, of course, is not how many undelivered messages you composed but *why* you never sent those messages. The answer is that you were afraid of the response you would get, afraid that you might be laughed at or ridiculed. In most interactions that involve either giving or receiving negative feedback, the emotional consequence of that feedback assumes great importance. This consequence can be either real or imagined, but either way it creates stress for most people.

In negative-feedback situations we often become concerned either with how the other person will respond to receiving the comment or with how the other person will perceive us when we are giving it. A fear develops that the other person will wind up feeling negative about himself or about us.

Consider Peggy, in the following example. Peggy's sixteen-year-old son Erin was repeatedly leaving his dirty dishes and clothes all over their apartment. She would continue to pick them up, and he would invariably deposit more. Peggy justified not telling Erin how she felt by saying to herself, "Well, we're never home together for very long, and I want that time together to be a happy time." The straw that broke the camel's back, however, came on an evening when Peggy had a special dinner party planned. She had spent a considerable amount of time the evening before in shopping and cleaning, and this evening she arrived home with just enough time to prepare the dinner and herself before the guests arrived. The apartment was a mess, with dirty clothes and dishes deposited everywhere—and no sign of Erin. Feeling frustrated and angry at always having to pick up after her son, Peggy decided it was time to do something. What had delayed that decision?

Peggy, like many of us, suspected that her son would respond to this negative feedback by accusing her of calling him a "lazy slob." She anticipated that the consequence of her interaction with Erin would be a confrontation regarding her opinion of him as a person. She dreaded even bringing up the subject because of her fear that doing so would result in a battle regarding their feelings toward each other, so she contemplated not discussing it at all.

Imagine that you are Peggy. Your son walks into the room, and by looking at him you can tell that he is upset. He says in a rather loud voice, "This house is such a mess, that it's impossible to invite anyone home with me" or "There is never anything good to eat around here." Your immediate response is to think that your son sees you as a poor mother. He must think you are really incompetent, and this makes you feel pretty bad. You imagine that your son feels you are an inferior person.

Both of these examples demonstrate that the anticipated consequences of the interpersonal exchange have an influence on the message being communicated. Without establishing the validity of the negative feelings about themselves, the people in these situations are allowing these feelings to interfere with the communication process. The focus of the exchange is shifted from the negative feedback (message) to the personal feelings (emotional consequence).

Negative feedback can be a positive step toward solving the problem at hand; however, one must focus on the message being relayed, *not* on the anticipated emotional consequences of the exchange. Try taking the following steps when giving negative feedback.

Describe the situation clearly. Identify precisely the behavior that you would like to see changed. For example, your son does not pick up after himself, and you are left with the total responsibility for house care. The target behavior is shared participation. While you are describing the situation, focus on present, not past, behavior. You would probably like to say, "I clean the house, but you leave clothes and dishes and other articles lying around after you use them. I end up spending more time cleaning up after you. You're old enough to participate. We had agreed on responsibilities. You do this all the time. I'm just a maid around here." Such a statement, however, will get in the way of clearly stating what is going on now. What counts is that you are upset because your son has left a mess for you to clean up.

Express your own feelings. Remembering two points when expressing your feelings will keep the exchange from becoming an emotional battle. First, take responsibility for your emotions. You might say, "I feel frustrated and angry when you don't pick up your things." By using "I feel" messages, you don't accuse the other person of causing your response, and he or she has no need to react defensively. You are simply stating how you feel. Second, share how you are feeling about the event *without* allowing the feedback process to act as an emotional release.

Specify the changes that you would like to see occur. Simply stating what you do not like does not guarantee that the other person will know what you want. It is appropriate to ask for a change in the other person's behavior, and the more specific you can be about this, the more likely it is that it will be understood by the recipient. Avoid being demanding, as this indicates to the recipient that he has no choice, causing his response to be of a defensive or aggressive nature. Simply state what you would like to have occur, such as: "I would like to request that you pick up after yourself and share the responsibility of our home."

State what you perceive to be the possible consequences of a change in the other person's behavior. Tell the other person what the outcome will be if your request is granted. For example: "If you do your share of responsibilities in our home, Erin, I will have some help and some time to relax, too." The consequences, or outcomes, are best stated in positive terms, avoiding "you had better do it, or else . . . " attitudes. Threatening the recipient with punishment, while it may create temporary compliance, will not do much for consistent cooperation.

So far, we have focused primarily on how to *give* negative feedback. We also need to learn how to *receive* negative feedback. All of the same concepts apply. Your goal as the receiver of the feedback is to objectively focus on the message being sent in order to begin the resolving process.

When someone is critical of you, first use an active listening response: "You sound (*upset*) with me about (*my not picking up my things*)." If the other person responds that this is, indeed, the case, continue with what you perceive to be the problem: "It sounds like you would like me to (*pick up my things*). I think that is reasonable" (or unreasonable, if that is the case). Remember that if you need more information, ask for it. If you need help, ask.

Imagine that you are Erin in the scenario above. Respond to the negative feedback given to you. Was your response something like this?

> Erin: "You sound upset with me for not picking up my things. It sounds like you would like me to participate more fully in the responsibilities we had agreed to. That's a reasonable request. I do enjoy our home when it is orderly. Also, I know we all find it easier to ask friends over on short notice when we keep with a system. Besides, I do want you to have more time for yourself, mom, and for us. I'm sorry about the extra work I caused you yesterday afternoon. I'll try to do better."

Does this response sound a little too good to be true from a sixteen-year-old? Teenagers can and do communicate with sensitivity and compassion when they have the skills to receive negative feedback properly. But they need to know how. Keep in mind that rarely do adolescents teach these skills to one another. They need to learn them from their parents. As with other skills, these are best learned by the parent modeling these skills again and again. We should be deliberate in our approach when teaching skills to children. Use the model until you gain proficiency in the skill.

IT'S NEVER TOO LATE TO BE A GOOD PARENT

Have you ever waved goodbye to your child as he was leaving for a trip and felt a tug at your heart, wishing you had done more for him? Or felt remorse at a comment you made and wished you could somehow take it back? Parents can remedy their previous neglect. It's never too late.

Parents always learn from their own children. Think about what you have learned by being a parent. Don't you have a treasure chest of memories and skills you never imagined you would have? Of course you do.

Parenting is a learning process for parents as well as for children, so trial and error comes with the territory of nurturing children. I know I have learned valuable skills from parenting. Here's what I have learned from being a parent:

I learned what responsibility meant. I learned that I could accept the duties and obligations of being a parent and could be depended upon to fulfill them.

I learned how to listen not only to my child's voice but also to her feelings and behaviors. I learned to hear what she was saying rather than what I would prefer to hear.

I learned patience, endurance, and sacrifice. I learned that I possessed unsuspecting strength within myself, which I discovered when I had to nurture her when I myself was sick or had other impending responsibilities.

I learned empathy, for in trying to understand my child I had to put myself in her place.

I learned the joy in giving of myself like no other experience I've known. I see my child prospering as a healthy, intelligent person as a result of my efforts.

I learned how to think independently in the face of unforeseen illness and accidents, when I had to make tough decisions on my own.

I learned how to share love. I have learned that giving my child love taps into a reservoir of unending love.

My child taught me what she needed. By listening and observing I learned what kind of parenting she needed—and that it might be different from what I had expected. I didn't know all this before she was born nor during her very early years. I realize now how much I've learned from nurturing my child.

A major premise of this book is that the parent serves as a reservoir of love and care, experience and knowledge, and that he or she is the best source of knowing the individuality and specialness of the child. Because of this, the parent *is* the primary catalyst for helping the adolescent meet the challenge of growing up physically healthy and personally competent in our ever more complex world. Certainly, it is critical that the adolescent accept responsibility for self; also, we as a society, as educators, as childcare professionals, and as other responsible adults have a stake in providing effective models for the child. However, it is still the parent who serves as the ultimate guide and model for ensuring that the child will be successful in *learning* appropriate ways to "be in the world."

And remember, you don't have to tough it out alone. Get information and surround yourself with supportive others. Parent-education classes can be one very positive way to improve parenting skills. The childhood education movement has produced more information about human growth and development than was ever available before. We now know more about the physiological, psychological, and emotional development of children than ever before.

Support from friends, neighbors, and extended families is important for attaining skills in parenting as well as for reducing the stress in parenting situations. The feeling that you have too many responsibilities and too little time and energy to fulfill them is not an uncommon feeling among parents. Parent support groups can be helpful in reducing the feeling of isolation and in allowing for the sharing of common and successful approaches in helping teenagers deal with stress.

As the title of this chapter promised, you have been reading about your role, about what you as an adult go through in parenting. You have seen how having a child can put stress on both you and your marriage and can also be one of the most rewarding experiences possible. You learned how to react to your child and thus how to help guide him or her through the stress of growing up. Now it is time to consider the child. What is he going through? How does he view his life? The more you understand how an adolescent feels, how he responds to the confusing world around him, the better prepared you will be to react to any problems that may arise and to handle the everyday crises that are just a part of adolescence.

CHAPTER THREE

Do You Remember Adolescence?

There he is, standing outside the door of the gymnasium, shaking like a leaf. "It's just the gym," he tells himself, "just a big building with smelly floors and squeaky doors." So why are his palms sweating and his heart pounding?

"Does my hair look okay? Damn, I know it's too short. It figures I'd get a pimple right on my chin, where everyone will notice it. I don't know why I let Mom talk me into wearing this outfit. I look like a nerd. Everyone is going to laugh at me. No one is going to want to dance with me. I'll die if Terry comes over to talk to me. I'll die if no one comes over to talk to me."

Surely these are the ravings of a maladjusted, neglected, tormented soul who has been misused and abused by life. Wrong. It could easily have been you yourself, just a few decades ago, going to your first dance, enjoying "the best days of your life." Ah, for the good old days.

All of us who have "grown up" vaguely remember what it was like to be an adolescent. Yet, we also forget. Time blurs the difficult side of human experience, leaving mostly a certain nostalgic glow as we reminisce about the exhilarating and unforgettable moments of yesteryear. Sometimes we even long for those days irrevocably gone. Back then, we recall, we were happy, endlessly energetic, carefree, and full of hopes and dreams! Needless to say, we were also—and maybe predominantly—plagued by uncertainty, confusion, ambivalence, and moody introspection. We were filled with anxious moments of despair and frequent episodes of stress.

The period of adolescence often represents a special time of stress for both parents and teenagers. Research shows that the teen years are without a doubt among the most confusing and stressful times of life because the developmental tasks are so great. Many youngsters characterize their adolescent years as the most unhappy and turbulent in their life, despite their having been told by some adults that the teenage years are the happiest time of life.

What is it about this phase of life that causes teenagers to describe it as the most unhappy and turbulent time and parents to refer to it as the most trying of times? That is what this chapter is addressing. Here you will learn about the physical, mental, and emotional changes an adolescent is going through, how they affect his behavior, and how that behavior affects him, you, and your entire family. You will learn how an adolescent views his teenage years, as well as how his self-concept is changing and evolving during that time. Practical information will be given that will answer the one question parents and teenagers always have in common: "What's going on here?" Most important, this chapter will show you how to accept these changes and to help your teen accept them too.

Before we examine these issues, it might be helpful to gain a perspective of how young people themselves view the adolescent experience. "I'm strong," says Robert. "I am capable of living an independent life. Yet my parents treat me like a child. I'm watched and questioned. I just wish I didn't need them." Sixteen-year-old Karen expresses it this way: "Adolescence is like needing a loan from the bank. It's awful to have to borrow because there are strings attached, but you do need the loan. Adolescence is like that. You hate to live under someone else's conditions, but you do need their love."

Seventeen-year-old Dean puts it another way. "You're just trapped. I know my dad wants me to become a lawyer like he is and even go into practice with him. It's his dream, but I just don't share it. He feels I'm ungrateful, telling me that if his father had offered him such a position, he would have taken it and been

thankful. I don't really believe that, and sometimes I don't respect
him at all. It wouldn't be so bad if he didn't want to do my thinking
for me. He tells me he knows how it feels to be a teenager. How
can he know? He hasn't been a teenager in today's world. Parents
expect you to value their decisions just because they are older. I've
got news for them—older is not wiser!

"They tell me I'm grown up, but they don't really believe it.
They treat me like I'm an overgrown child. They tell me they've
given me so much, and they want so much for me. I feel like
an $80,000 investment! They tell me they love me, but I wonder
why they really don't know me then. I don't think they know
who I am."

Each of these adolescents is addressing the same general concept: responsibility. An adolescent is leaving his comfortable, secure, unconditional acceptance of and by adults and entering a
new phase where he is responsible for his own actions. No longer
can he simply be "mama's little man," secure in the knowledge
that his parents will make everything right, that he has only
himself to please and consider. Suddenly, he is responsible to
others. He has control over not only his own life but also the lives
of others, in the way that they respond to his actions. This is a
dramatic realization for a young person to make and takes getting
used to, in much the same way that you had to get used to being
responsible for the life of your baby when you first became a
parent. It wasn't easy, but you survived, and with your love, understanding, and help, so will your teenager.

BEING A TEENAGER TODAY

Teenagers today are working through the adolescent stage in
an ever-changing society. As they go about gaining the experience
necessary to meet the tasks and demands required of the adolescent phase, they face changes in the larger society that give inconsistent messages about what it means to be an adult and how
adults should function.

At some time in your life, you may have made a decision to get
into better shape. You changed your diet and exercised regularly.

If you were fortunate, your body did, indeed, change. Remember how painful and exhausting those changes were? Shaving an inch from your waistline or adding an inch to your biceps took its toll on you physically and emotionally. You may have had little energy left to do things you really wanted to do, and you probably went around snapping at everyone.

The teenage years are a time when a youngster undergoes much greater changes. If it takes a lot for an adult to simply lose a few pounds or firm up a few muscles, imagine how your child feels when he grows four inches in a year, or gains thirty pounds, or suddenly sprouts hair where there was none before. These changes, which are out of his control, are intense, demanding, and frightening. In a diet or exercise program, you have a goal and control over your changes; you know when they are going to begin and end. Your teenager can't see the light at the end of the tunnel and has no idea what's coming at him next. Naturally, this lack of control causes insecurity and stress.

While your teenager is going through these very dramatic changes, he or she naturally needs extra love and support from you. However, parents are often busy building careers or caring for other children, and they may not give that little extra effort. Parents may often provide very little support for their teenagers simply because they are too busy reshaping and retooling their own lives in a society in flux. This means that the teenager not only has to cope with his changes but also has to do so pretty much on his own.

Once, adolescence was regarded as a grooming ground, a place to learn to be an adult. Today, society has changed so rapidly that we expect our children to become adults instantaneously.

"There's no place for teenagers in America today," says David Elkind, author of *All Grown Up and No Place to Go*. "It was generally recognized that young people needed time, support, and guidance in learning how to become adults. The period of adolescence provided time needed to adapt to the many changes they were undergoing."

Today, teenagers are thrust into a new role of premature adulthood without adequate preparation and are expected to confront life and its challenges in an adult way. Many facets of life that were once regarded as being for adults only—life's mysteries, contradictions, tragedies, and sexual, physical, and social responsibilities—are no longer off-limits to children. In part, the new age of television and video has erased the dividing line between childhood and adulthood, since it does not segregate its audience but communicates the same information to everyone, regardless of sex, age, or level of education. Have you noticed how children on television are depicted as small adults? What we see is a projection of the adult child—a new kind of person with an "obsessive need for immediate gratification, a lack of concern for consequences, and an almost promiscuous preoccupation with consumption," says Neil Postman, author of *The Disappearence of Childhood*.

This new transformation makes the behaviors, attitudes, desires, and even physical appearances of adults and children nearly indistinguishable. Young people are now committing crimes once attributed to adults only; clothing styles for children copy those designed for adults; children's games are becoming *sports,* complete with adult rules and regulations. Children commonly use language once reserved for adults and not even to be uttered in the presence of children.

Why should we be concerned that there are fewer opportunities for young people to experience childhood? A simple answer is that premature adulthood has its problems. It forces children to cope with outside tasks and conditions when all their energy is already needed just to handle the basic demands of puberty. Another effect is stress overload. Coping with an abundance of freedoms, fewer personal family relationships, and the loss of a sense of security and, perhaps, of their expectations about the future, disconnected teenagers experience more debilitation and an inordinate amount of stress, as we will see in the coming chapters.

Because society expects a child to metamorphose instantly into an adult, there is a natural tendency on the part of parents to treat children as adults. This can have dire consequences. If we feel helpless or assume that the teenager is a kind of adult and needs little, if any, adult guidance and direction, we impair the child's ability to construct a secure personal identity, leaving him or her more vulnerable and less competent to meet the inevitable challenges of life.

Parents, too, have mixed and somewhat inconsistent attitudes toward young people. On the one hand, we urge our teenagers to learn about relationships and love but to do so mostly without touching. On the other hand, we often remind young people of how bold and entrepreneurial we were at their age—there was no prolonged adolescence for us, we say, as we tell stories of our own teenage years. When *we* were young, we say, we hit the work force as active, self-assertive youths. At least, that's how our stories go now. Too often we glorify youths who have found ways of growing up fast without any of the conflicts so many of today's young people inevitably feel as they contend with their confused sense of what is desirable.

While we all like to feel that we have options and can do as we please when it comes to important matters, we recognize that having too many options is as bad as not having enough. Remember the turmoil you experienced when you were selecting a career? Today's adolescent is bombarded by a wide number of options and choices. He is likely to be confused as he confronts a wide variety of options in ideologies, careers, and lifestyles from which to construct his future. That a teenager has more career options doesn't mean he will make better choices. In fact, the abundance of choices causes stress in that it contributes to ambiguity.

In addition to the difficulty of career choice and employment options, a young person faces an uncertain future that is further beclouded by possible annihilation through overpopulation, pollution, or nuclear warfare. There is a sense of hopelessness in making decisions premised on a future that may not be. We adults often look at a young person and assume he should know how fortunate he is to have his whole life ahead of him. What we forget is that from the adolescent's perspective, he doesn't know what the future holds. And if he is hurting now, he thinks that the future will be nothing but pain. "If childhood is the happiest time of my life," laments Roger, "adulthood must be awful."

There is no one "healthy" way for adolescents to go about taking steps toward their future life. This baffles parents, who, because they themselves have gone through adolescence, want to help their children. At the same time, teenagers struggle for independence as they begin the task of separating from the parents.

Our teenagers need to know that as their parents we want to help. They also need to know that we recognize that to grow up is to become reliant on one's own momentum, even if pain is felt. But what can we do in the face of such developmental changes and of the tensions in a child who is at the same time a young man or woman? Fortunately, acute adolescent turmoil doesn't last forever! Your teenager won't always be irritable, moody, sullen, rebellious, hard to reason with, and suspicious that you are quite possibly a major source of his discontent!

The story of Dean, whom you met earlier, is a fine example. Dean visited me nearly two years after the previous interview. As a second-semester freshman in college, he had gained some distance so that he was more at ease with himself and better able to see humor in his adolescence. His is one of the best descriptions of what adolescent stress is all about and provides insight into how it ought to be viewed by parents. "I realize now that there were moments when no matter what my parents said, I would have disagreed with them. I was determined to go my own way, and I wouldn't let anyone persuade me otherwise. But I know that I needed someone to disagree with, someone I could talk with who wouldn't walk away just because I was being a tough talker. When I have children and they grow up to be teenagers, I only hope that I'll have patience with them and not forget that it's not so much what you say, it's your attitude. If you're sending signals that you care and you want to help, to be there, to stand by, then that's what a teenager needs. He may try to pick a fight with you, and he may scream or cry or cuss or whatever. But he needs you there, and you can't forget that. You shouldn't become passive or take abuse, just as you can't rise to every piece of bait thrown at you. I guess you have to keep remembering that with time, a lot changes. Soon this person who seems so completely wrapped up in himself and has no perspective will get a sense of humor about things. And the next thing you know, he's growing up. Then everybody can take a deep breath. I'm beginning to take a deep breath myself, about myself. That's when you know that you won't be a teenager too much longer."

PROFILE OF AN ADOLESCENT: WHAT DO TEENAGERS REALLY WANT?

Adolescents have some pretty strong ideas about what they want and need from parents. Here is how more than 2000 adolescents in a recent poll described "the ten things I want most" from parents:

I want my parents to think I'm somebody (special).

I want my parents to be warm and friendly.

I want my parents to be more concerned about me.

I want my parents to know the me that nobody knows.

I want to express my views and have those views be valued.

I want to go to school with kids I relate to. (Adolescents see parents as controlling this.)

I want to be part of a happy family.

I want my parents to lighten up.

I want to learn more about my emotions.

I want to live in a world at peace. (Adolescents see parents as controlling this through such acts as voting.)

What, if anything, are parents to do? How can we and our adolescents bridge the gap between us, living in harmony and loving and respecting one another all at the same time? Before we can help, we must have a sense of what the adolescent experience is about in today's time.

An adolescent is a person who:

1. Is leaving behind the stages of childhood and working through the stages of adolescence
2. When scared or frightened, slips back into the security of being a child
3. Is undergoing a rapid and intense period of physiological and psychological changes
4. Wants to be independent but does not have a backlog of per-

sonal experiences to use in functioning independently in the society of which he is a part

5. Needs to express his personal needs and to have these needs taken seriously

6. Has not yet formed a cohesive value system that would support him in what to "live for," so this tremendously important anchor of security is not yet within his grasp

7. Is locked into financial and emotional dependence on his family

8. Is trying to make decisions of lasting importance about career exploration, life values, and relationships

9. Vividly notices when there is a discrepancy between the rules and values espoused by adults and adult behavior

10. Has the same intense emotional needs and feelings as adults but limited understanding as to what these emotions mean or how to successfully cope with them in a manner acceptable to adults

11. Has a strong need for adult mentoring and guidance as he constructs a personal identity and tries to acquire a sense of selfhood that will sustain him

12. Feels lonely and alone when parents are physically and emotionally absent; needs them to
    • show love and attention
    • listen and show empathy and patience
    • offer guidance and direction
    • allow experiences for positive growth through exploration
    • encourage separation and independence
    • help him cope with the crises at hand
    • model what it's like to be an adult

13. Without adult nurturing becomes unable to construct a secure self-identity and becomes less competent to meet the challenges inevitable in daily life

14. In the absence of effective adaptive coping skills, becomes debilitated by the ravages of stress

15. When the family situation does not feel nurturing or supportive, has very few options and may in actuality be trapped and helpless or may turn to peers for the fulfillment of these needs

16. Is at risk for high incidence of poor health, alcohol and drug abuse, sexual abuse, family violence, sexual promiscuity, alienation, and suicidal tendencies
17. Is by law a minor

PASSAGE THROUGH PUBERTY

Sometimes we naively assume that the tension and stress between parent and teenager arises out of adolescent "rebellion." While rebellion can certainly contribute to the tension we feel, it is for the most part a symptom of an underlying cause. Much of the stress and tension experienced during the adolescent years is a result of new stages of growth and development and derives from the learning experiences necessary for your adolescent to get on with the tasks and demands of the growth process. During this time a teenager has several important tasks to attend to. These include passage through puberty (that is, sustaining the body and mind through a time of rapid and intense physiological and psychological growth), developing formal operational thinking skills, forming an identity, acquiring a sense of self, and acquiring socialization skills that can sustain him during the adolescent period and move him closer to adulthood.

Adolescence has been termed a period of crisis, a necessary turning point, and a crucial moment when development occurs—rightly so, because several important events occur during this period. The most obvious are the physiological changes. The growth in size, growth of body hair, voice changes, and other outward manifestations of growing reproductive capacity all send strong signals to your adolescent (as well as to his parents and to the immediate society) that, physically, he is maturing and becoming an adult. If all this makes *you* nervous, imagine how the teenager feels as he or she changes into a whole new person!

The outward changes of physical development are constant reminders to your adolescent of how "different" he is from his peers. As he experiences his own changes and observes those of his peers, he forms a strong opinion of his physical self. Coming to terms with his changing body image is not easy for him; these new changes seem rather mystical.

Most adolescents have relatively little information about the wide range of normality or the timetables for the appearance of the various physical manifestations that affect their total body images. In a very real sense, it is the lack of accurate information about the changes during the stage of puberty that causes stress for the adolescent. For girls, the perils of puberty include not understanding the internal and external changes they are so very much aware of and the future of their bodies—potential height, weight, menstruation, breast development, hair growth, body shape and configuration, facial features, and skin conditions. For boys, the perils of puberty include many of the same concerns as those of their female counterparts—height, weight, hair growth, body shape and configuration, skin conditions, and facial features, along with such concerns as wet dreams, spontaneous erections, masturbation, and sexual fantasy.

The changes associated with puberty are overwhelmingly stressful because there are no hard-and-fast answers to the questions, no absolutes. "Why does Jon grow facial hair at thirteen and I still haven't at sixteen?" "Why am I the only one in my class to have a menstrual cycle?" "Why am I so different?" "Am I normal?" "Will I always look like this?" "Will I always sound like this?" "Will I ever feel happy?" These are all questions for which adolescents appear to have few satisfactory answers.

HORMONES: THE BANE OF ADOLESCENT BEHAVIOR

During puberty, hormone levels increase dramatically. These are responsible for setting in motion all the physical changes that transform a child's body into an adult's. The increasing levels of hormones accompanying adolescence bring out many emotional and behavioral changes.

Research at the National Institute of Mental Health is uncovering the link between hormones and adolescent behavior. In an effort to "delineate the course of puberty," psychologists Edith Nottelmann and Elizabeth Susman and their colleagues are studying hormone levels and their relationship to the physical development and behavioral characteristics present during pubertal years. Three groups of hormones were found to rise dramatically during puberty. Together, they are responsible for the dramatic changes occurring in adolescence. These findings are exciting because historically, much of the research on adolescent adjustment and almost all widely disseminated surveys on adolescent problem behavior have reported findings based on chronological age or grade in school. Physical-maturity measures were limited to height and weight, and comparisons were made in relation to age grouping in school grades.

Although chronological age often stands as a developmental marker for processes that are not well understood, such studies are severely limiting when one is looking at the changes occurring in adolescence. Pubertal development, it has been found, is more closely associated with an internal time clock than with chronological age. What this means is that we may be inadvertently hurting our adolescents by adding to their insecurities. A child who is more or less mature than his classmates but who is with them because of his chronological age is going to feel "weird." Every day, he will compare and contrast his abilities, skills, and knowledge with those of his classmates . . . and feel ever more different, out of the group.

Since hormonal changes are a natural part of growing up, and in most cases are inalterable by us, why should we bother understanding and recognizing them? We do so in self-defense.

By identifying hormonal states and fluctuations, we can more accurately predict behavioral changes and thus find ways to offset them. Research also suggests that boys are more at the mercy of hormones than girls and that, to some extent, hormones affect girls and boys in opposite ways.

That changes in hormone level contribute to mood stability is probably not surprising to many parents. As Phyllis, the mother of fourteen-year-old twin girls, laments, "It's good behavior one hour and deplorable behavior the next, happiness at 10:00 and guerilla warfare at 11:00. It's hard for me to keep up with their moods. At first I was concerned with their mental health, but now I'm just worried about mine!" Says one of the twins, "My moods change so often that I feel like I'm going crazy. All I do is apologize for my behaviors. I'm not in charge, my body is. It's an awful feeling." If the woes of Phyllis and her daughters sound familiar, take heart, for your adolescent is "normal" and is simply hard at work with the tasks and demands of puberty.

For the most part, you can see the changes your teenager is going through. You see his growth spurt (and its effect on your bank balance in terms of clothing replacement); you watch him proudly start fingering all three of his chin whiskers. There is, however, a major change going on that you don't see. Believe it or not, his brain is growing.

BRAIN GROWTH

Your teenager's brain will increase in size by about one-third during these already tempestuous times. The final pound of the adult three-pound brain is "added on" when the adolescent is between the ages of twelve and sixteen. This growth involves further development of the nervous system and enhances the brain's efficiency and capability. The growth does not occur continuously but rather in sequences of short periods of rapid growth (during which the neural networks needed for new cognitive functions, such as speaking and reading, are created) and longer periods of practically no growth (when the new functions are integrated into the total, or cognitive, system). On the average, children experience a rapid brain-weight increase of from 5 percent to 10 percent between the ages of two and four, six and nine, ten and twelve, and fourteen and sixteen. This growth spurt occurs during a period of about six months sometime during each two-year period, generally earlier for girls and later for boys. During the ten-to-twelve growth spurt, female brain growth is about three times that of males; during the fourteen-to-sixteen brain-growth period, the situation is reversed, favoring males.

Now that you know and understand the enormity of the changes your teenager is going through, you are more compassionate and tolerant of his mood swings, of his seemingly erratic personality. But sometimes just knowing and understanding isn't enough. If your child shouts an obscenity at you when you simply remind him to do chores, are you really going to stop and say, "Oh, that's all right dear; I understand—it's just that your brain is growing"? Of course not! You're more likely to snarl back or

ground him or take some other punitive action. Compassion
doesn't always translate well into day-to-day situations. How can
you help your child and yourself through these times?

1. PROVIDE INFORMATION

Accurate information about what's going on can help your child
feel comfortable and better accept the individual changes he may
be experiencing. Because they are experts in this area, pediatricians are an excellent first source of information. Additionally,
your family pediatrician knows your child and so will be able to
talk with him about the anxious feelings he is having. School
nurses are also a ready resource for parents. Ask your pediatrician or school nurse for a list of recommended reading. A number
of excellent books for both parent and adolescent are also listed
in the resource section of this book.

2. PERSONALIZE, DON'T GENERALIZE

Sharing your feelings about adolescence with your child can be
very helpful to him. Your ability to empathize with your adolescent contributes to your parent/child relationship. One approach
that I used to help my questioning adolescent gain a perspective
about the changes that occur in facial features over time, for
example, was to frame for her a series of my own pictures from
early childhood right up to the present. Next to it I placed a
similar array of photos of her father, followed by photos of herself
from birth to the present. This proved to be an invaluable tool in
helping her accept her appearance as the one belonging to her
right now, and it also illustrated for her the marked changes that
occur not only throughout adolescence but throughout other life
stages as well.

3. MONITOR REST AND NUTRITION

During this stage of pronounced growth, your adolescent has an
enormous need for adequate rest and nutrition. Researchers have
found that about 90 percent of teenagers do not get enough sleep,
which affects their ability to function at a high level during the
day. Dr. Carskadon of the Stanford University Sleep Center be-
lieves that teens need more sleep than children and recommends

that adolescents between the ages of twelve and seventeen get nine or more hours of sleep each night.

Proper nutrition is also essential to good health and is a significant factor in overall well-being. Studies suggest that the nutrition of teenagers is so imbalanced that they are at risk. The Department of Health and Human Services has found that adolescents consume less than 60 percent of the recommended daily allowances of food nutrients. It is a well-established fact that the breakfast meal is an important part of eating habits in the health equation, yet it is estimated that well over 70 percent of adolescents go to school without eating breakfast. Habits for good nutrition start in the early years. The fitness and nutrition sections in the last chapter of this book will provide suggestions for helping teenagers.

NEW WAYS OF THINKING: FORMAL OPERATIONAL THOUGHT

Along with physical growth, your teenager is going through a stage of mental and intellectual growth. He is learning to expand and change the ways he thinks. Because these changes occur so suddenly, they catch both parents and teens off guard.

Such remarks as "Did you hear what I *said?*" and "Oh my God, I can't believe I said that!" are commonly heard from adolescent children. The unaware parent may simply assume that the "rebellious streak has struck" and levy undue punishment. Doing so only adds to the tension between parent and adolescent. Take heart (and hold on). Your adolescent is climbing one step further up the ladder to adulthood.

Now that your child is a teenager, he has a number of important learning functions to address, the most critical being formal operational thought—learning how to conceptualize "what might be" as opposed to "what is." This more abstract level of thought allows him to go beyond the here and now to comprehend the abstract (such as in philosophy, algebra, and calculus) and to appreciate simile, metaphor, and parody.

There are a number of outcomes of formal operational thought, and flashing a new vocabulary is one of them. When I began writing this book, I asked my daughter and her friends to share with me some slang terms, to tell me some of the expressions that they use daily. What a mistake that was! In the months since I made that seemingly innocuous request, I have been stopped in local stores, at my daughter's school, on the street, anywhere her friends recognize me. From every direction I have heard, "Oh, Dr. Youngs, I have another really awesome word for you. Have you heard . . . ?" Apart from being accosted by adolescents at every turn, I have been surprised by how quickly the slang changes. No sooner did I get several expressions down than I was told "That's not 'live' anymore. *Geez,* Mom!" Heaven forbid that I should include a passé slang expression here.

This experience taught me how important having their own vocabulary is to teenagers, what an integral part of their day-to-day peer interaction it is. One reason young people readily develop their own lingo or slang is that it allows them to practice their new mental abilities and at the same time enables them to define their own tastes, values, and preferences, in their own way. These new abilities give rise to the use of humor and wit, useful in moving outside themselves to view, examine, and define aspects of themselves that are too delicate and too painful to confront in a more serious manner. This doesn't mean that an adolescent is fully aware of his new skills, though he, too, is amazed at his newfound wit.

All of a sudden your adolescent is an astute social critic as well. "That's unfortunate," you say, "because he now criticizes me, too!" Since formal operational thought enables your adolescent to go beyond the real and into the possible, it opens up for him the world of the "ideal" and of "perfection." The concept of "ideal" may result in his gaining a new view of his parents.

It is not uncommon for adolescents in this phase to fantasize that they were adopted but that their real parents (who just happen to be extremely rich and very famous) are coming for them soon. Just like their parents, adolescents are unsuspecting and unprepared for the behavioral changes that follow. One dad remarks, "Yesterday I was his beloved parent. Today, nothing suits my son's tastes. The house is not 'rad,' the car is not 'awesome,' and we are no longer 'totally uptown.' We were walking down the street and a friend of his approached us. My son introduced me to his buddy as 'a friend'! When I asked him about it, he said, 'Geez, Dad, you're wearing *cords*. They went out of style years ago!' "

And if parents are open for attack, peers are geared for guerilla warfare. Adolescents can be quite cruel with one another. Ridiculing comments are all too common. Obviously, such remarks are painful for the adolescent who receives them.

New thinking skills also provide your adolescent with the ability to argue. No doubt you have already learned this! During their early teens, children develop the ability to marshal facts and ideas to make a case. "Do it because I told you to" is no longer considered to be a logical explanation. Rather, your child wants to know the *reasons* she should or shouldn't do something. "You can't have Jenny stay overnight on a school night because you have homework, and besides the house rule is no staying over on a school night" will be met with a reasoned and logical response: "I study better with Jenny's help, and that dumb rule was made two years ago when I was just a kid." Such arguments should be seen for what they are, as an effort by the adolescent to use and exercise her new powers of argument. You might reply, "It's good to know you enjoy studying with Jenny. Should you decide to invite her over for the early part of the evening, I'd be happy to accommodate that. But she will not be able to stay over during the week."

ASSERTIVE CHOICE

You have just read about five outcomes of formal operational thought. There is a sixth one that is not necessarily a natural outcome but is definitely a desirable one. This is a type of thought that we want our children to learn, a skill we want them to master. The following information will help you to learn about assertive choice so that you can pass on your knowledge and newfound skill to your teenager.

One of the most common sources of stress is not being able to tell someone else what we are feeling and thinking. An important reason for teaching your teenager to develop assertiveness skills is to enable him to confidently confront situations that would typically produce anxiety, frustration, and guilt and would otherwise cause him to deny his own feelings and emotions. This confidence is especially important if he is to be effective in making difficult decisions. Assertiveness skills comprise a blueprint for confidence: they provide effective communications, and they enable your child not only to be receptive but also to assert his rights without using intimidation or being intimidated. Assertiveness skills are necessary for managing the conflicts of everyday life.

There are times when you want to tell people how you feel, what you think is important, and what you can and can't do. You want to tell them that you have listened to them but that you cannot do what they want. You want to tell them what irritates or doesn't irritate you, how you work best or how you don't. And you want to do this in a way that is accepted by other people and that gets your point across effectively. It doesn't do you any good to yell or to have people guess what your needs are. They will likely guess wrong, and as a result your needs will not be met. It also doesn't do much good to hope that if you are nice to people they will somehow know what it is you need and give it to you.

Assertion is "owning" what you need, including your emotions, and not putting the responsibility for that ownership on someone else. Assertion is also talking about things in such a way that people will listen and not be offended, giving them the opportunity to respond in return. It is a manner that is direct, self-respecting, self-expressive, and straightforward.

Your adolescent needs to learn to assert what it is that she really wants to say. Perhaps your teenager's best friend has learned that by shouting, pouting, ridiculing, and being intimidating she can get what she wants. Or, she may have learned that by being a sweet, likable "I'll-do-anything-you-want" type of person she can get others to continuously respond to her in the way she wants. Whether she is overly passive or overly aggressive, the behavior is inappropriate. To be assertive means to value yourself —to act with confidence and speak with authority. Let's examine these characteristics.

THE PASSIVE TEENAGER

The passive teenager appears to be a calm, complacent individual who never makes waves and is always willing to do for others. The problem with this type of personality is that the person is not being true to what he or she needs but rather is responding to the needs of others. Eventually, the child will feel that nothing she does is of value, that nothing she says has any effect. This often leads to anger, for when the passive person is denying herself, she is usually "keeping score" of all that she misses, and just when you least expect it she blows up.

You've probably met such a person. When she finally reacts unfavorably to something you have said or done, she brings up incidents from weeks, months, and even years ago.

Donna was asked by her friend Sue to purchase a gift for the upcoming party of a mutual friend. Donna agreed to do it, even though she had other plans that night. She canceled her plans to select a gift that should have been purchased by Sue. The following week, Sue asked Donna to pick up a book from the library for her. The next Tuesday, Sue asked Donna to call a mutual friend with the message that Sue wouldn't be attending a social function. With this, Donna finally exploded. "Why don't you do it? I'm sick of doing you favors. You've asked me for one favor too many!"

Sue was shocked at Donna's outburst. She had no idea that Donna was displeased with her. After all, she had never complained before, and in fact had seemed more than pleased to be of help. The passive person tries very hard to conceal her anger, but the truth is that it usually controls her. The angrier she gets, the more prone she is to explode. And when she does, the anger is usually blown out of proportion.

Dealing with the passive personality is not easy, because you never know when that person is being direct with you. Being passive may at times be necessary, but when it becomes a modus operandi it can be self-destructive and interfere with interpersonal relationships.

THE AGGRESSIVE TEENAGER

At the opposite end of the spectrum is the aggressive person. These are the personality types who find it necessary to have an inordinate amount of control over themselves and everyone else. They may justify their tactless behavior by saying, "Well, at least they know where I stand!" or "I just tell it like it is and let the chips fall where they may." They achieve their goals at the expense of others. Aggressive people want to be in control at all times and will do whatever is necessary to accomplish this. Being in control at all times implies taking the control from others, and this is just what the aggressive person thrives on. As a result, the recipient of such a person's words or actions is often humiliated and usually hurt. No one likes dealing with the aggressive personality. As a result, an aggressive teen is often shunned and avoided. No one likes to be bullied, and the aggressive person is not tolerated for long.

THE ASSERTIVE TEENAGER

We now come back to assertiveness. How do you know an assertive teenager when you see one? There are both nonverbal and verbal cues. The first nonverbal cue is eye contact. The assertive teen uses direct eye contact. This doesn't mean staring someone down and not blinking; it just means looking the other person in the eye and holding the contact fairly steadily throughout the conversation.

The second nonverbal cue is the use of hand gestures. Gestures are most effective when they help emphasize the content and importance of what the speaker is saying. It does not, of course, mean making wild gestures with the hands.

Posture can also indicate assertiveness: sitting or standing straight (not hunched over) and not hiding in the corner of a room. Projecting one's voice—not yelling, but speaking up and not mumbling—is being assertive. It is common to see people make assertive comments and then ruin the effect by either dropping or raising their voices at the end. For example, in your role as parent you might say to your child in a firm voice, "I want you to clean your room immediately." This by itself sounds fine. However, if instead of waiting for a response you then ask, "Okay?" you are destroying the assertiveness of your statement.

Other phrases that can detract from assertiveness (particularly when delivered in a whiny voice) are those such as "You know?"

COMPARISON OF ALTERNATIVE BEHAVIOR STYLES

PASSIVE (Nonassertive)

CHARACTERISTICS	Allow other(s) to choose for you. Emotionally dishonest. Indirect, self-denying, inhibited, win-lose situation, which you lose. If you do get your own way, it is indirect.
YOUR OWN FEELINGS IN THE EXCHANGE	Anxious, ignored, helpless, manipulated. Angry at self and/or other.
OTHERS' FEELINGS IN THE EXCHANGE	Guilty or superior. Frustrated with you.
OTHERS' VIEW OF YOU IN THE EXCHANGE	Lack of respect. Distrustful. May consider you a pushover. Do not know where you stand.
UNDERLYING BELIEF SYSTEM	I should never make anyone uncomfortable or displeased . . . except myself.
OUTCOME	Others achieve their goals at your expense. Your rights are violated.

or "You know what I mean?" Being assertive involves knowing when to stop talking.

One hallmark of assertive behavior is the making of *I* statements, such as "I feel, I like, I wish, I would appreciate, I need." The passive teenager puts responsibility on someone else, often finishing a statement by asking, "Don't you think so?"

ASSERTIVE	AGGRESSIVE
Choose for self. Appropriately honest. Direct, self-respecting, self-expressing, straightforward. Convert win-lose to win-win.	Choose for others. Inappropriately honest (tactless). Direct, self-enhancing. Self-expressive in derogatory manner. Win-lose situation, which you win.
Confident, self-respecting, goal-oriented, valued. Later: accomplished.	Righteous, superior, disparaging, controlling. Later: possibly guilty.
Valued, respected.	Humiliated, defensive, resentful, hurt.
Respectful, trusting, know where you stand.	Vengeful, angry, distrustful, fearful.
I have a responsibility to protect my own rights, and I respect others but not necessarily their behavior.	I have to put others down in order to protect myself.
Outcome determined by aboveboard negotiation. Your rights and others' rights respected.	You achieve your goal at others' expense. Your rights upheld; rights of others violated.

Statements that affirm what you are feeling and what you need imply taking responsibility for your own decision making. The assertive teen has control and has the choice to be more assertive or nonassertive in a given situation. Assertive choice gives you options.

Successful communication is that in which you are honest with yourself; you are direct and straightforward and in control of the situation without causing anyone else undue pain. People respect honesty, even if it is criticism, if it is presented in a way that is understood.

Are *you* more often assertive, aggressive, or passive?

Now that you have learned what assertiveness is, how to acquire it, and when to use it, you are ready to share your knowledge with your teenager. As has been emphasized, you as a parent are a leading role model for your child. If you learn and use assertive choice, your child will do the same.

As part of our own assertiveness, we must differentiate between acceptance and approval. You can tolerate unlikable behavior or remarks without sanctioning them. For example, James's father might say, "James, I can't stop you from swearing and using vulgar language when you are away from me, though I would prefer that you didn't. However, it is not appropriate in the house and will not be tolerated." This demonstrates a respect for the teenager at the same time that it acknowledges the family's rights. The communication-skills section in chapter 2 provides additional suggestions that will help you and your teenager keep channels of communication open with respect and dignity.

TEACHING YOUR CHILD HOW TO THINK ABOUT THINKING

Adolescents think that parents and the events in their lives cause them to feel the way that they do. Thus, they often blame someone else for their feelings of stress and emotional upset. In doing this, however, they often neglect an important factor, and that is that the way we think determines our behavior and thus our responses to stressful situations. From time to time, we all engage in faulty or irrational thinking. What we say to ourselves before, during, and after an incident greatly influences our feelings and behaviors.

Cognitive restructuring is a fancy name for a technique for dealing constructively with feelings of stress that arise from irrational or faulty thinking. The concept of cognitive restructuring can best be understood by first considering the relationship among thoughts, feelings, and behaviors. Perhaps you have heard someone say, "I can't help the way I feel—it just happens." This assumes that thoughts and feelings occur independently and are not directly related. However, the opposite is true. Rarely does a feeling "just happen," and we *do* have the capability to change the way we feel. It is not so much the presence of irrational ideas that leads to disturbing emotions but the absence of coping skills.

One way of examining the relationship among thoughts, feelings, and behaviors is shown in the following example, in which *A* refers to the activating event. Let's say that you reprimand your adolescent for having failed to follow through on a responsibility (in this case, for not completing homework and taking care of pets). Following this reprimand your child may feel upset, angry, or defensive. *C* represents your child's feelings about the event and also includes behaviors. For example, upon being held accountable for homework and pet care, a child might become defensive and shout, "Why do I do all the work around here?" In this case, the adolescent mistakenly assumes that *A*, the event, has led directly to *C*, feelings and behaviors. Let's examine this more closely.

A ACTIVATING EVENT
(parental reprimand)

"I know you wanted to see the television special at 6:00, Jon, but you won't be able to. It's 5:50 and your homework isn't done, and your pet hasn't been cared for, as was your responsibility to-night."

C FEELINGS AND BEHAVIORS
(upset, angry, defensive)

Jon assumes that his mother made him upset and angry and that he therefore has a right to be defensive. After all, she did reprimand him. Something very important, however, occurs between *A* and *C*, producing *B*, self-talk. That self-talk influences feelings and behavior. Let's look at Jon's thinking:

B   JON'S THINKING

"Mom is made at me. She thinks I'm lazy, bad, and irresponsible. She knows how much I wanted to see that television special. If she cared, she would let me watch it."

While Jon's mother did initiate the process, it is Jon's thinking that produced his feelings. The self-talk can be rational or irrational, functional or dysfunctional. Since even the best of us make errors and are unable to always live up to our self-expectations, it is important to look at the sources of B and at our most common self-statements. These self-statements can become habitual responses to stress (for example, smiling or drinking) and need to be changed, like other undesirable habits. A different and more positive scenario of self-talk on Jon's part might be as follows:

B   JON'S THINKING

"I wish I had completed my chores. My homework is due tomorrow, and my dog depends on me for care. It's not too much work, and I did commit to doing it before the program."

Now let's see how this thinking would affect Jon's behavior.

C   FEELINGS AND BEHAVIORS

Disappointment. "I really am sorry. I knew I should have completed my chores before my friend came over, and I should have told him I would have to visit another time, since I had a pretty tight schedule tonight. I should apologize to my mom and explain what happened. I really do want her to trust me and to feel that I can be counted on. I think I'll ask if I can watch the program as soon as I care for my dog and see if I can complete my homework after that."

This example shows that one event can be perceived in a variety of ways and can result in a number of different emotional responses. It is not so much the stressful event that makes us tense, then, but rather how we think of that event.

Sometimes even when we are aware that thoughts somehow lead to feelings, we fail to realize that we actually have the ability to change unwanted or irrational thoughts voluntarily so that different emotional feelings will result. By helping our teenagers learn and practice cognitive restructuring, we can reduce the stress between parent and child. We can also increase relatively positive feelings. Part of managing stress means learning to understand our thinking and feeling processes. Recognizing that the way we think determines the way we feel requires some changes in our usual way of dealing with ourselves and our interactions.

ESTEEMING THE SELF

Caught up with the many transformations he is undergoing in his body, facial structure, feelings, and thinking powers, your adolescent quite naturally becomes focused on self. He develops a kind of delusion of uniqueness: "No one feels the way I do about anything; no one has ever had this problem." Or, "This is unbearable. You can't solve this problem. No one can." He may fear that he is not "normal." Tormented by issues that seem private and personal, such as the need to belong, to be accepted, to be special, and to be loved, he has yet to learn that many fears, anxieties, doubts, and needs are universally shared by all.

As a natural consequence of focusing on self, your teenager will also develop a self-concept. If his opinion of himself is unrealistic or untrue—for example, if he feels unworthy or unlovable—these feelings will influence the way he treats others and are very influential in later life. If he is unable to love himself or finds himself unworthy, the teenager may have difficulty in forming close relationships, or he may distance himself from people and actually not allow for the opportunity to feel worthy or to be loved. In this sense, the self-concept can become a self-fulfilling prophecy.

Your teenager will need to learn the importance of self-concept and its contribution to his well-being. He must also assume the responsibility for being in charge of its care. Self-esteem is made up of the positive and/or negative thoughts and feelings we have about ourselves.

Positive	*Negative*
I'm attractive.	I'm not good looking.
I'm smart.	I'm dumb.
I'm fit.	I'm fat (skinny).

I learn from my mistakes.	I'm afraid to fail.
I'm fun.	I'm boring.
I'm a good friend.	Why should anyone like me?

The more positive feelings your child has about himself, the higher his self-esteem will be. Conversely, the more negative feelings he has, the lower his self-esteem.

High self-esteem is very important because it enables the person who possesses it to:

Accept challenges. When you have high self-esteem, you're not afraid to develop your abilities. You're willing to risk trying new things. If you don't try, you can't grow.

Enrich your life. Happy people are a joy to be around. By being happier with yourself, you'll be eager to meet new friends. By being more comfortable and open about yourself, you'll develop closer relationships.

Maintain self-confidence. Believing you can do something is half the battle; it allows you to involve yourself completely with whatever you're doing. Wholehearted effort helps improve performance.

Remain flexible. Change isn't always easy. It's unfamiliar and frightening at times. However, a positive self-image makes it easier to accept new ideas and ways of doing things.

The following are among the common effects of low self-esteem:

Lack of self-confidence. People with low self-esteem often have little confidence in their abilities. They may assume that they are doomed to fail again because they have failed before.

Poor performance. Lack of self-confidence may result in a person's making little or no effort toward realizing projects or goals. However, failures that result from a lack of effort are not a true reflection of a person's abilities.

Distorted view of self and others. Some people won't give themselves credit for their accomplishments and may think others look better in comparison. They may also believe that things "just happen" to them, that they don't make things happen.

Unhappy personal life. Negative people are not fun to be around. People with low self-esteem find it hard to develop close relationships. The result may be a lonesome and unhappy personal life.

THE SELF-ESTEEM PROFILE

Is your teenager easily hurt by criticism? Here's a profile to help you and your teenager examine her self-esteem. Have her answer yes or no to the following questions, then read the scoring profile below. One thing to keep in mind is that most teenagers feel bad about themselves from time to time. Therefore, in answering these questions your teenager should think about how she feels *most* of the time.

Do you accept constructive criticism?

Are you at ease meeting new people?

Are you honest and open about your feelings?

Do you value your closest relationships?

Are you able to laugh at (and learn from) your own mistakes?

Do you notice and accept changes in yourself as they occur?

Do you look for and tackle new challenges?

Are you confident about your physical appearance?

Do you give yourself credit when credit is due?

Are you happy for others when they succeed?

If your teenager answered most of these questions yes, she probably has a healthy opinion of herself. Whatever the level of your child's self-esteem now, you can help her take positive steps to improve it.

Are you very shy or overly aggressive?

Do you try to hide your feelings from others?

Do you fear close relationships?

Do you try to blame your mistakes on others?

Do you find excuses for refusing to change?

Do you continually wish you could change your physical appearance?

Are you too modest about personal successes?

Are you glad when others fail?

If your teenager answered yes to most of these questions, her self-esteem could probably use improvement.

Here's how you can help your teenager personally care for her self-concept.

Acceptance. Help your adolescent identify and accept strengths and weaknesses. Everyone has both.

Encouragement. Take a "can-do" attitude. Help your adolescent set a reasonable timetable for personal goals, and offer encouragement along the way.

Praise your adolescent for, and encourage her to take pride in, her achievements, both great and small. Experiences are personal. We must each enjoy our own.

Time. Teach your child the importance of taking time out regularly to be alone with personal thoughts and feelings and of getting involved in activities she can enjoy by herself (for example, crafts, reading, or individual sports). She must learn to enjoy her own company.

Trust. Encourage your adolescent to pay attention to her thoughts and feelings, to act on what she thinks is right. Doing what makes her feel happy and fulfilled will be a rewarding experience.

Respect. Help your adolescent value herself and not try to be someone else. Help her explore and appreciate her own special talents.

Love. Your adolescent must come to love herself. This is done by accepting and learning from mistakes and not overreacting to errors, and by accepting her successes and failures as those who love her do.

THE ACTUAL, IDEAL, AND PUBLIC SELVES

You can help your adolescent lessen the discrepancies between the emerging self and the "old" self. An area that may cause both intrapersonal and interpersonal stress for your teenager involves the differences that exist between the actual, ideal, and public "selves." The actual self is the opinion he holds of himself; the ideal self is how he would like to be; and the public self is the person he shows to others—the image projected in public. "Putting up a good front," or projecting an acceptable image, is something we all engage in from time to time. When the discrepancies between public and private selves are too great, however, the stress experienced can be enormous. When a teen's actual and ideal selves are different, he may experience varying degrees of an inner stress that is reflected in his dealings with others.

You can help your adolescent examine the characteristics of each of his own "selves." Have him list on a sheet of paper eight to ten words or phrases to describe each "self."

1. Actual self (his private opinion of himself).
2. Ideal self (how he would like to be).
3. Public self (the person he projects in public).
   - In what ways do your actual self and ideal self differ?
   - How different are your public and private selves?
   - In what ways does this cause stress for you?

How might you go about bringing your selves closer together? For example, could you change some of your self-imposed demands, unrealistic expectations, or irrational beliefs or learn to be more assertive?

Remember, also, to be supportive of your teenager. While you may enjoy teasing your teen by saying such things as, "Oh, you're *unique,* all right. Actually, I think *bizarre* would be a better word for you!" It is important to realize that your child takes this feeling of uniqueness seriously. In the same way that you would be frightened if you thought you had a disease that no one else had ever had and for which there was no cure, your teenager may be frightened by his uniqueness. You would want reassurance; your teenager is no different.

One way to help your child get such reassurance is to have him join a support group. Support groups for teens (also mentioned in other chapters) are excellent because they allow the teenager to share his concern with others his own age. The sharing of concerns helps the teen develop a better sense of the fact that the problems from which he suffers are common, experienced by many others.

BEFORE IDENTITY CRISIS: IDENTITY

Another outcome of your adolescent's new stage of growth and development is that he begins to take a different and more complex view of himself. "Who is this person?" he wonders. "Who am I?" The need to share and articulate values, ideals, plans, and expectations begins to shape the teenager's identity. The adolescent phase is a time for discovering the true self, for identifying and articulating feelings that are constant over time ("What do I stand for?" "What do I believe in?").

The search for identity may lead your adolescent to adopt—at least temporarily—moral, religious, and political ideologies that are different from yours. In order for him to develop a mature and differentiated ego identity, it is necessary for him to question and challenge the value systems, goals, beliefs, and ideals with which he has been reared. Understanding this facet of adolescent development can help you feel less anxious about your teenager's scrutiny and occasional rejection of the standards you have set. This search is often as painful and stressful for your child as it is for you.

You should recognize that your teenager's need for growth and autonomy and your needs for maintenance and continuity of family structure may conflict with each other at this time. "Where did

I go wrong?" you may ask. Be assured that this situation does not necessarily mean that there is serious conflict between you and your teenager. The process of adolescent identity formation is a natural (rather than rebellious) state.

Whether it is a natural part of growing up or not, your child's attempts to influence your attitudes and behaviors to a greater extent than was common in childhood and the resultant disturbance in the equilibrium between you causes stress. Rules once accepted are challenged. Now that your adolescent is capable of conceptualizing ideas, attitudes, and feelings, you notice that your parent/child relationship begins to change. Sometimes a parent feels ambivalent about allowing a dependent child to become an independent adult. A parent may send her child mixed messages: "You're a child, but not a child; a young adult, but not a young adult"; "Grow up," but later, "Act your age."

This confusing pattern is characteristic of an adolescent's life. When the child moves into his teens, the outside world does make demands on him, and it does so in no uncertain manner. His teachers expect him to produce, almost to the extent that an adult must produce at work. While guarded and treated like a child at home, he is told by the outside world to "shape up and be productive." The messages are double signals.

To minimize the stress and tension for everyone, here's what you as a parent can do:

ACCEPT CHANGE

Throughout their children's adolescent years, parents must be oriented to the inevitable need to modify or change. If a parent is unwilling to transform rules to allow for change and growth in the "new" teenager, the stress between parent and child will be monumental.

COMMUNICATE/NEGOTIATE

Shared communication is a real key. Even if you have clear and explicitly defined rules for maintaining stability in your family, it will be necessary to negotiate new ones. We have already examined a number of communication skills to help you in this process.

EMPATHIZE

As your adolescent puts childhood aside and moves into the adolescent stage, he sometimes experiences loss. He may become confused or frightened by the complexity of tasks, demands, and (unknown) changes confronting him and slip back into the security of being a child.

There is another situation that further complicates the process of identity articulation in the adolescent: messages from peers.

PARENTS VERSUS PEERS: WHO IS NUMBER ONE?

Is there a parent in the world who hasn't had this experience? Your child comes out of his room wearing a new sweater and asks you your opinion. You say, "Oh, you look so *cute* in that!"—and then see only the dust as the teen runs back into his room to change. Even if you had been wise enough to choose an adjective other than "cute," chances are your opinion, if it carried any weight at all, was a negative factor (that is, if *you* liked it, he would run to change it). But let your teen model that same sweater for a friend and hear, "Radical, man!" and you won't be able to pry that sweater off him until his wedding day! In short, your opinion is beginning to matter less and that of his peers, more.

A number of studies have shown that as children begin puberty, parents feel great concern and helplessness. They see themselves as having less influence on their children than peers do. The children, however, consider their parents to be the greatest influence on them, although they also say that they do not know their parents' views on a number of topics. Research confirms that many parents feel poorly equipped to deal with the biological, psychological, and social changes of their children during the early adolescent period. Whatever the underlying reasons for this insecurity and weakening of parental authority, when accustomed parental guidance is withdrawn the young person is thrust toward uncritical acceptance of the peer group as a model and a major coping resource.

While this allegiance to the peer group may be useful in alleviating the adolescent's immediate anxieties, it has serious limitations. It is not a substitute for parental guidance. The peer group at this stage is usually too shallow and rigid to afford the necessary direction for growth and development. When the peer group is organized around drugs and/or acting-out behaviors, other fears are realized.

Peer pressure in and of itself has no power. The peer group is powerful only when teenagers turn to their peers for the fulfillment of needs not met at home. Fourteen-year-old Dee, the only child of divorced parents, felt lonely. Her mother worked until nearly 6:00 each night, and Dee got home from school at 3:00. When her mother was home, she spent a considerable amount of time with the man to whom she was now engaged. Seeing her mother so happy and in love made Dee feel even more alone; she longed to belong to someone, too. She turned to her peers, and she went along with any antic as long as it meant that she would be accepted. Her mother was shocked and outraged when the school called and alerted her to Dee's role in setting two fires in the girls' restroom. Said Dee, "We did it the first time as a joke. My friends dared me to do it again, and they said I wouldn't be invited to join the club if I didn't. I thought, I have to belong to the group."

This example shows a negative peer-group influence. However, when children are able to assert themselves without feeling intimidated or fearing recrimination, then the peer group serves as a constructive experience. Peer groups help shape the common experiences of the adolescent culture, thus determining the framework in which the adolescent gains appropriate experiences. What is acceptable? What is not? Some of the adaptive tasks for which positive peer support can be especially valuable are

- Preserving a satisfactory self-image and sense of being valued by others
- Appraising and reappraising of the meaning, degree of threat, and opportunities of new situations
- Learning about new roles
- Preserving reasonable emotional balance by having depend-

able sources of reassurance and comfort in distress, as well as resources for reduction of tension by encouragement to express feelings freely

- Obtaining new information, developing new perspectives and new alternatives for dealing with situations; learning from the pooling of others' information
- Having someone of his own (belonging)
- Learning appropriate behavior, seeking role models whose behavior can be adapted or adopted
- Obtaining reliable feedback about behaviors, plans, and goals and modifying the level of aspiration
- Acquiring growth-promoting skills (for example, through practice in moderating aggression, learning to be assertive, and using social skills
- Validating identity and values
- Identifying a supportive group for engaging in hobbies, sports, or recreational activities that are unfamiliar or that seem difficult
- Learning the formal role of socialization

In general, the influence of peers is closely tied to learning how to socialize. The coming together, customs, and rituals are all signals indicating that one belongs to the group. But moving from childhood to adolescence creates a sort of culture shock for your teenager. Friendships were once easier—a child who was good at baseball found acceptance in the sports group. If you had a bicycle, you were a part of the street fun. Now that your child is an adolescent, the rules among friends have changed. Alas, this, too, is a new experience, and often not always a positive one. Initiation rites as well as acts of rejection and exclusion can be devastating to young people. The need to belong is a compelling force and a powerful human need. To avoid becoming a victim of negative peer influence, your teenager will need a strong sense of self.

When was the last time your teenager asked you, "Is it okay if I go to the concert with my peer group?" Wouldn't you find it difficult to keep a straight face if your adolescent brought home a youngster and said, "I'd like you to meet Don, a member of my peer group." A teenager would almost never use such a cold, clinical term. She would simply talk about her "friends." Because your child's friends are such a critical part of her life, it is important to understand the nature of friendship and how it affects all of us.

There is no doubt that peer friendships play a very important role in the lives of adolescents. We talk a lot about the importance of friendship, but we never seem to formally identify for children the characteristics of friendship that, if understood, can lead to more satisfying relationships (and a better sense of well-being).

The friendships formed by your adolescent fall into two categories: external and internal. Delineating the distinct elements of each of these categories can help you to assess the value placed on friendships by your teenager and provide you with insight into the skills she will need to interact with friends.

EXTERNAL FRIENDS

This category is characterized by convenience and availability.

1. *Physical proximity.* The availability of someone who lives down the street or is in your child's French class increases the frequency of interaction and provides friends with opportunities (mostly of convenience) to "use" each other in times of need. This *situational friendship* may not possess the elements necessary for building a deep relationship.

2. *Cooperation versus competition.* Adolescents, like adults, tend to like others who cooperate with them in their attempts to attain personal goals and rewards. Similarly, they tend to dislike those who hinder or contradict their quests for self-fulfillment. It is not uncommon for an adolescent to develop a friend for the duration of a project and to drop her as soon as the project is over. Baffled by the change, neither child will be able to fully articulate what has happened.

3. *Esteem fulfillment.* Teenagers side with those who "like" them, see them in a positive light, and "promote" them (talk well of them). This gives testimony to the adolescent that he is functioning in a logical and acceptable manner. It does not mean that

the friendship is mutual, however, only that the friendship serves the purpose of developing esteem. John, for example, may value Jimmy's company because Jimmy is constantly boasting about John's successes.

INTERNAL FRIENDS

The second category is characterized by mutual feelings in each of the following areas:

1. Respect. Friends respect each other in the sense of assuming that each exercises good judgment in making choices. ("I'll check with Melody. She always does what's best.")

2. Trust. They share mutual trust in the sense that each assumes that the other will act in light of his or her friend's best interest. This promotes a loyalty. ("I know that I can count on her —she never lets me down, just as I'm always there for her.")

3. Understanding. Friends have a sense of what is important to each other and why a friend does what he does. They are not puzzled or mystified by each other's behavior. ("I can usually figure out what's wrong when he's upset.")

4. Enjoyment. They genuinely enjoy each other's company, even in times of working through difficulties. ("I always feel so good about myself when I'm with her.")

5. Acceptance. They accept each other as they are, without trying to change or make the other into a new or different person. ("She appreciates my style. She appreciates me.")

6. Confiding. They share experiences and feelings with each other. ("She tells me things that no one knows about her.")

You can help your adolescent understand the value she places on friendships. If she understands more about her interactions with her peers, she can better become responsible for her communication with others. This also helps your teenager to develop positive feelings about herself and her ability to successfully manage her peer-group relationships.

MUSIC AND OTHER "NOISE"

Music has a profound influence on *all* of us. To a teenager, music represents many things: peer-group acceptance (knowing all the lyrics to the same songs as your friends), rebellion ("Anything mom and dad can't stand can't be all bad!"), and uniqueness ("No one else can really understand these lyrics—they describe my life perfectly!"). Music to a teen is not just the noise it may be to you; it is a way of life. We must recognize that and respect it.

The issue here is not what constitutes "good" music—I happen to enjoy some of my daughter's music—but what is the detrimental effect of certain sounds on your child's physical and psychological well-being. The work of numerous researchers has proven that whether you hear a sound consciously or unconsciously, your body responds to it, especially at the cellular level. While some sounds can keep us well and "in tune" with ourselves, others can make us literally ill. The notion that it is possible to harness the positive forces of sound to create good health (physical and psychological harmony as well as balance) and to minimize the negative effects of harsh, unnatural sound vibrations merits attention. It is particularly so with teenagers, since sound occupies a good number of hours in their day.

Radionics is the study of vibrations and their relationship to the health and vigor of the body, particularly the muscles and organs. Musical rhythms affect both our hearts and our brains. Both soft and hard rock produce physiological and psychological tension. Our responses to musical tempo are thus linked to our body's own rhythms. Human hearts normally function at a rhythm of about 70 to 80 beats per minute. Most music is paced at this tempo, which we perceive as moderate. Slow music slows down heart rate and pulse. Insistent rhythms arouse a range of agitated feelings (such as tension, excitement, and sexual arousal). Sedate rhythms cause a range of soothing feelings (relaxation, calmness, sensuality).

It is *not* a good idea, for example, for your teenager to wake up to raucous albums early in the morning or to play such albums last thing at night. Morning is a time, however, for some uplifting music. And at night, relaxing music can help your teen prepare for a restful sleep.

Show your child how to relax with music. Put on a tape or record that fills the environment with relaxing, comforting sounds. Select the album or albums that will appeal to and still soothe your adolescent. The National Music Association (NMA) has compiled a catalogue listing highly relaxing and meditative soothing music to bring about body and muscular relaxation. This list can be found in most major music stores. With your teenager, use soothing music with the relaxation techniques recommended in the stress-prevention chapter in this book. As the music plays, take note of what is happening to your bodies and minds as they grow calm and relaxed. Discuss how your physical bodies and your emotions react to different kinds of music. Keep in mind that you are teaching your teen to listen selectively and to use sound in a positive, health-promoting way.

Sound contributes to stress when we perceive it as noise. Noise —a psychological concept defined as undesirable sound—produces annoyance if it interferes with listening, distracts from task performance, or breaks our pattern of concentration. The degree of annoyance is determined by the extent to which we are willing or able to alleviate the causes of the annoyance.

A child may be able to control some of the noise in and around his home. However, this may not be the case in school. Recent research indicates that noise in a school environment has a wide range of adverse health effects on adolescents—including, according to the former surgeon general of the United States, William H. Stewart, adverse physiological changes in the body's cardiovascular, glandular, and respiratory systems and in neuromuscular functioning. Apart from dramatic physical impacts, noise-induced stress can significantly lower the quality of an adolescent's emotional life. Too much noise can close in on her, making her irritable, frustrated, and tense. She won't understand why she is in such a bad mood all the time and thus becomes even more frustrated. The cycle feeds on itself, making the bewildered adolescent less able to manage conflict and change.

In the case of noise-induced stress, the first step is awareness.

Determine or help your teen determine what sounds are closing in on her and making her life miserable. You can do this by having your teenager keep a log to help her pinpoint the noise, recognize how the noise makes her feel, determine whether she is overreacting to it, and develop coping skills. Identifying the exact noise is the first step toward eliminating or reducing the stress. Also, knowing the cause of her bad moods will be reassuring to her. She'll see that she's not really a bad-tempered person but just a normal person reacting to a bad situation. The following format is a simple one your teenager may want to use to get started.

Nature of Sound _____

Time of Occurrence _____

Frequency _____

My Feelings _____

Coping Mechanisms _____

Let's take a look at how a sixteen-year-old might fill out this log. Marcy spent the morning shouting at her sister, bursting into tears when her mother told her to clean her room, and snapping at her friends on the telephone. At the suggestion of her mother, Marcy sat down and wrote in her noise journal. It reads as follows:

Nature of Sound: My baby brother George keeps screaming and screaming. It seems as if he is never going to stop!

Time of Occurrence: George has been crying all morning. I think he is teething. He has cried every morning this week. He has the room right next to mine and wakes me up every morning.

Frequency: Constantly. George never seems to shut up. I can't even have telephone conversations with my friends because of his noise.

My Feelings: I'm mad at George. I know he can't help crying, but I wish he'd stop. I'm mad at my mother, too, for letting

him cry. Why doesn't she do something to make him stop? If
I cry, she makes me stop right away.

Coping Mechanisms: I could leave the house, take a walk, or
go ride my bike just to get away. I could tell mom how much
I hate that crying and ask her to do something. Maybe I could
sleep in my sister's room or on the couch so that I wouldn't
be awakened each morning by George's crying. Maybe I could
take a little more time to talk to him and soothe him.

This procedure will move both Marcy and her mother toward a
constructive approach in reducing Marcy's anxiety and increasing
her well-being. The log is also a good springboard for talking about
how sounds in your home affect each member of your household.
Does your teenager's favorite record album have much the same
effect on you as Marcy's teething brother had on her? If so, and if
you share it in this manner, your teenager is more likely to show
empathy for others and consideration for their feelings and needs.

In this chapter we have been learning more about your teenager's growth and development and about how these special demands create stress for both you and your teenager. But not all
of the stress she experiences is of her own doing. In addition to the
expected normal stresses of being a teenager in a family, teenagers can undergo extra stress as a result of today's family situations. In the next chapter we will look at the family.

CHAPTER FOUR

War and Peace: Family Stress

Many of us who are parents of adolescents today may have wonderful memories of our own youth, memories of two-parent families whose members pulled together and supported one another. Imagine your teenager twenty years from now, recalling her teenage years in the bosom of her family. Will she see a loving, supportive family scene, or will the picture be one of chaos? Will she see a family unit sitting at a table having dinner together, or individual members grabbing quick sandwiches and going their own ways? Most important, will she get the same warm, secure feeling you probably have from your own memories, or will her stomach tighten from feelings of anxiety? Will there be anger and bitterness? What kind of memories of her family are you building for your teenager?

This chapter is about the dark side of the family unit, the side that causes stress in teenagers. Instead of being a strong foundation on which a child can confidently build her life, a family may be a desert of shifting sands. In the next few pages, we are going to discuss how today's families differ from yesterday's, how you can identify whether your family is adding to your adolescent's already full load of stress, and how you can help to eliminate or lessen family stress.

ARE HAPPY FAMILIES ALL ALIKE?

In advertisements for a study it was conducting on the family unit in search of the "happy family," *Newsweek* magazine stated that "the 'family' is changing. Once upon a time families were all alike. Happy. But today even the happy family isn't the same . . . the family just isn't what it used to be. Today the family has become a barometer of the social, psychological, and sexual upheaval that's shaking up our nation." If *Newsweek* is correct, this could explain why, more and more, families are seen in all shapes and sizes—married families, unmarried families, single-parent families, teenage-parent families, stepfamilies, and midcareer-parent families. No family is exempt from the influence of social change, and no doubt each will experience stress as it goes about "being a family."

Major changes have taken place in the ways in which we live together. In 1955, 60 percent of the households in the United States consisted of a father who worked outside the home, a mother who was a housewife, and two or more school-age children. In 1980, that kind of family unit existed in only 11 percent of our homes. In 1986 the figure was 7 percent—an astonishing change. Nearly 74 percent of women are in the work force, and that percentage will undoubtedly increase. Of our 80 million households, almost 20 million consist of one adult and one child, with adolescents making up 14 percent of these children. There is evidence that a similar trend is in store for the future. According to the Census, 61 percent of the children born in the United States in 1980 will live with only one parent before they reach the age of eighteen; this has now become the *normal* childhood experience. Of every 100 children born today,

17 will be born out of wedlock

48 will be born of parents who will be divorced before the child is eighteen

6 will be born to parents who separate

4 will be born into families in which one of the parents will die before the child is eighteen

25 will reach age eighteen "normally"

A child often acts as a good barometer of what is taking place in the home. When family problems or stress occur, a child may act out or demonstrate through his behavior how he is feeling. For example, a sixteen-year-old boy who is not allowed to express any anger toward his father may vent that anger at school by getting into fights with other students. A thirteen-year-old whose parents are going through a divorce may not be able to express her anxiety directly and might develop physical symptoms of that stress, such as stomachaches.

Sometimes we have difficulty detecting family stress because we focus too narrowly on the behavior of the child and do not attempt to trace it back to where it began. Thus, the teenager who is continually getting into fights in school may inappropriately be seen as "going through a rebellious stage," while the real source of trouble is ignored. The adolescent who is developing stomach problems may be checked out by the family doctor, given a clean bill of health, and, if the problem continues, seen as a child who has a fear of going to school. Because of the broad spectrum of events that can contribute to these types of problem behaviors, it is necessary to do more than just look at the behavior of the child. It is critical to seek the causes of the undesirable behavior and to determine whether family stresses are contributing to the child's problems.

ASSESSING FAMILY STRESS

You love your child, and are hopeful that your family is a haven for him to come home to. But what if you're wrong? What if you, with the best intentions in the world, are creating an environment that fills your child with insecurity and stress? "Wait a minute," you say. "I know my child is under stress, but our family isn't the cause of it."

How can you tell whether your child is experiencing family stress? One of the first things to do is to examine the behavioral and emotional manifestations of the stressors. A child typically demonstrates these by misbehaving, withdrawing, suddenly doing poorly in school, or developing psychosomatic problems.

Once you have determined that your child is stressed and is exhibiting the classic symptoms of a nervous and anxious adolescent, it is important that you identify the sources of that stress. Go back and look for its beginnings, using the following questions as guidelines:

1. Is the origin of the stressor from within the family system (mother goes back to work) or from outside the family (loss of a job)?
2. Does the impact of the stressor extend directly to all family members (divorce) or only to some members (adolescent has argument with friend)?
3. Is the onset of the stressor very sudden (illness), or does it emerge gradually (pregnancy)?
4. Is the degree of severity of the stressor intense (a death) or mild (nonserious illness)?
5. Is the length of adjustment to the stressor short-term (child starts school) or long-term (terminal illness)?
6. Can the stressor be expected (child becoming an adolescent), or does it occur unpredictably (an auto accident?)
7. Does the family believe the stressor is one that can be dealt with (adjusting to a new home), or is it beyond control (inflation's effect on the family finances)?

It is important to ask these and other questions that explore the changes and events that have occurred within your family in the recent past. In addition to this, parents should be aware of developmental issues that may be occurring. Is your child spending more time away from the family because of a need to establish a personal identity? Is your child's sudden drop in grades due to a growing social interest? These questions need to be answered in order to prevent emotional overreacting or miscommunication between you and your child.

There are three broad categories of stressors that can cause problems for teenagers in families. These include the rapid growth and development of the teenager, external factors (especially a parental separation, divorce, or remarriage), and family dynamics.

GROWING PAINS

As a child progresses through the various developmental stages of infancy, childhood, adolescence, and young adulthood, he manifests changes in his behavior and emotions in relation to his physical growth that affect not only himself but everyone else in the family as well. Chapter 3 examined some of the important developmental stages for adolescents as these relate to the stresses inherent in the tasks and demands of those stages. These are very natural and common events (such as identity crises in the adolescent) that can contribute to varying degrees of stress within the family. When parents and their children are aware of the changes and the likely types of behaviors to expect within each of these stages, the family is better equipped to cope effectively with the stresses that arise.

Of course, it is not the adolescent alone who shows the stress of proceeding through the life cycle. Parents themselves go through the stages of young, middle, and older adulthood. The needs of family members may overlap and complement one another, or they may conflict or compete with one another. Parents may be going through one kind of developmental stage while the adolescent works through another. Often, parents are heard to say, I wish I had been more settled in my career (or my marriage or with myself) when my children were teenagers. They needed me more at that time than any other. I just wasn't able to give them what I could now that I'm more established (more self-secure and self-assured).

In recent years, we have become more aware and more sensitive to the key emotional and social (psychosocial) crises that each of us experiences throughout the stages of our lives. Normal family stages, then, are an important and often overlooked source of stress. Just as with catastrophic stress, this type of stress requires adjustment and adaptation by family members.

HOW COULD THEY DO THIS TO ME?

A second major source of stress for teenagers is events external to the child. Factors outside the teenager's control may contribute to his anxiety and insecurity. Examples of such factors are

> the family moves to a new city
>
> a parent changes jobs
>
> a previously nonworking parent acquires a job (or a parent loses a job)
>
> the parents separate, divorce, or remarry

This final factor is the predominant cause of external family stress for today's teenager. An adolescent today has a significant likelihood of living in a home in which his parents separate, divorce, or one or both remarry. These factors are wholly outside the teenager's control. How the family deals with such a situation determines the level of stress the teenager experiences as a result of it.

SEPARATION AND DIVORCE

Only a few generations ago, divorce was considered tragic, a family humiliation. No one talked about those who got divorced; family members who failed their relatives in this way were sometimes disowned. Now society accepts divorce almost casually, and we don't often stop to think about how divorce affects teenage children. The number of youngsters affected by divorce more than doubled between 1970 and 1980. Nearly 60 percent of the teenage population has experienced the effects of the separation or divorce of their parents.

Much of the stress an adolescent suffers in separation and divorce is a result of a sundering of the once-existing mother/father love relationship. The child and his parents have been separated either totally or partially, depending upon the custody and visitation arrangements. Being separated from brothers and sisters is an additional stressor, as is being disconnected from a set of grandparents. Mourning these losses takes time for a teenager, and a great deal of commitment is required on the part of adults to help him adjust. The impact of separation and divorce on a teenager is compounded in certain instances, as follows:

1. Parents only tell the teenager that there are marital problems after one or the other of the parents has moved out of the house.
2. Parents don't allow their adolescent to express his feelings about the new circumstances of his life.
3. The adolescent has recently undergone another loss (for example, a recent move to a new city, enrollment in a new school, a best friend's moving away, or any other traumatic experience requiring the child to make major transitions).
4. The adolescent receives no family and/or professional help to work through the loss.

A young person brought up to love and respect family may now feel torn apart. An adolescent facing this family crisis alone, or feeling alone, is particularly vulnerable, because it comes at a time when he is evaluating the desirability of relationships for himself. He may be wary of marriage and of having children, feeling doubtful about subjecting children to what he himself has gone through ("I would never want to put a child through this"). Sometimes an adolescent feels guilty and takes on the responsibility for the family's conflict: "It's all my fault. If I had behaved better, this wouldn't have happened."

THE SINGLE-PARENT FAMILY

In 1985, 11.1 million children—one out of every four—were living with only one parent. Single-parent families are most likely to be headed by separated or divorced women. The family life of teenagers in the single-parent family varies a great deal. The teenager may be abandoned (emotionally or physically) and left alone to work out his own crises. He may be treated by the parent as a friend, someone whom the adult can confide in. He may be expected to accept his parent's actions and to condone them without question. The single parent may somehow be impervious to what such adult behavior does to the teenager. "My dad and I check in on the weekends," says sixteen-year-old Tony. "I don't ask about his life, and he doesn't ask about mine." "My mother and I double-date," says seventeen-year-old Rebecca.

There are, of course, teenagers who find living in a single-parent household better than living in a two-parent home. As Brandon comments, "It's much easier to get one adult to make a decision than it is two. When my parents were married, they would often fight over making decisions. It got so bad that I quit asking because I was afraid I would start an argument between them."

HIS, HERS, AND THEIRS: BLENDED FAMILIES

Then there's the blended family. As the number of divorces in this country continues to rise, so will the number of remarriages. Every year in the United States a half million marriages occur in which at least one of the partners has children from a previous marriage. Each day nearly 100 teenagers become stepchildren. Sometimes the impossible does happen: everyone gets along well and learns to love one another. All too often, however, the predictable happens, and the child does not adjust well to his new lifestyle and experiences significant stress.

Imagine how you would feel if your child came from school this afternoon with three of his friends and said they would be living with you from now on. The matter is not open for discussion, he tells you. Starting immediately, you are going to have to share your house, and more important to you, your child's love, with these virtual strangers. What would your reaction be?

Pretend for a minute that you are not brave enough to argue or talk back. Pretend that you are a youngster whose parent has just remarried, bringing into the household another adult and a few assorted children. You had just begun to get used to the fact that there are only the two of you, and now the place is suddenly full of outsiders.

An infant or a young child can transfer his affections relatively easily. Young children adapt more easily. Teenagers, however, tend to want things to remain the same; they seek stability. You and I might go crazy if we had to listen to the same record every day or go hang around the same store in the mall week in and week out or eat the same lunch 365 days running, but a teenager thrives on such things. While a parent might see a divorce as a blessed and long overdue release, a teenager sees it only as a rejection. Then, just as he has learned to close up the pain of being left by one parent, we expect him to open up again to a relative stranger.

The child's view of remarriage is very different from an adult's view. While the new couple may be happy and excited about providing the youngster with a "family life" again, for a teenager there exists a new set of realities. His hope that his biological parents will get together again is dashed. He wonders if he will ever again see the absent parent, and, if so, whether that parent will feel that the child has "sold out" if he expresses feelings of caring toward the new parent. An only child may acquire step-siblings, or a youngest or oldest child may be displaced by a step-sibling who appropriates a coveted position. While the parent now has a new bond of love and friendship, the teenager, in contrast, experiences new losses. He now needs to share his remarried parent with another person and often other children as well—none of whom he has chosen.

Many of these factors became a part of the confusion and aliena-tion felt by fifteen-year-old Charles. Here's how he describes his experience: "When my mother and I lived alone, we were so happy. We were friends. We did things together. Sometimes, John —that's her new husband—would come along, but we used to discuss it and decide if we wanted him along. Mostly, my mother dated him when I had activities, like play practice or something.

"I know that my mom is happy now, but I miss her—us—so much. We still live in the same house! Now, she spends all her time with John. I used to be the man of the house. Mom even said I was. Now John is. Mom has changed, you know. Decisions she once made are now made by the two of them, and sometimes she lets him decide.

"John has a seven-year-old son who lives with us on the week-ends. Since we only have three bedrooms and one has been made into a study, he has to sleep in my room. I hate it. I hate him. He's such a brat. John spoils him, and my mother fusses over him like he's her own. It's sickening. I want my old life back. Mom said life would be better for us, that we would be a family again, but Mom and I *were* a family, and it's the one I want. Then, our life worked. Now it's compromise after compromise, and I'm the one who always loses. Mom always decides in favor of John's kid. She thinks that I should understand and accept it. But I don't think it's fair. She sold out on me! I want John to go away."

You can help lessen the stress your child feels as a result of gaining an instant expanded family. The following four-step approach is a start.

1. Listen. When your child tells you of his feelings about his new parent or sibling, listen. Let him talk as long as he wants and get it all out. Don't make him feel guilty about saying negative things. Don't you sometimes say negative things about his friends? You may have learned to love his best buddy with the tattoo, but no doubt you had a few things to say about him first.

2. Point out the advantages. A teenager is in his "me" stage. He wants to know the bottom line: "What's in it for me?" Point out to him what benefits he will get from having another parent ("Just think, Charles—I'll have someone else to nag besides you; you won't get picked on as much!"). Let him know how good having a little brother can be ("If you play your cards right, Jeremy would probably be willing to clean your room in exchange for your taking him to the movies once a week"). The point is, take the time to sit down with your teen and tell him, in terms that mean something to him personally, how the new family unit can support and help him, too.

3. Reassure him. When you had your second child you probably spent a great deal of time with your first child, reassuring him that you still loved him just as much. Now that your teenager is a "young adult," you may unrealistically think that he knows how much you love him and that nothing will ever lessen that love. Why should you think that? Don't you still get a twinge of fear when your spouse stares at an attractive person for just a little too long? Imagine how much worse that feeling of insecurity is when the person is brought into the family unit. Keep talking to your child; tell him over and over how much you still love and need him.

4. Help him accept change. Usually it's not the differences that cause problems but rather getting used to the change. Change is never easy for any of us. However, change is considerably easier when members of the new family:

- see a need to change
- know how to change
- are actively involved in the process
- can see the personal benefit of changing
- are committed to the change
- are encouraged and supported in changing

Remember that change doesn't occur overnight, and that what feels okay one month may not feel okay the next. Be realistic. Allow your teenager to express these views without guilt. Accept the fact that he may change his mind.

LOOSENING BONDS

One of the most stress-producing differences between remarried families and biological families is that in stepfamilies, the parent/child relationship has preceded the new-couple relationship. In first marriages, couples have a period of time in which to be together and assimilate values before making the necessary adjustments in becoming a new family. In remarriages the natural parent/child relationship may be strong, while the new-couple relationship is more delicate and requires adjustment and compromise. The presence of a teenage child who has feelings of loyalty and protectiveness toward both biological parents, and who may be secretly wanting a bigger piece of all this new affection and intimacy going on, can add a dimension of turmoil that corrodes rather than enhances the teenager's capacity for adjusting to the new family.

Ron had two boys, ages twelve and thirteen, from a previous marriage. After his divorce, Ron spent weekends and vacations with his children, enjoying sports of all kinds. Ron dated Nicole only when his children were not with him. After Nicole and Ron were married, Ron and the youngsters continued their usual activities together, and Nicole would go along. The children tried desperately to be the focus of their father's attention, even to the point of asking that Nicole not join in activities Ron had planned for the whole family. Both boys resented Nicole and would often sulk when she was along.

If you are a stepparent who has been resented and shut out by children, or a natural parent who has seen your normally polite teenager turn churlish, you have lived through this same experience. At the time, you were probably thinking of yourself, feeling sorry for yourself for being treated so badly. What about your teenager? He not only had the stress of knowing that he was behaving badly, making you ashamed of him, but he also feels put upon.

Happily, even a situation as anxiety ridden and seemingly inflexible as this can be changed. Ron and Nicole did so in an intelligent, planned manner. The result was a lessening of their teenagers' stress and the happy coincidence of the lowering of their own anxiety levels at the same time.

Ron and Nicole began to plan periodic weekend trips to a favorite family resort. While they were there, Ron and the boys went off hiking together. At other times both the adults and the children would swim and play together. While Ron and Nicole shared private time together, the teenagers entertained themselves. In this way, new relationships formed, former relationships were preserved, and family integration began to take place. The children began to feel less "dumped on" and more accepting of their new stepmother. Their manners improved as their stress lessened, making a cycle that fed upon itself and made everyone more comfortable.

Many blended families seem to start with the unrealistic assumption that the new parent and the stepchildren will come together and love one another from the start. After all, the child loves his or her parent, the parent loves the new partner, and the new partner loves the parent, so all should love one another. This unrealistic expectation can lead to deep disappointment and guilt in the family and stress for both parents and adolescents. Mary can certainly relate to this. "Just two weeks after our wedding, two of Jim's three youngsters, ages fourteen and sixteen, came to live with us. Both of our families had established different behavior patterns. My two children, ages four and seven, were used to my strict rules, but Jim's youngsters were accustomed to more freedom. The first year was the hardest. Since the teenagers were at that breaking-away stage, they had no interest in forming a loving bond in a new family. Negotiating rules and coping with their jealousy and resentment were the most painful aspects. You have to be flexible, get used to each other's rules, and then negotiate on the important ones." Mary is right. Caring has a better chance to develop if there is less pressure to feel "instant love."

THE TEENAGE TRAITOR

For teenagers, to love and care for a stepparent often seems disloyal to the absent, idealized parent. Sara, for example, encouraged her mother to date, but she changed her attitude when her mother remarried eighteen months later. A child may have to hear from the biological parent that loving a stepparent doesn't take away from the child's love for the absent parent. Whereas children in biological families may try to keep their parents together, children in stepfamilies feel a strong loyalty to the natural-parent spouse and may try either consciously or unconsciously to drive the new couple apart. Loyalty to the biological parent is a very strong emotion, and adolescents feel compelled to show it.

Teenagers fare best when they are free to develop "full" relationships with both parents. It is important that, where possible, the teenager continues to see both biological parents. The more courteous the relationship between the divorced spouse and the stepfamily, the more easily this sharing of children is managed and the less strain there is for all concerned.

Even if the adults in both households are able to work together with regard to the children, feelings of competition and insecurity are very difficult to avoid. Children in two households may find themselves on continual emotional ups and downs. "I'm thrown back and forth between two houses," says Weldon of his natural parents. "It's really hard to shift gears and remember what the ongoing saga is in each house. It's really hard to get into a family routine. Besides, it's really inconvenient, but no one seems to take my inconvenience seriously."

Adolescents, experiencing normal conflicts about their own identities and their place in the family, have a particularly difficult time in managing loyalties between families. The question of "Who am I and where do I fit in?" is a more acute one for teenagers than for their younger siblings.

Teenagers are particularly susceptible to overt sexual displays. Aware of the sexual relationship between the newly married couple, some may feel like Donna, who said, "If Mom had treated Dad like that, they would still be together."

You can help your child adapt to the stressors caused by the need for them to share your love. The following steps are a good start.

Communicate. Talk about feelings. Parents as well as their teenagers often pine over the loss of the once close relationship between them. When the situation is openly discussed, solutions are more likely to be found. Discuss your feelings about how each of you is faring. Often, stepchildren will offer complaints to just one parent. "Mom, he always introduces me as his daughter," complains Shelley. "But I'm not his daughter. My real father is the only one who can call me his daughter. I wish he would stop."

Be consistent. Parents must be willing to talk to each other in private to arrive at an agreement on troublesome issues. A mother may say, "It's okay with me if it's okay with John." But when John, the stepfather, says no, he becomes the bad guy. Another mother may tell her new husband that she wants him to discipline her young son—but when he does, she objects, saying, "Leave my child alone!" Good communication skills can alleviate the sending of confusing and double signals.

Seek assistance if necessary. Blended families have become so complex that the Stepfamily Association of America offers counseling referrals, support groups, and educational publications with advice on legal, financial, and practical ways of lowering the stress of stepparenting. Additionally, the resource section lists a number of excellent sources for parents and adolescents.

FAMILY DYNAMICS

The third category of family stressors includes the physical and emotional difficulties that may be experienced by a family member, be it parent or child. The most prominent stressors in this category are sibling stress (especially where physical or emotional handicaps are involved), scapegoating, family violence, teenage pregnancy, homosexuality, and drug and alcohol abuse. We'll be talking about the teenager's perceptions of several of these. Homosexuality and drug and alcohol abuse will be discussed at length in separate chapters.

The way one family member copes with any stress greatly impacts other family members as well. When adolescents develop formal operational thought, for example, each family member is forced to adapt to the adolescent's new demand to question nearly everything about family functioning, much as family members must adapt when an infant is teething. Siblings fear that the adolescent is "unhappy" or "insane," while other children in the family withdraw into their own worlds. Just as sullenness or moodiness of an adolescent may be felt by the other siblings and by parents, an argument between parents is felt by the adolescent and frightens him. Also, the tensions experienced by the parent of a child under the influence of alcohol or drugs may be felt by other family members.

Deep in his heart, a teenager truly loves his brother or sister. However, the teenager rarely shows those feelings. He is more concerned with how the sibling makes him feel than with how the sibling feels. A brother or sister who does something wrong or who is somehow "different" can be a major source of stress for a teenager. Thomas and his brother were good friends and were just one year apart in age. They shared many of the same friends. When his younger brother was hospitalized for drug addiction, Thomas's school life nearly came to a halt. He began to do poorly in school, stopped bringing friends home, resigned as president of the social club, and nearly became a recluse. His once outgoing and bubbly personality took on a sullen and introspective nature, and he began a pattern of overeating. "Can you imagine," said Thomas, "how it feels to be so disgraced, and in your own school? I had it all. Now I'm so embarrassed. My brother has ruined my life." Another major stressor for teenage children is having a retarded or physically handicapped brother or sister. "Riding the school bus with my ten-year-old retarded sister is the most humiliating experience I've ever known," said Jean. "Other kids make fun of her appearance. She stares blankly into space and chews on her tongue, rocking back and forth. It's more than I can handle." Jean is experiencing more than normal sibling stress. All of us who have a brother or sister have run screaming from the room at one time or another, certain that heaven put this creature on earth just to torment us. Jean has those normal problems, plus the added ones caused by her sister's handicap. To make matters even worse, she carries around the burden of guilt. It's one thing to avoid a sister who is just a normal pain in the neck, but it's quite another to avoid a sister who has a special problem.

Sometimes the problems are self-induced. A teenager may be embarrassed by the appearance or actions of family members. For example, a sibling who drinks or uses drugs can be a major source of stress for an adolescent on several fronts. First, the teenager is embarrassed by her sibling. She may be at a party and see her brother drunk and obnoxious, making a fool of himself. Second, she may resent having to be responsible for her brother. No sixteen-year-old likes to have to get out of bed and drive over to a party to pick up a sibling who is too drunk to drive. Third, she may worry that she, too, will take up drinking to excess or will take some drugs that she won't be able to stop using any time she wants. Fourth, she may feel that she has let her parents down. Perhaps she is the older sibling and feels she should have kept a better eye on the younger one. And fifth, she may feel that she is supposed to keep the sibling's problem a secret. A teenager who has to hide a sibling's problem from their parents is under a great deal of stress. The fact that the problem is not of her own making is even worse. "My sister wears so much makeup. She looks cheap. My friends look at her and then me and wonder. I wish she'd stop painting her face and fingernails in such colors."

Even though children must be accepting of individual differ-

ence—including their own siblings—we underestimate their
need, and their ability, to discuss how each is viewed and accepted
by the other.

Another problem is scapegoating. "It was Barney's fault!" "But
Mom, Ellen made me do it!" At some stage in life, nearly every
child goes through the "not me" phase, blaming actions on someone or something else. This scapegoating can also take place
within a family. Sometimes a family unconsciously faults a teenager for family problems. The adolescent can develop increased
feelings of rejection and alienation from other family members.
The young person who either assumes the responsibility for family problems or who feels to blame for them has a tremendous
burden to carry.

All too often, our children tend to bear the brunt of our fears
and our inabilities to accept responsibility for our actions. Our
children become the scapegoats for these frustrations. As parents
we must try to avoid these incidences and face up to the situations
that we have created or that have been dealt to us, without placing the blame on our teenagers.

Fifteen-year-old Janet, a cheerleader, spends most of her free
time practicing for her school's games. Janet's mom has diabetes,
and depending on her blood-sugar level she is either relaxed or
extremely nervous and volatile. In addition, the mother is unhap-
pily married and derives most of the joy in her life from her
relationships with her daughters, Janet and Ann.

Last Thursday, Janet rushed home from school, grabbed a
snack, and headed for her room. Her mother, feeling tired and
forlorn, asked Janet about her plans for the evening. When Janet
described the plans, her mother pointed a finger at her and began
accusing her of being disrespectful and impertinent. Suddenly she
began gasping for her breath. "You're going to be the death of me.
Can't you see that I'm sick? Must you always do what you want
to do?"

Clearly, Janet had served as a scapegoat for her mother's feelings of loneliness and her inability to deal with her own illness.
Had the mother been in control of her emotions and had a handle
on her condition, she would not have blamed Janet for her illness.
What she really wanted was her daughter's time and attention.

Instead, she tried to manipulate Janet by blaming her for the problems. Accusations such as those made by Janet's mother can cause teenagers to shun their parents rather than grow closer. As parents, we must be in touch with what we expect from our children and not give out incorrect messages.

Janet's case is not uncommon. Teenagers are often blamed for many of their parent's burdens. Sixteen-year-old Patrick is an average student. In the evenings, he works at a local hamburger shop. He is saving up for a car and for his college tuition. Patrick's dad has a drinking problem, and as a result he is often dismissed from the various jobs he manages to be hired for. When the father isn't working, he focuses negative attention on Patrick. No matter what Patrick does, it doesn't seem to be good enough for his father. "You look terrible!" "Get a haircut!" "This is the best grade you can get?!" "No, you can't borrow the car! I'm not going to provide you and your buddies with a car so you can go off to some side street with a six-pack!" Patrick does not drink and feels that his father's accusations are unfair. He feels the impossibility of getting his father's affection. Patrick is clearly the scapegoat for his father's inability to confront his own alcoholism and his accompanying feelings of failure.

Not all cases are as complex as these, but in many families the guilt syndrome is common. As parents, we need to allow for our own bad days, our own fears and failures, and not blame them—directly or indirectly—on our children. Such blame would only further alienate our children from us. We would be teaching them how not to accept responsibility instead of helping them to admit their strengths and weaknesses so they can develop stronger senses of self.

A teenager in a family with a history of alcoholism, battering, or sexual victimization faces additional stress. A young person in such a family is always in a bind. He can't go outside for help without betraying his own family and exposing family secrets. The young person is often afraid of retaliation or, at least, of further rejection from other family members, and he or she may grow up with a distorted view of what loving and caring mean. In such a family, whether the adolescent is a direct victim or not, the models of behavior observed are confusing and damaging.

There is a strong correlation between the adolescent's traumatic experiences and the gradual development of his self-perception as a worthless and unlovable person. The escape from these feelings takes many routes, most notably those of alcohol or drug abuse, truancy, arson, fighting, stealing, cheating, thrill-seeking, sexual promiscuity, pregnancy, or running away from home. These escape routes often lead the teenager into problems more overwhelming than any he or she was trying to escape. They are signals of a need for help. If there is no help and family support, the intensity of the emotional trauma the adolescent experiences is often repeated in his own family when he reaches adulthood. Research shows that children of family violence have a greater chance of victimizing their families as well.

THE CAPABLE FAMILY: RESISTING FAMILY STRESS

Ah, for the good old days of 1950s television, where every family had a mother who cooked in high heels and pearls and a kindly father who was all-knowing. In just thirty minutes once a week, the Perfect Parents could solve all their children's problems, no matter what they were. You and I are lucky if we can get our teenagers to just *listen* to us for thirty minutes, let alone accept our advice!

Alas, families are not perfect. We sometimes seem to create more problems than we solve, give our children more stress than support. Since it is the family that is a cause of that stress, it is the family that must help the teenager learn to cope with it.

The coping process starts with your identifying the stressful situation. The goal is to perceive the problem as an appropriate family concern, to accurately identify the family problems, and to share decision-making powers among family members. Families differ in the extent to which they promote the development of coping skills in children. Research has found that children who are good copers tend to have parents who are warm, loving, supportive, conscientious, and good at communicating. While respecting their child's independence, such parents hold firm to their convictions about what is right, explaining their reasons to the child and yet insisting on proper behavior. This authoritative style of child-rearing has been contrasted to both the authoritarian (controlling without warmth) and to the permissive (noncontrolling but warm) styles. The maximum of support with the maximum of challenge seems to be the goal. Families that produce effective, competent children often follow this principle, whether or not they are aware of it. They neither maintain strict control nor allow their children total freedom. They're always opening doors for their children—and then encouraging them to move on and grow. This combination of support and challenge is essential if adolescents are to develop into capable young adults.

Along with teaching a child general coping techniques, you and your family can help in specific ways.

Supervision. The happiest teenagers are those with supervision. A common mistake is for parents to think that teenagers are old enough to fend for themselves. While that may be true for short periods of times, it is not fair for your adolescent to be expected to fend for himself. If your work schedule does not permit you to supervise your child, possible solutions would be to change your schedule for greater flexibility or to provide other adult supervision. As do families with young children, families with teenagers will need to take into account difficult work shifts, and work responsibilities. While this may sound unfair, it is important to keep in mind that teenagers require supervision, too.

Quality and quantity of activities. Teaching adolescents to have a healthy and zestful life experience requires an approach to living that maximizes rational self-fulfillment and minimizes stress and burnout. This includes fostering in adolescents the enjoyment of the love and support of family and friends, enjoyment of constructive and productive work, the importance of spiritual fulfillment, and the added self-fulfillment possible through meeting new and exciting growth challenges. The following activities bring adolescents closer to success in those endeavors.

- Nature and outdoor activities promote mental, physical, and spiritual wholeness in addition to providing many opportunities for creativity and learning.

- Social service caters to a person's basic need for moral, spiritual, and ethical expression and development. "Adopting" others within a helping context is one of the best ways to get on the outside of our own problems and stresses.
- Sports, games, and related activities satisfy the need for wholesome physical and mental activity in addition to promoting sound physical health. The social aspect of such activities is also important. A range of activities is possible, from active participation to spectatorship.
- Travel, although constantly growing more expensive, is financially accessible in some form to everyone. Travel offers well-rounded educational experience as well as mental and physical relaxation.

Effective skills in family functioning. You may feel that your family needs to acquire the skills that can allow it to become functional. Support groups for families provide a good outlet for teenagers to share their family experiences. The purpose of a support group is to provide an opportunity to share feelings, frustrations, and triumphs as well as strategies useful in coping with many kinds of stress. Although the family may, in some cases, need special therapeutic attention, just having the opportunity to share feelings with other families in discussion or therapy groups or to learn from informational materials is proving to be extremely helpful. Mutual support groups and courses for parents are appearing throughout the United States, and organizations are forming to act as support networks for families and to provide education for the community and for professionals who work with families. You will find that a number of local organizations offer counseling and support for members of families. Identify these and determine how they may be of use to your family.

One final bit of good news: What you always knew in your heart of hearts—that a loving family produces a loving and kind child —has been proven by research. In a study spanning nearly twenty years, psychologist Emmy E. Werner attempted to identify some of the individual, family, and cultural factors that may increase or decrease a child's risk of developing serious problems in adolescence. Werner and a team of physicians, nurses, social workers, and psychologists followed the development of more than 800 high-risk children (that is, children of divorced or troubled parents) through young adulthood. Nearly one-third of the children in the study experienced a difficult and turbulent adolescence. Of those, one in five developed serious problems by the age of seventeen. By late adolescence, fifteen percent had a record of serious or repeated delinquency.

Most of the children in the study, however, did not get into trouble. The researchers were deeply impressed by the resiliency of the overwhelming majority of the adolescents. Even among the high-risk children—those whose records showed at least four risk factors by age ten—one-fourth developed into stable, mature, and competent young adults. What is more, they expressed a high degree of faith in the effectiveness of their own actions.

How did these resilient teenagers differ from their more troubled peers? Two characteristics emerged: (1) They were from smaller families in which there were fewer siblings with whom to compete for attention; and (2) they had care-giving responsibilities.

Basically, care giving is the lending of emotional and physical help to someone who wants or needs it. Because of the care-giving responsibilities of these adolescents, who were held responsible for helping other family members, they were able to get the attention of other care givers (grandparents, siblings, babysitters, parents, and others). The emotional support of these care givers was a major protective factor in the midst of chronic poverty and/or serious family disruptions. These adolescents reported a higher degree of satisfaction in helping others.

Other studies confirm similar results. A long-term Harvard study has turned up some startling results about how to raise "happy" children. Begun forty years ago in an effort to understand juvenile delinquency, the study followed the lives of nearly 500 teenage children, many of whom were from impoverished or broken homes. When the subjects were compared at middle age, one fact stood out: regardless of intelligence, family income, ethnic background, or amount of education, those who had responsibilities in shared home and work projects as children, even if this meant only simple household chores, enjoyed happier and more productive lives than those who had not had such responsibilities. When these individuals reached adulthood, they were better off than their childhood playmates who had been less industrious. They earned more money and had more job satisfaction. They had better marriages and closer relationships with their children. They were healthier and lived longer. Above all, they were much happier.

CHAPTER FIVE

Sex and the Single Teenager

With the onset of puberty, teenagers undergo phenomenal physical and emotional changes. One of the most perplexing of those changes is an unfolding sexuality. Coping with sexuality can and does produce a great amount of stress for many young people and adults alike. But sidestepping the responsibility of helping adolescents become sexually responsible can produce even more stress, as statistics such as these affirm:

In contrast to the 1970s, when only about 15 percent of all teenagers were sexually active, today more than 50 percent of all teenagers are sexually active by the age of fifteen.

One out of every ten girls between the ages of twelve and sixteen becomes pregnant each year.

One-fifth of all babies born in this country are born to youngsters between twelve and eighteen years of age.

As parents, we cannot ignore these statistics. Sure, it's hard to discuss sexual matters with our children. The sexual question, a major factor contributing to the so-called generation gap, has typically posed many problems for parents and children. Values, attitudes, and behavior differ widely, but one constant remains: adults must realize that sexual interest and probably some form of sexual contact during adolescence is an inevitable and normal part of human development. We have a responsibility to talk to our children openly and honestly about all issues of human sexuality, including romantic or sexual rejection, the decision to have sex for the first time, the risks of pregnancy and sexually transmitted diseases, homosexuality, and sexual molestation. You will need to confront your feelings about your adolescent's becoming sexually mature. It can be both frightening and rewarding to see your child struggling to become independent, to find his own way, to make his own decisions, to "try on" certain adult roles when he still seems so young. What your teenager wants and needs most is for you to be approachable for information, guidance, and reassurance as he unfolds sexually.

BEING REJECTED AND REJECTING

Even if your teenager is voted the smartest, most popular, most attractive, and wittiest kid at school, he will probably experience rejection in one form or another. Rejection is a part of exploring relationships, terminating unsatisfactory ones, and establishing new ones. Being rejected is not a pleasant feeling and can be a very traumatic experience. Similarly, rejecting others can be an unpleasant experience. Because teenagers are still gaining social and interpersonal skills, they are often rude and cruel to one another, particularly in matters of rejecting others as suitable friends or dating partners.

You can help your adolescent with his feelings of rejection. Show concern. You must not take his feelings lightly. A parent can sometimes make the mistake of saying something unhelpful or unkind just when the child is feeling intense hurt. Such comments as "Don't take it so hard—she wasn't good for you anyway" or "You always got into trouble when you hung out with him. Good riddance!" are likely to be more damaging than enhancing. Be a good listener. Focus on your child's feelings and help him with them. Reassure him that the hurt he feels from being rejected *will* go away, and that in the meantime he can lessen the feelings of rejection by talking about his feelings with those in whom he can trust and confide. Stress how beneficial and healing

it is to be especially kind to himself right now, while he's coming
to terms with the hurt. This is a good time to focus on hobbies,
sports, or related physical activities. They will help the child to
release the anxieties and anger he may be feeling and to channel
these feelings constructively.

Share related experiences that can support and help your child.
"I remember when I was growing up," says twenty-two-year-old
Anu. "I came home in tears because the love of my life said I was
no longer his type. My mom patiently listened to my sob story,
then shared a similar experience of when she had been rejected.
It was comforting to know that my mom's love for me was unconditional. Somehow she managed to make me feel that the guy
wasn't worth all the time I was spending thinking about him. I
began to think that because he had left, I had gained!"

Part of sexuality is being able to deal responsibly not only with
rejection but also with rejecting others. Help your child understand that there will be times when he will not want to begin or
continue a relationship with someone, but that he must let the
person know courteously. You can use role playing to rehearse a
scenario for either rejection or rejecting another. Ask, "What will
you say? What will you say if she says no? What will you do if she
is with friends? What will you say next?" Role playing allows your
teen to think about his decision and how he will go about handling
it. It allows him to anticipate stressful interactions and negative
thoughts, images, and feelings about his upcoming task. It allows
him time to examine the coping strategies and behaviors needed
to handle the situation. Exchanging roles—you play the part of
your adolescent and he plays the part of the other person involved
—is also beneficial. This approach helps your adolescent generate
strategies and arguments that are most personally convincing.
Role playing provides you with an opportunity to assess your
adolescent's understanding of the situation and his capacity to
implement it under stress. It is through this form of conversation
that you not only help your child with his immediate dilemma but
also enhance the all-important parent/child relationship. Your
child comes to trust that you will be there for him, will offer advice
when he wants it, and will take his feelings seriously. He learns
that his actions, and the feelings of others, matter.

"BUT IF I DON'T HAVE SEX WITH HIM, HE WON'T GO OUT WITH ME AGAIN"

Teenagers, like us, want to touch and be touched, to experience a mutual closeness when attracted to a member of the opposite sex. These feelings lead to the desire for sexual intercourse. Peer pressure may exacerbate the issue. One friend may brag, "I have sex after the third date." Another may warn, "If you don't have sex with your date, he will never go out with you again." A girl or boy may thus surrender to intercourse and never learn what true intimacy is about. Sexual intercourse can be a marvelous, wondrous experience, but it demands that two people are mature enough to assume its responsibilities. When engaged in carelessly, promiscuously, or selfishly, sexual intercourse can be an emotionally scarring experience. This is why parents try to shield their children. However, we need to communicate openly with our youngsters in order to help them understand love and sex—the pleasures, the sorrows, and the responsibilities involved.

How can we help our youngster to identify sexual readiness? Since this issue is so complex and laden with emotion, many parents attempt to restrict their child's social activities and demand that the child abstain from sexual activity. Other parents may become too permissive, feeling that it is impossible to influence a teenager's sexual activity.

No doubt your views are based on your wishes for your child. You may want your child to wait until she is out of high school before she has sexual intercourse. You may wish that your child's first sexual encounter will be with that person who will be her permanent mate. As one parent told me, "Sure, we want our daughter to be sexually responsible, but let's be frank—we would prefer that she abstain from having sexual intercourse until she is eighteen years of age, and then that it be with someone who would also be an appropriate life partner!" You may want to help your son or daughter avoid making a mistake you yourself made, particularly if you married because of a pregnancy. Perhaps you want your child to remain "innocent" longer, to enjoy her activities and friends, and to acquire an education before she must cope with the complexities and the demands of relationships.

Ultimately, your adolescent is the one making the decision about whom to have sex with and when. As a parent you may wonder and worry about whether your teenager is sexually active, but today the question of when sexual intercourse starts is no longer the biggest concern. Adolescents are making their own choices, and the real issues facing many parents is that of whether their son or daughter is having a relationship for the right reasons and is using contraception. As issues of sexuality are openly discussed, you can guide your adolescent toward the attitude needed for responsible sex.

RESPONSIBLE SEX

Teenagers need to know how to assert their rights. They need to know not only that it's okay to say no to sexual intercourse but also why it's okay to do so. One girl said, "At school, I'm always asked if I'm a virgin. If I say yes, I'm considered a prude. If I say no, I'm considered loose. What am I supposed to say?" Assure your teenager that there is nothing wrong with being a virgin and that it's appropriate for him or her to tell friends it's none of their business if they ask. In chapter 2 we discussed assertive-choice skills. Review these skills with your adolescent. They can help your child to feel confident about asserting his or her own rights —in this case, to privacy.

Your teenager wants to know the answers to the questions, "How do I know when it's right? What if I really love (him or her)?" Again, take the time to hold these conversations. Your teenager is very interested in hearing from you.

Remember when your mother repeatedly said, "Be careful whom you date—you may be choosing your mate"? The way you cope with your own fears also contributes to the stress your teenager experiences. For example, if you fear that your teenager may become sexually active upon dating, you may become too restrictive. Or, as noted earlier, you may become too permissive. Each of these courses of action carries its own special problems. Dating is an important function in the adolescent stage. Apart from being both fun and stressful, it helps adolescents to develop social and interpersonal skills. It also offers the initial context for sexual experimentation and discovery and provides a base for the development of reciprocal relationships involving trust, love, and mutual concern. We need to examine our own fears surrounding these adolescent experiences and find appropriate ways to help our teenagers adjust to the transition they must make from adolescence to adulthood.

In helping teenagers learn how to view sex responsibly, parents must make every effort to discourage their children from equating sex with social gain or reward. A girl should not feel that she has to "repay" her date with intercourse, for example, nor should a boy think he has to "perform" in order to prove he is masculine. In counseling, many adolescents confess to having made love out of fear of being ridiculed or rejected. Part of sexual responsibility is being able to accept and deal with sexual rejection. Let your child know that there will be times when he wants to kiss or hold a partner and will be rejected, and that he must respect the other's decision.

Your child will need to know the consequences of sexual intercourse and must come to understand that sexual intercourse is a responsibility with those consequences.

CHILDREN HAVING CHILDREN: TEENAGE PREGNANCY

One consequence of increased sexual activity among teenagers is a comparable increase in teenage pregnancy. One out of every five children in the United States is born to a teenage mother. Every day in America, forty teenage girls give birth to their third child. Although young women are able to conceive, the pelvic girdle does not attain its full size until the adolescent reaches the age of seventeen or eighteen. This puts the teenage mother and her infant at physical risk. Teenage mothers tend to give birth to children who are premature. Prematurity leads to an increased chance of major health problems resulting from an insufficiently developed immune system. "Children Having Children," as *Time Magazine* titled its December 6, 1985, issue, or "premature motherhood," as it is called by others, has some other negative effects. The death rate for infants of teenagers is 2.4 times that of infants born to mothers seventeen and older, and the maternal death rate of children under fifteen is 2.5 times that among mothers age twenty and older.

Pregnancy flings the teenager into parenthood. Being a teenager with a baby is a displacing experience that seriously impairs the efforts of both the teenage mother and father to develop a healthy sense of personal identity. As David Elkind reminds us, "To be in the place of a parent while still being in many respects a child, to be in the place of nurturing when one's own needs for nurture are still strong makes the formation of a consistent, whole, and meaningful definition of self difficult, if not impossible, to attain." Teenagers are simply not prepared to cope with parenthood.

Teenage pregnancies sometimes seem to have "storybook" happy endings, with the boy and girl getting married and appearing set to live "happily ever after." Unfortunately, this is not often the case. Understandably, most young mothers and fathers are unprepared for the time, money, patience, and commitment a baby requires. Many feel trapped, and they are. "If only we knew how emotionally taxing and physically fatiguing this would be, we wouldn't have let this happen," says Bobby, a sixteen-year-old father. "I love Carrie and our baby, and I want them to have more. We are living with my parents and trying to finish school, but it's hard. Carrie is often up late at night with the baby and goes to school tired and drained. I'm sometimes tired and irritable from holding down a job and completing high school. Sometimes I find myself drawing two columns listing the pros and cons of quitting school, so I can work full-time to support the three of us, or of quitting my job, so I'll have time to study and improve my grades to get into college in order to earn more.

"My life has changed, and not for the better. It has become so complex. My high-school friends talk mostly about upcoming football and soccer games, but I don't have the luxury of playing sports now. The time I once spent in practice now belongs to getting financial security for Carrie and the baby. Where I once worried about money for having a good time on the weekends, I now worry about how I will ever afford a place of our own.

"I spend a considerable amount of time trying to repair the relationship with Carrie's parents. They feel we were irresponsible and blame me for 'ruining' Carrie's life. It's been five months since the birth of our baby and they still aren't talking to me. Carrie is sixteen, and they wanted her to have an abortion so that she could continue living out their plans for her. We love our baby, but it has changed us, too. If I had known how much and how fast our lives would change, I wouldn't have let this happen."

Bobby's story illustrates several of the stresses that teenage pregnancy can cause. The teenager becomes an adult too quickly. He experiences a responsibility for others at a time when he is still learning to be responsible for himself. He is set apart from his friends, unable to take the time or effort to join in their activities. He cannot take the time to do things he used to enjoy, such as sports. Because of these deprivations, he begins to resent those whom he most loves. Then he feels guilty, as if he is a bad person for doing so. And, as if all those problems aren't enough, he also has to face the stress of parental disapproval and disappointment. That's a lot of stress for a person who just got his driver's license a few months ago!

Bobby and Carrie were fortunate, to a degree. They were able to remain together, get married, have their baby, and have a tolerable living situation. Bobby is secure in his love for his wife and child and is a loving, supportive part of their lives. Not all teenage fathers are so lucky.

For the most part, teenage pregnancy is still viewed as the young mother's dilemma. Often, decisions about the mother and child are made irrespective of the teenage father—that is, the teenage father is often not allowed by angry parents to see the mother or child again. This special problem carries problems of its own, producing in young fathers feelings of loss, rejection, and alienation. The perspective that teenage boys are interested only in sexual gratification and have fleeting casual relationships with their girlfriends is far from accurate. Boys usually know their girlfriends for a year or more, are emotionally bonded by feelings of affection and love, and have been having sexual intercourse for ten months or longer. More than three-fourths of the fathers continue dating their babies' mother for two or more years after the baby is born. Contrary to the myth that young fathers prefer to leave after learning that the girl is pregnant, many young fathers do not want to abandon their girlfriends and babies. The pregnancy can thus cause overwhelming stress for teenage fathers as well. "Elaine and I had been together for a year when her parents learned she was pregnant," explained sixteen-year-old Gary. "They said they would kill me if I ever showed up at their house again. After a month of trying to call and get through, I became so depressed that I contemplated suicide."

The feelings of young fathers have been routinely neglected by parents. Many teenage fathers report that the girls' parents don't accept them, don't approve of them, or refuse to speak to them. They are generally excluded, primarily by the girls' parents, from decisions made about their babies. Often, the teenage father is not told if and when the baby has been born, whether the child has been adopted or turned over to foster care, or whether the pregnancy has been terminated by abortion.

Many explanations have been offered for teenage pregnancy. Among these is lack of information about pregnancy and birth control. "I had no idea I could father a child at age thirteen," says Matt, "so we didn't bother with contraceptives." Another explanation involves the teenager's desire to have someone of her own to love, and to be loved and wanted in return—"I just need someone of my own," says fourteen-year-old Kathy. "My mother and new stepdad have each other, and my dad lives out of state. Who is there for me? I was always so lonely. My baby will need me, and I won't be alone. Somebody will finally care." Finally, there is the need to be regarded as an adult. "My mother treats me like I'm a child, but I'll have her know that I can be an adult, too. When my baby is born, she will have to deal with me like an adult," says sixteen-year-old Tracy.

You must not be passive in teaching your teenager about the consequences of sexual intercourse. All adolescents must know

1. How pregnancy occurs
2. How pregnancy can be prevented
3. What should be done if a girl becomes pregnant

You must communicate with your adolescent. Start now. A twelve-year-old child is not too young to learn, and a seventeen-year-old is not too old to review. Assure your child that he or she can turn to you for information and for help when needed. Don't feel that you have to know all the answers. Get help if you need more information. Contact your child's pediatrician, your family doctor, a school nurse, or a family crisis center for help and referral services. The reference section at the end of this book provides additional information.

The dramatic increase in teenage pregnancy has also resulted in an increase in abortions among teenagers. Nearly all states have reported an increase in teenage abortions. Abortions among U.S. teenagers under fifteen has risen 220 percent in recent years. In 1985, New York reported 1200 teenage abortions for every 1000 teenage live births. Abortion has become a viable alternative for young people. Yet abortion, for whatever the reasons, is always sad and often emotionally damaging. Preventing children from having to face abortion is a powerful reason for parents to teach children about responsible sex.

Because the emotional trauma of abortion can cause life trauma, parents want to eliminate its possibility from their teenagers' experiences. Your teenager needs to understand exactly what abortion entails and should not view it simply as a way to resolve a pregnancy. "We figured if anything happened she could always get an abortion" is not a healthy attitude for teenage couples to have. Abortion should not be something that serves as a backup for teens but rather should be fully understood, with all of its ramifications. Teens must know this before they become sexually active. We can aid this understanding in many ways. If you feel you need assistance in helping your teen, obtain professional counseling. Health-care centers can help you. Learn as much as possible about abortion on your own, then be prepared to stimulate and answer your teenager's questions. Purchase materials or photocopy articles on abortion, make them available for your child to read, and discuss them. And remember, your sons need this information just as much as your daughters do.

SEXUALLY TRANSMITTED DISEASES

Part of being responsible in sex is being informed about all of the consequences of sexual relations. Aside from the risk of pregnancy, young people need to be informed about sexually transmitted diseases. We need to talk openly, honestly, and intelligently about syphillis, gonorrhea, herpes, and AIDS.

Educate your youngster to be aware of the signs and symptoms and of ways to lessen the risk of contracting disease. You may not know all the answers and may need to turn elsewhere for help. The reference section at the end of this book lists resources that provide the hard facts you need in order to have a credible discussion with your child. Pediatricians, gynecologists, and school counselors may also be able to either provide information or refer you to someone else who can help. It is important not to turn away from difficult questions or from those you are unsure of.

THE GAY TEENAGER

When your child was being brought to you in the hospital, just before the first time you held him, what went through your mind? You probably uttered a spontaneous prayer that he be whole and healthy, that he have all his fingers and toes, that he be of good mind and spirit. It is likely that the farthest thing from your mind was the question of whether he would be gay or straight.

Are you going to love your son or daughter any less if he or she is gay? Of course not. You may find that the sexual preference of your child is hard to accept, but since you love him, you are going to do your best to understand.

How much do you know about homosexuality? Homosexuality means sexual attraction to persons of the same sex as oneself, whether male or female. The word comes from the Greek *homos,* meaning *same.* Female homosexuality is usually called *lesbianism,* after the island of Lesbos, where the Greek poet Sappho lived in the sixth century B.C. and addressed some of her most ardent lyrics to other women. There are also people who enjoy having sex with both males and females, with possibly a slight preference for one or the other. These people are called *bisexuals.*

Terms such as *homosexual* or *lesbian* or *gay* refer to persons who are exclusively or primarily attracted to members of their own sex and who enter into sexual and affectionate relations with them.

Because many gay people still hide their sexual orientation, their actual numbers are not known, but they are certainly in the millions. The Institute for Sex Research, founded by the late Alfred Kinsey, estimates that between puberty and old age about 37 percent of all males and 23 percent of all females engage in some homosexual activity.

In ancient history, at the time of the early Greek and Roman civilizations, homosexuality was an accepted practice; it was considered a natural part of sex. However, as time passed, people began to consider *sex in general* a hidden activity, and homosexuals were singled out for ridicule. Laws were passed that condemned homosexuality and labeled homosexual acts as criminal. Homosexuals concealed their actions and "went into the closet." In many countries, the homosexual's right to live the same kind of life as everyone else, regardless of sexual preference, is slowly being acknowledged and restored. But this is not the case everywhere, and there is still tremendous prejudice against the homosexual in many communities.

Many heterosexuals believe that homosexuality is a matter of choice. Yet homosexuals do not speak of having chosen but rather of having *discovered* their sexual orientation. Some do not even like to call their homosexuality a preference, since this would imply a choice. They call it a state of being, with feelings they are powerless to change. All they can choose is what to do with these feelings.

The fact that some homosexuals "discover" their sexual orientation rather late in life lends credence to the notion that there is a choice. However, such persons have tried desperately to live by society's rules—some even to the extent of marrying and having children. But after much frustration and pain, many such people realize that they have been merely going through the motions required by heterosexual roles. The idea that homosexuals can change their sexual pattern if they so choose adds to the social pressure on them.

A few gay people have tried to change to heterosexuality. Seeking social acceptance, sometimes under heavy pressure from parents, they have undergone lengthy and expensive treatments that in some cases appear to have achieved that change. Whether the adaptation to a heterosexual lifestyle ever becomes truly spontaneous and fulfilling is open to question. To their own surprise, the Kinsey researchers uncovered not a single instance of a person who had been "cured" of homosexuality by therapy.

If homosexuality is not a matter of choice, where and how does it originate? This is still an unanswered question. We simply don't know enough to pinpoint the causes with certainty. The pattern seems to be set in early childhood. Roughly 10 percent of the population in every country the world over is gay. There are many theories about the origins of homosexuality, but its universality suggest these possible explanations:

It is genetic. Gay adults contend that they knew they were gay even when they were children but didn't realize the full meaning of their sexual orientation until they reached adolescence. Most lived their adult lives recognizing and accepting their gayness and never deviating from it. It is estimated that three of every ten gays fall into this category.

It is caused by sexual trauma in childhood. Research links incest and child abuse to gayness. More than a million children are reported sexually molested each year. Cited also is molestation by other children, such as an adolescent babysitter. Five of every ten gays are categorized by sexual trauma.

It is a conditioned response. Some psychologists link gayness to limited opportunities in childhood for social contact with peers of the opposite sex. During the adolescent years, when sexual impulse is heightened and sexual experimentation is probable, same-gender sex is more likely to occur, thus making it easy to continue. These teens do not bother to try to establish sexual relationships with those of the opposite sex; instead, they tend to follow the same sexual pattern in their adult lives, and as a result they are unhappy and harbor confused feelings within themselves. It is believed that two of every ten gays develop a predisposition for sexual preference through this means.

Did you know that it is not uncommon for all adolescents at one time or another to think they are gay? During adolescence, most teenagers engage in some form of homosexual activity. While you may find this surprising, this fact has been known for some time and is accepted as normal. This does not mean that your child is a homosexual, even though your teenager may think he is. Maybe he became involved in same-sex sports and assumed that because he enjoyed these activities, he is a homosexual. Your adolescent may have had homosexual dreams or homosexual fantasies. He may have masturbated with persons of the same sex. Again, this does not mean that he is homosexual. Many gays agree that they were not *completely* sure of their sexual preference until they had been mature adults for some time.

If you or your child are disturbed about this, wonder whether the child is gay, or need information to put your mind at ease, the parents' FLAG organization (found in the resource section in this book) provides information free of charge to anyone interested. Both you and your child need to learn to cope with his homosexuality if it exists. Additionally, there are FLAG organizations in most cities that can also direct you to organized groups existing in cities near you. In my talks with homosexual teenagers, I found that the hardest part for them was not accepting their own homosexuality but rather telling their parents. It is devastating, for some parents at least, to discover that their son or daughter is gay. No rationalization or philosophy can ease the pain they experience. Being gay is not something that the teenager is doing to hurt the parents, nor is it in any way the parents' fault. Homosexuality is not an illness or a sexual perversion but rather a different sexual orientation. What has to be remembered is that the vast majority of gay people are responsible, productive members of society whose sexual preferences are a matter of their private, not their public, life.

Up until now, we have discussed you—*you* need to learn more about homosexuality and to clarify your feelings on the topic. But what about your child? What is he feeling right now? Your teenager is undergoing a tremendous amount of turmoil. He is facing a situation most teenagers abhor: being different. Your child is no longer just one of the guys; he's different. He may feel frightened, scared that others will find out his secret and shun him. At a time when he wants more than anything to belong, to fit in, he is petrified that he will be excluded from the group. This fear is real and can be paralyzing.

At the same time, the gay teenager may feel pride. If he has done any research on his own, he may know that many famous and respected people were gay. He may decide that since his preferences are not going to change, he might as well be proud of who he is. After all, haven't you always told him, "Be yourself"?

Lee's male friends are always trying to hang around with him because Lee seems to attract the best-looking girls. "Man," says Lee's best friend John, "I don't know what you do, but they just can't get enough of you!" Naturally, Lee just laughs and accepts his role as "leader of the pack." None of his friends knows that he'd give anything to have boys, not girls, hang around him. Lee is gay.

"I've always been attracted to guys," says Lee. "No way could I tell my parents. They'd be mad or ashamed. I used to feel really down all the time; now I just feel scared. How am I ever going to have a best friend if the word gets out that I'm gay?"

While gay men are ridiculed in our society, gay women are noticed less. Since women tend to be emotionally demonstrative anyway, kissing and hugging one another frequently, it is easy for a lesbian's friends to justify to themselves that "Jessica's just really affectionate."

Says Jessica, "I'm sixteen, the age when I am supposed to be talking on the phone for hours with my girlfriends about good-looking guys. Instead, I find myself thinking about my girlfriends and wondering what it would be like to be with them. I told one girlfriend of my feelings once, and she looked at me as if I were disgusting. I'll never tell anyone, ever again. For sure I won't tell Mom or Dad. They'd stop loving me entirely and probably kick me out of the house. As long as I'm a 'good girl' and hide my real feelings, the only one who's miserable is me."

Both Lee and Jessica follow patterns that are typical for gay teens: fear of divulging their different sexual preferences, worry about not being loved or accepted, loneliness. As parents, we hope to foster a sufficiently accepting and loving atmosphere to make our child feel that he or she can share anything with us. But think for a moment: Have you ever said those very words to your adolescent? When was the last time you actually said, "We can talk about anything, you and I, because I love you so much." Have you ever taken the time to sit down and discuss sex and sexual aberrations?

SOME DELICATE MATTERS

INCEST

Incest is a criminal offense and is considered an illegal act in every state in the United States. This kind of relationship is frowned upon by almost all religions and societies; it is often called the universal taboo. Incest is a particularly frightening problem because it can involve sexual relations between an adult and a child in the same family. At least half of the one million youngsters sexually abused each year have had an incestuous relationship. Incest is a sexual relationship between close family members: brother and sister, father and daughter, mother and son, uncle and niece, grandparent and grandchild. One consequence of the increasing number of "blended" families today is a proportionate increase in incestuous relationships involving a stepfather and teenage stepdaughter.

It's not easy for youngsters to expose sexual victimization. The young person is often afraid of retaliation or at least of further rejection. The child involved in incest is often only six or seven when the relationship starts, so young she is confused by what is happening. Sometimes she thinks that all children are expected to agree to an adult's sexual demands. By the time she understands that this is not true, she is too ashamed or frightened to tell anyone. The adult usually continues to molest the child again and again, threatening to hurt the child or send her away if she does not agree to the relationship.

Incest often causes the young person to grow up with a distorted view of what loving and caring mean. For most young people, gradually breaking away from parents and finding new love relationships is a painful yet necessary step in the process of self-definition. In some cases, however, this process of breaking away and of self-definition is made difficult and extraordinarily stressful when the teenager has been the object of sexual advances by another family member.

Studies strongly suggest that incest does have lifelong repercussions. The most commonly reported outcome of incestuous experiences is sexual acting out and promiscuity. Other young people who have had incestuous experiences may become homosexuals as an expression of their extreme emotional pain and confusion. In addition, if and when incest is discovered, the teenager must suffer the guilt of being responsible for the adult's punishment and for the disruption of the family. Some teenagers leave home rather than face this possibility. Teenagers involved in incestuous relationships account for a large number of runaways each year.

Incest, like homosexuality, is an indication of the enormity of stress that teenagers may encounter. Unlike homosexuality, however, which has become more socially acceptable, incest is a terrifying prospect. It is not something teenagers want to share with their friends or, for that matter, with anyone else. Incest is a barrier to discovering the self, for it embeds in the person a sense of being vulnerable, of not really being in charge of one's own body.

A child needs to know that if he is involved in an incestuous relationship and cannot find anyone close enough to talk to, he should look in the phone book under the listings for social service organizations or mental health services or call information for the name of an organization that can help. Many listings will have the terms *child abuse* or *family counseling* in their descriptions. The resource section in this book provides additional information.

RAPE

Despite the fact that intercourse is usually an act of love, in the case of rape it is a way of expressing hate and inflicting pain. It is an act of violence, punishable by law. Teach your adolescent that some instances of rape can be avoided by protecting herself. Review safely rules with your child, including those concerning hitchhiking and going out alone at night. Without using scare tactics, alert your child to the high incidence of danger involved when these commonsense rules are neglected. Again, be sure your child knows that she can turn to you for help. Additionally, crisis lines and crisis centers have been established in each state and in most cities. Review with your child the information she might need and the steps she should take if she ever needs emergency help. With a knowledge of safety rules, your teenager will be more likely to be able to protect herself and to be of help to others.

VERY SECRET SUBJECTS

Masturbation and sexual fantasies are two sexual subjects that parents and their adolescents find embarrassing and difficult to discuss with each other. The word *masturbation* means handling or massaging one's genitals for sexual pleasure and to reach orgasm. For hundreds of years masturbation was considered a sin, and myths arose and circulated about its dangers. People were led to believe that if a male ejaculated as a result of masturbation he would become weak and listless, would not have enough sperm left for reproduction, or would slowly go insane. The tales were so numerous and widespread that people were filled with guilt and fear about masturbation.

Today, we know that masturbation by both males and females is a natural part of growing up. Masturbation is one of the ways in which a child learns about his or her own body and is considered a harmless outlet for sexual tension.

Some young people, usually during adolescence, find that they become overinvolved with masturbation, to the point that it interferes with other activities. Your adolescent may masturbate more when upset or disturbed about something instead of trying to determine the source of his unhappiness and do something about it. Often a little counseling with an adult the teenager trusts can help the teenager understand why this is happening. What your child wants and needs to know is that masturbation will not hurt him or anyone else.

Your teenager may also be concerned about the unusual kinds of daydreams he is having. He gazes off into space and imagines he is kissing or loving someone he knows or wants to know. The daydreams involve all sorts of people and all kinds of situations. Another word for daydreaming is *fantasizing*. Sexual fantasies are a normal part of being a sexual human being. Most people have sexual fantasies throughout their lives and accept them as an enjoyable aspect of sex.

THE JOY OF SEX: A DEVELOPMENTAL VIEW OF SEXUAL UNFOLDING

When your teenager was a young child, you probably thought he had nothing more on his mind than being mischievous and making your life as hectic as possible. There was more going on, too.

Even very young babies have sexual urges. A young child will inevitably direct his sexual impulses toward the adult of the opposite sex who is closest to him. Early sexual urges might be likened to feelings of infatuation or fondness.

In midadolescence, the developmental task is to ready the body for sexual reproduction. This stage of puberty produces some of the most dramatic sexual changes in the individual's life: the growth of pubic hair, the development of breasts, the menarche, the ability to have erections and nocturnal emissions (wet dreams), and the discovery of arousal through manipulation (masturbation). As the body moves closer to sexual maturity, sexual impulses are stronger. The adolescent's desires cause him to look at his parents with renewed interest. This is a very frightening thing for the teenager. He is impelled to move abruptly away from these threatening feelings by devaluing the parents, seeking shelter in anger, reaching out to substitute figures. This time he reaches into his same-age, same-sex peer group.

Now boys pair up with boys and girls with girls. This is preparatory to moving out, in a year or so, into relationships with the same-age opposite sex. For now, the child of twelve or thirteen feels much more comfortable with friends of his own sex, even though he may be eager, although not quite ready, for heterosexual relationships. There is safety in numbers. When a boy goes calling on a girl, he takes the gang along. Standing on the corner, he whistles boldly at passing girls, backed up by his buddies. Girls cling together too. The girl hangs out with other girls in search of reinforcement of her own role. Being with other girls confirms her femininity.

A year or two later, after your adolescent has gained what he may think is sufficient skill in maneuvering in the opposite-sex relationship maze, he moves from his same-age, same-sex group into same-age, opposite-sex groups. If he experiences rejection (unbearable teasing or ridicule or repeated failure in social skills), he will turn his affection back to adults again, though not to his parents. A coach, movie star, or rock idol becomes the focus of his affection. When the teenager feels secure again, he will venture back to the same-age, opposite-sex group. When this feels comfortable, he will move again, this time into more adultlike love relationships. This is how you, too, prepared for sexual maturity. You can help your adolescent understand his unfolding sexuality. In addition to providing information about the issues already discussed in this chapter you can do the following:

Strengthen gender identification. During early adolescence, physical maturation is a particularly sensitive matter. For this reason your adolescent needs understanding and support from you. This is very important. Assure your adolescent that these physical changes bring him closer to an image of himself as a sexual adult. This serves to strengthen his gender identification.

Recognize self-involved behavior for what it is. Many of the changes produced by his unfolding sexuality cause more self-involved behavior because his body is transforming very rapidly. These body changes tend to produce some strong but ambivalent feelings within the adolescent, particularly with respect to the need for peer approval. For example, it is reassuring for a fifteen-year-old boy to observe his facial hair in the mirror, but it is embarrassing for him to be teased about it by other adolescents. Or a thirteen-year-old boy, on assessing his body height and weight, may be aware and pleased that some growth toward maturity has occurred, but he may feel deflated and concerned about himself when he observes that twelve-year-old girls are more physically developed than he is.

Inform your adolescent. In addition to his understanding his sexuality, it is also important that your adolescent be fully informed regarding these changes and how the sexes and individuals differ in growth characteristics. He needs to know *why* each change is occurring. The meaning and normalcy of such events as nocturnal emission and menstruation are major examples. Your teenager feels anxious about the many physical and emotional changes now taking place. Changes such as wet dreams, menstruation, and feelings associated with masturbation may evoke feelings of fear, joy, embarrassment, or relief. He will vacillate from feeling unique and alone with all of the changes to feeling a need for peer comparisons as he accepts his new identity. Feeling awkward and unattractive, he will want assurance from you that he is loved, accepted, and, most of all, normal. Expect, too, that he will seek approval from his peers as to how these new changes fit into the peer social environment.

Don't withdraw affection. Uncertain as to how to relate, you may alter your response to your adolescent or withdraw at a time when he needs you most. You may become less physically affectionate, withholding kisses and hugs. You may become more cautious in touching your adolescent for fear that these actions will cause him to develop sexual desires toward you or will help cause promiscuity or homosexuality. You may view the impulsivity and emotions of your teenager as frightening (and they may look frightening to the teenager as well). Your caution may be due to memories of your own adolescence or to your feelings of being unsure of how you can best help your teenager. Communications may be less open at a time when it is vital for you and your child to relate to each other. A parent of a thirteen-year-old boy said to me, "I stopped kissing my son as often as I used to. I thought he was getting too old for that type of thing. I didn't realize that my sudden withdrawal made my son feel that he had done something wrong. One day he asked me if I was mad at him!" Because your actions are closely monitored by your teenager, he feels such rejections more acutely.

Listen, care, communicate. To cope with the monumental changes during the adolescent years, you will need to talk with your teenager about human sexuality and the responsibilities of being a sexual individual. Remember that his peers often provide erroneous information, so most kids are taken by surprise.

Modeling. Children learn by what they see. Your adolescent acquires a good many of his attitudes by what he sees at home. Perhaps this is a good time for you to reexamine your own relationship and to analyze the ups and downs, the good times and the struggles. Your adolescent has a natural curiosity about love and love relationships. He is busy forming an ideal of what he wants a relationship to be. Be aware of the messages he receives from you when he observes your own relationship.

Get more information for your adolescent. In early adolescence, which may range from the ages of nine to fourteen in girls and ten to fifteen in boys, there are hormonal changes that may be so intense that the adolescent feels his body is out of control. Midadolescence generally ranges from about thirteen to sixteen for boys and eleven to fourteen for girls. However, there are considerable variations among individuals. In boys, midadolescence can start as early as eleven and end as late as eighteen. In girls, it can start as early as ten and end as late as sixteen. More and valid information about various dimensions of sexuality during these times can help your adolescent to gain a healthy perspective on issues pertaining to each stage. Attending a sex-education class or reading current literature on the subject can be a useful way for your child to gather additional information.

Get help. Sometimes it is easier for parents and teenagers to disentangle themselves from their anxieties and difficulties about these issues if they seek help from a professional. Often the task of the therapist is to help the family members talk with one another about sex. Counseling may be one way for some families to overcome their fears and resolve their difficulties.

If you don't talk to your teenager about sex, he will look for answers to his questions elsewhere. You can't help and guide your adolescent if you don't know his feelings and confusions. If you work them out together, you can be assured that your adolescent is progressing toward sexual maturity. Only then can you feel confident that you have prepared your teenager to take on the responsibilities involved.

TALKING SEX WITH YOUR TEEN

Where do you begin talking with your teenager? Young adults are just waiting for someone to take an interest in their lives, especially someone who loves them and has experienced much of what they are going through. Don't worry that talking about sexual intercourse will encourage sexual experimentation; information usually discourages rather than encourages adolescents to become sexually active. Remember, too, that they are encouraged and pressured by their peers. It's up to you to provide the knowledge and the balance they will otherwise lack.

We all want our children to experience mature love. Part of their attaining that goal is in their knowing what is involved in a caring, loving, responsible relationship. Your teenager will not know what a mature relationship is unless you share with him what you know that to be. Liken it to your relationship, if this is appropriate. This is always a special conversation because you can reveal what you learned in the early love relationships you had when you were an adolescent. Share how you learned mature love and how you knew when you had finally discovered it.

Teenagers are eager to learn all they can about human sexuality. They want and deserve realistic and personal answers. When offered an opportunity to discuss sex seriously, teenagers talk freely and sensibly. They look for standards and meaning. They want to come to terms with their sexuality. You can help your child to integrate sexuality into his or her life as a meaningful dimension.

In talking with your child, you will need to define clearly four essential concepts: *sex, human sexuality, sexual intercourse,* and *love.*

Sex is the state of being male or female. Human sexuality is the way a male feels about being male and a female feels about being female. These feelings produce the need in humans to touch, kiss, and be close. The need to be together in a loving way is a natural and instinctive feeling. It is a biological urge that ensures the continuation of the human race. Sexual intercourse is the act of mating, a joining together of the male and female reproductive organs. The function of sexual intercourse is reproduction. Love is true intimacy—a deep, committed, caring devotion that endures over time. Love consists of two basic elements, *eros* and *agape*. *Eros* refers to passionate love, while *agape* describes the stable and committed relationship that exists between two individuals who care deeply for each other. We hope that our children will enter into relationships that have both of these elements. When there is too much or not enough of one, the imbalance creates an unsatisfying relationship.

Parents and teenagers who can talk about sexual issues are much more likely to cope successfully with the inevitable stress produced by the developmental life-stage changes of human sexuality. Look for opportunities to talk about the many aspects of human sexuality with your teenager, and be sensitive to his confusions and anxieties. Look for opportunities to have meaningful discussions—for example, when your adolescent discusses the boasting of one of his classmates or talks about the "hot and heavy" couple at school. In contemporary society boys and girls have more use of cars and more freedom. There is maximum temptation and minimum supervision, and parents must thus be realistic.

Chances are that your child may disagree with or challenge much of what you say. This is natural and to be expected. Even if your opinions differ, share with your adolescent your experiences and wisdom. Doing so will provide him with alternatives.

Sarah, a seventeen-year-old, was furious with her parents for disapproving of her new boyfriend, Mike, twenty-four. Her parents warned her that she was probably not ready for the type of relationship that Mike might want. They urged her not to date Mike exclusively. Sarah felt her parents were overreacting and making unfair judgments about Mike. Later, when she was pressured into a sexual relationship, she realized that her parents had been right. If Sarah's parents had forbidden Sarah to continue to see Mike, she might not have learned to trust her parents. Though her parents offered firm counsel, they left the decision to Sarah. A short time later Sarah stopped seeing Mike of her own accord, and she felt secure about her decision. Her actions may have been different had her parents demanded her to stop seeing Mike without allowing her to participate in the decision.

Your teenager is gaining maturity, trying to discover what everything means. After you have shared your values with your teenager, she will make her own choices. You can't shield her from the world forever. She may still mistake sexual intimacy for mature love, and that, too, is what learning is about. Sexual intimacy is a powerful, exciting feeling. But sexual maturity is gained from understanding the issues and the consequences of love relationships through experience. It is not a textbook education. By being open and accessible and by providing your child with the information he or she needs, you can better prepare your adolescent for sexual maturity in a healthy way.

CHAPTER SIX

School: The Toll of a Thirteen-Year Career

Here's a quiz for you. What looks like a job, feels like a job, and takes its toll on a person like a job? What demands seven to eight hours a day of intense concentration, five days a week? What has people in positions of power overlooking your performance, and people below you depending on you for help? A job? Sort of. The correct answer is: going to school.

I have always been amazed at how relatively little we know about the cumulative effects of schooling, learning, and educational environments on students, and how much less we know about the child's experience during the years he spends in school. Children do spend a large portion of their waking hours in educational settings. The average student spends approximately 15,000 hours in educational environments from kindergarten through twelfth grade. From the time young people are five years of age until they are eighteen, nearly eight hours each day during the week are spent in the school environment. In the end, each child will be a twelve- or thirteen-year veteran of a mandated educational experience. Yet surprisingly little attention has been give to the overall impact of the school experience on children, and neither students nor their parents receive a "school manual" similar to the job manuals that companies often give out to inform employees of company policies and of the many facets of organizational life.

When I asked adults about their primary memory of school, the word most commonly used was *pressure*. Instead of hearing the terms I had expected, such as *happy* or *fun*, I heard *intense* and *frustrating*. When you were a teenager, did you think that it was cruel and inhuman punishment to make someone sit in classrooms for seven hours a day and study such "useless" subjects as science, literature, and geometry? Why should you suppose your teenager feels any different about school than you did? Take a few moments to talk to your child about her feelings and about yours. You may find that you have more in common than the car that you argue over!

THE STUDENT STRESS PROFILE

As parents, we can and must undertake the challenge of helping children to learn adaptive ways of dealing with stress in school. There are a number of methods and approaches for dealing with school stress, and many of these will be suggested in this chapter. Others will be dealt with more systematically and in greater detail in the final section of this book, which deals with stress-reduction methods. However, an important point that must always be kept in mind in coping with and managing school stress is that the responsibility for maintaining health should be a reflection of the basic relationship between your teen, the school, and you.

The school experience can and does represent a great many of the stressors your child experiences throughout his childhood. While you shouldn't remove all stress from your adolescent's life, too much stress can be harmful to his well-being and personal development. How do you know how much school stress is too much, what is "good" or "acceptable" stress, and what is "destructive" stress? How can you determine just how much school stress your adolescent is under right now?

The following stress profile is designed to help students and their parents understand, on a self-evaluative basis, the areas and frequency of their school stress. After your child has completed all forty-nine items, your child should transfer the scores to the scoring profile. Discuss the results of the profile so your child under-

stands what her scores mean. Both general and category scores
are useful in discussion.

STRESS PROFILE FOR STUDENTS

*Directions: Circle one number for each item. 1 = never; 2 = some-
times; 3 = frequently.*

INTERPERSONAL
 1. When in school, I like to be by myself.   1   2   3
 2. Peers do not include me in their activities.   1   2   3
 3. I worry about what other students are thinking about me.
                                                     1   2   3
 4. I frequently tell other students what to do.   1   2   3
 5. I am easily influenced by peers.   1   2   3
 6. I like to be the leader of the group.   1   2   3
                              Total Items 1–6_____

SELF-CONCEPT
 7. I feel that other students do not like me.   1   2   3
 8. I worry about what my family thinks about me as a
    student.   1   2   3
 9. It bothers me to back out of a possible fight with other
    students.   1   2   3
10. I see myself as a loner in the school environment.
                                                     1   2   3
11. I do not feel good about myself in school.   1   2   3
12. Other students act friendly toward me.   1   2   3
13. Other students would describe me as calm, cool, and
    collected.   1   2   3
                             Total Items 7–13_____

SELF-CONTROL
14. I feel I can't control what happens to me.   1   2   3
15. I let other students tell me what to do.   1   2   3
16. When I do something wrong in school, there is very little I
    can do to change it.   1   2   3

17. In school, I am blamed for things that are not my fault.

                                                      1   2   3

18. When another student is angry with me, there is little I can do to change his mind.   1   2   3

19. I let other students take charge of things.   1   2   3

20. If there is a fight, I feel like I want to join in.

                                                      1   2   3

                      Total Items 14–20_____

COPING SKILLS

21. In school, I often lose control of myself.   1   2   3

22. If I see a fight at school, I feel threatened.   1   2   3

23. I get upset when I see fighting in school.   1   2   3

24. In school, I am often so angry that I feel like hitting someone.   1   2   3

25. If someone is angry with me, I can avoid getting into a fight by working it out with him or her.   1   2   3

26. When I get angry in school, it's usually for a reason I can understand.   1   2   3

27. When there is a problem, I feel like letting other students decide what to do.   1   2   3

                    Total Items 21–27_____

PROBLEM SOLVING

28. I have trouble solving my school-related problems.

                                            1   2   3

29. I try to get my own way.   1   2   3

30. I get upset or angry when things go wrong.   1   2   3

31. I can't tell friends how I feel about things.   1   2   3

32. I try to avoid facing school problems.   1   2   3

33. I need a friend to help me with my problems.

                                            1   2   3

34. I don't think planning ahead makes things turn out better.

                                            1   2   3

                    Total Items 28–34_____

SCHOOL

35. I worry about school.   1   2   3

36. I feel nervous at school.   1   2   3

37. I wish I did not have to go to school.   1   2   3
38. I have trouble doing my schoolwork.   1   2   3
39. I am not interested in schoolwork.   1   2   3
40. I do not have good friends at school.   1   2   3
41. When I am in school, I wish I were someplace else.

                                                    1   2   3
                        Total Items 36–41_____

PHYSICAL/BEHAVIORAL SIGNS OF STRESS

42. I feel upset at school.   1   2   3
43. I feel I can't find time to relax or rest.   1   2   3
44. I feel I can't stay still.   1   2   3
45. I get sad or depressed.   1   2   3
46. I get stomachaches or headaches.   1   2   3
47. I find myself overloaded with too much to do.

                                                    1   2   3
48. I have trouble sleeping at night.   1   2   3
                        Total Items 42–48_____

SCORING SHEET
STRESS PROFILE FOR STUDENTS

Copyright © 1980, Christopher F. Wilson

Instructions for Scoring

1. After you have completed items 1–48, total the scores in each section and enter it in the corresponding box on the following page. See sample scoring sheet.
2. Add up all your category scores and enter the number in the box after Total Overall Score. If you divide the total score by 7, you will find your average score for the total test, and this should be entered at the bottom of the scoring chart.
3. Plot your score on the dotted line with an "X" and draw a line between your scoring "X's" so that a clear profile of your stress evaluation is visible.
4. Check your level on the same line as either low, moderate, or high.

STRESS

LOW ------------- MODERATE ------------- HIGH

	SCORE	7 8 9 10 11 12 13 14 15 16 17 18 19 20 21
Interpersonal	☐	. . . .
Self-concept	☐	. . . .
Self-control	☐	. . . .
Coping skills	☐	. . . .
Problem solving	☐	. . . .
School	☐	. . . .
Physical/Behavioral Signs of Stress	☐	. . . .
TOTAL OVERALL SCORE	☐	LOW ------------- MODERATE ------------- HIGH

THE STUDENTS' WORLD OF WORK

For your teenager, being a student is his occupation, learning is his role, education is his career, and school is his organization. These facets encompass his world of work. Have you ever asked your child, "How was your (school) day?" and he replied simply, "Fine"? Not knowing what his answer entailed, you probably let it go at that.

The demands on the youngster-as-student in the school organization and the adult in the work setting are quite similar. This comparison is useful for a number of reasons: if we can better understand what causes stress for teenagers in school, we can empathize with them, because we are familiar with work related stress. This information can prove useful both in helping your teenager develop an understanding of the sources of stress in the school environment and in delineating the skills and techniques he is likely to need for managing stress in all work settings. By understanding the sources of school stress, you can provide a more supportive environment. Allowing your teenager to express his views about the pressures and consequences of his work helps him to cope with his school-related fears.

Researchers have identified four factors responsible for contributing to organizational stress. These include (1) the tasks and demands intrinsic to the job, (2) the organizational climate and culture, (3) personal safety needs, and (4) the balance between organizational demands and personal life. These four can be likened to much of the stress adolescents encounter in the school setting. As you read each one, try to remember your own school days, times when you felt flooded with these problems, stressed by matters out of your control. Discuss them with your child to see which specific factors are the most troublesome for him and to find out whether you can help him put them in perspective.

INTRINSIC STRESS

Students contend with multiple subjects in school, with a different teacher for each course and a new group of peers in each class period. The typical school experience is for the student to rotate to a different course every fifty-five minutes, six or seven times each day. How many times have you heard your child complain, "Why do my teachers have to give us tests on the same day? I think all the teachers sit in the cafeteria and think up ways to give us huge homework assignments that are all due at once." Think of how you would feel at work if you had six reports all due on the same day and had absolutely no flexibility to stagger them.

A student experiences additional stress when the curriculum is either too demanding or is not challenging enough for his or her level of ability, particularly when the teacher is unable to spend adequate time with each student. Again, think of how you feel at work when you are given an extremely difficult assignment and left to do it on your own. If you couldn't get anyone to spend some time with you, answer some questions, or give you some pointers, wouldn't you be frustrated and upset?

Imagine sitting in a boxlike room, possibly with no windows, with harsh overhead lighting. Surrounding you on all sides, almost touching you, are about forty other people, many sniffling with head colds or making hawking or other disgusting noises. They are constantly elbowing you out of the way, trying to get all the attention focused on themselves. You are on a hard wooden seat with no cushion, trying to keep your knees from banging a metal rod that connects a flat writing surface to the chair. If you have long legs, you try to toss them somewhere where they won't be knocked by everyone who passes. Now, do you feel like concentrating on advanced physics or English literature? Most likely, all you want to do is get out of there as quickly as possible. But suppose you can't? Suppose you have to stay there for seven hours today, seven hours tomorrow, and seven hours a day for the next several years? Feeling stressed yet?

For students, poor physical working conditions seem to be one of the major factors contributing to "job" stress. Learning is a challenging task even in the most optimal of conditions. It is compounded by the numbers of students in today's classrooms and the incidence of disruptive behavior by other class students. Says John, "I'd compare my school classes to the zoo: each student spends so much time trying to get recognized that each behavior is more bizarre than the next. Even the teacher has to compete for attention."

"Okay, enough!" you may say. "But how can I take on my child's organization? Isn't that a bit like taking on city hall?" The answer is yes, and it's probably less satisfying. But something can be done by the school itself, by you working with your child, and by you working with the school. Let's examine each of these.

Class size may be the single most important factor in reducing job stress. In classrooms where the numbers of students do not exceed twenty-two, students are more likely to receive the individualized and personalized instruction needed to meet the challenges of learning. Teachers of smaller classes are better able to modify the curriculum and to be more innovative, and students are more likely to understand what they do as purposeful. Students develop a better sense of self-worth because the teacher has more time for each student. Limiting classes to fewer than twenty-two students will boost teachers' morale and students' motivation. Until we do this, we simply are not taking education seriously as an important event in the lives of our children. Parents need to choose this alternative above all others and then insist that schools implement it.

You can't always change the way the school operates, and you may not always be able to influence the way the teacher treats your child. The one area over which you do have control is communication between you and your teenager. There are several suggested actions you can take.

Help prepare your child for the job. Every child needs a quiet study area, safe from interruption, equipped with a good light. During study time there should be no TV or stereo, no major interruptions. Discourage lengthy phone calls during study time. Agree on a regular time for studying.

"What helped me most," said Rob, "was how my parents helped me get organized. My father designed a bookcase and a desk that was really handy. My mother helped me set up a file and showed me how to use it. They gave me a gigantic month-at-a-glance wall calendar to record my work assignments. It was easy for me to notice when I was able to schedule social activities. I felt like a professional doing a job."

Remember, each child is different. Your adolescent may be able to complete all her studying and homework in a single session, or she may do better if she studies for twenty minutes, takes a break, and then comes back to it. The important thing is that she recognize her own style of doing productive work. We all have a preferred work style, an optimum pattern for producing our best work. You can help your teenager identify her work style by pointing out the rituals that you go through before you are ready for productive work—for example, organizing your desk and sharpening all your pencils (even those you don't use!).

Teach your teenager time management. One of the greatest pressures on your youngster is time. For most junior-high and high-school students, there never seems to be enough time to cope with the work of several courses, time for friends, extracurricular activities, family, and self.

Teach your child to break large tasks into smaller ones. If she has to write a report, can she schedule the research for this weekend and the writing for the next weekend? Instead of cramming the night before, can she study for a big test over two or three days?

Learning to budget time is both possible and essential. A very important step in learning to manage time is to set up a daily or weekly "to-do" list. It should not be a long and detailed list but should contain those things the student wants to accomplish each day (or week). Priority setting is important. Show your adolescent how to delineate the four to six tasks that are the most important and then prioritize them. Set a timetable and estimate the length of time necessary to perform each task. The chart on the following page has proven helpful for students.

Show active interest. If you ask, "What did you do in school today?" and your child answers, "Nothing," ask more specific questions based on what you know is being taught. Even if you don't get much information, you're telling your child that you care about school, that he should, too, and that school is purposeful in one's life. Ask your teenager what he is learning. Does he feel he is showing improvement? What contributed to the good grades as well as to the poor ones? That is, is the "A" a mark of achievement, or was the work too easy? Find out if he feels you are supportive. Ask these questions even though you may feel you know how it's going. Think about how disappointing it is when a supervisor at work assumes you are doing well, so he or she doesn't bother asking. Or, worse, it may be assumed that because you have done well in the past, you will continue to do well—and at *all* tasks. Remember, school is tough for "A" students too.

TODAY'S DATE	TASKS	DATE DUE	TIME NEEDED TO ACCOMPLISH TASK	WHOM WILL I ASK FOR HELP IF NEEDED?	SPECIAL MATERIALS NEEDED
1.					
2.					
3.					
4.					
5.					
6.					

Children do as their parents do, not as they say. If you get excited about new books and new ideas, your teenager will too. If you act as though anything worth doing is worth doing well, that's how your child will approach his or her educational career.

Determine what on-the-job skills your adolescent needs. Use clues from report cards, teacher conferences, and aptitude tests to become familiar with your child's strengths and weaknesses so you'll know where you can help. Is your teen lacking a particular skill that is holding him back from current work? Can you obtain special tutoring for this problem? Is there a physical problem, perhaps with eyesight or hearing, or is there some learning disability?

Help your adolescent with homework judiciously. When children become students, parents often become tutors. This can be a very frustrating and tension-filled experience for both parent and child. Not all parents are able to tutor their children. If you find that you are unable to help your child, for whatever reason, find an outside source. Children do enjoy working with outside help, and this helps to alleviate the tension of additional constraints on parental time. If you do decide to tutor your child yourself, here are some helpful hints.

- *Do* emphasize to your child that the work is for his benefit, not yours.
- *Do* encourage him to do his best work, but recognize that this work may not necessarily be "A" level.
- *Do* let him know regularly that you are proud of him for doing his best.
- *Do* allow him time to relax.
- *Don't* communicate the idea to your child that he is letting you down.
- *Don't* blame him for doing poor work.
- *Don't* say or imply that you are ashamed of him.
- *Don't* condemn him as lazy.

If you have a good health-insurance policy, you just may be ready to begin tutoring your child. First, try this approach. "Michael, I talked to your math teacher this morning. She told me you were doing very well with simple equations but were having some problems with graphing. Let's work something out so I can help you with that graphing for a little while." This opens lines of communication. You can learn a great deal about your child simply by listening to him.

Your tutoring sessions should be enjoyable and satisfying for both you and your child. During the sessions it is better to sit next to your child rather than across from him. This way it is easy for both of you to see the lessons, and it encourages a friendlier atmosphere. If after the first session you find that the tutoring is unpleasant for you or your child, stop immediately and go back to listening to your child. Remember, the child's initial reaction may be based on fear of not being able to do the work. Be nonjudgmental.

For some children the major difficulty is not in mastering the subject matter but in following directions, so be sure that the directions you give are not difficult to follow and are presented slowly and clearly.

Plan the lesson in small steps that require frequent answers. This keeps the child's attention on the work and gives you a closer look at where the difficulties lie. For example, if you are doing addition problems, present them one at a time rather than asking the child to do a page of fifteen or twenty examples all at once.

When your child speaks to you or when you are speaking to him, be sure to look at him. It is sometimes easier to *see* confusion and frustration than it is to hear it.

Don't skip any problems. Wait for an answer to each one. This helps the child develop the habit of working on difficult items rather than passing them by.

You know how much your adolescent dislikes the bitterness of failure, so minimize your use of the word *no* and of phrases such as "That's not it" or "That's wrong" while you are tutoring. Instead, respond to a wrong answer by restating the question and supplying your child with more clues to help in getting the correct answer. After the child gets the correct answer, it is very helpful to go over the question in its original form without the clues but with praise.

LEARN MORE ABOUT YOUR CHILD'S JOB

Get involved. Become familiar with the courses your child is enrolled in, and know what's being taught and what's expected. What books will be read? How much homework will be required? What major long-term projects can be anticipated? Is your child likely to need help with any projects?

MEET YOUR CHILD'S "BOSS"

Meet your child's teacher at the beginning of the term. In fact, many parents feel quite uncomfortable about contacting their child's teacher and anxious if the teacher calls to request a meeting. For many of these parents, such feelings may be related to the fact that the "teacher" is still associated with their own childhood, when the teacher may have been a strong authority figure who defined what was right or wrong and who judged them. Parents also need to realize that teachers often come to parent-teacher conferences with their own apprehensions and uncertainties about how they will be viewed by the child's parents. Understanding the perspective of the teacher as well as the feelings that you yourself may have will help to make your relationship with the teacher not only productive but also enjoyable.

Many parents hold the belief that parent-teacher conferences occur for one of only two reasons: their child is behaving badly, or their child is having serious problems keeping up with schoolwork. While these reasons are sometimes accurate, they are not the only conditions in which conferences occur. In fact, conferences may serve quite a variety of functions, and may be held for the following purposes, among others:

- to report on the child's progress
- to compare the teacher's understanding of the child with that of the parents (when the teacher has noticed something in the child's behavior that could be of concern)
- to ask parents for specific help (for example, when a child is having difficulties with schoolwork that may be related to the home environment)

Parents should feel free to take the initiative to schedule conferences if they have specific questions or if they want to know generally how their child is doing. If you think there is a problem, make an appointment with the teacher immediately.

Watch for the overinvolved teenager syndrome. Children can experience job burnout just as adults can. It may be due to an after-school job that takes up too many hours, or it may be caused by too many clubs, dates, or other activities. Is your teenager trying to do too much at once? Discuss with your child which activities can be cut back. Your child will be relieved that you have intervened.

CLIMATE AND CULTURE

The conditions in schools have been deteriorating for such a long time that some of us may not be able to identify the characteristics of a good school climate. Schools with positive climates are characterized by people-centered belief and value systems, procedures, rules, regulations, and policies. People care, respect, and trust one another, and the school as an institution cares, respects, and trusts people. In such a school, people feel a high sense of pride and ownership that comes from each individual's having a role in making the school a better place.

Schools with positive climates are constantly changing as people reshape them in accordance with human needs. In such schools, school improvement is everybody's business. As the climate of the school becomes more positive, some highly undesirable symptoms of poor climate tend to disappear. Discipline problems, vandalism, defacing of property, and violence subside. Attendance and achievement improve. The number of dropouts declines. People are more respectful of and helpful to others, and they assume more responsibility for the climate in the school.

A note of caution: this situation doesn't happen by itself. Among the many important factors that contribute to a positive school climate are community involvement and interagency cooperation. An individual student, parent, educator, law-enforcement official, or community leader cannot repair breakdowns in discipline or end campus violence. It requires a collective effort. The challenge to provide positive, orderly, and crime-free schools requires strong parental involvement, administrative support, and the active involvement of the educational organization and its surrounding community.

Every organization has a culture as well as a climate. The basic principle is that people, not machines, make organizations work and that group culture ties people together and gives meaning and purpose to their everyday lives. A culture is a people system of informal rules that spell out (rather rigidly) acceptable patterns of human behavior. Sometimes a culture is fragmented and difficult to read from the outside. In a business organization, for example, some people feel most loyal to their bosses, others feel more loyal to the union, and still others care only about their work or their colleagues. Sometimes the culture of an organization is very strong and cohesive; nearly everyone knows the goals of the organization and is working toward them. Those who do not may feel emotionally alienated and leave on their own.

The sheer numbers of students in today's school environment have drastically altered the nature of the cultures there. Since there is so little sense of belonging to a school anymore, and since a teenager wants desperately to belong to something, he turns to his peer group. Yet being a part of a peer group is not always a happy experience. The fact that children suffer emotional duress in peer groups is mostly due to their lack of any training in what the "rules" are as well as to their lack of a coping skills to deal with the rejection that is often encountered.

Becoming a member of a peer group usually follows a pattern for the adolescent. Assessment comes first. Adolescents begin to decide which groups they would like to join, and they may or may not make overtures to the desired groups. At the same time, members of various groups (not necessarily the desired ones) may make bids for their friendship. Adolescent groups, like organizational groups, tend to carefully select their members according to very specific standards. Popularity and acceptance may be based on such characteristics as good looks, athletic ability, social goals, religious affiliation, ethnic-group membership, and special talents. These criteria may not be publicly stated, but they are informally known.

Becoming a member of a peer group presents a number of challenges for your adolescent. Along with his strong need to be liked and included, he will have to decide which group he would like to identify with. No matter what group he chooses, he must be willing to suppress some of his own individuality and to focus instead on characteristics shared with his peers. Most peer groups expect members to conform in order to bolster the group. If a youngster is not able to handle the expectations of the group, he may be forced to choose between an unhappy, self-imposed membership, or face rejection and withdraw. He then looks for an alternative peer group. Sixteen-year-old Jack wanted desperately to belong to a select group of school athletes who were popular and generally the focus of attention. The desire to belong to the group motivated his earning good grades, and his dedication and hard work at football practice. When he was cut from the team, and thus generally ignored by the members of this group, Jack felt devastated. After repeated attempts to belong to the group met with failure, Jack lost interest in achieving good grades. Poor grades made membership ever more elusive. Jack was now out of the group, and Jack chose to turn to another group for acceptance. Once again, he took on the trappings of a new group's identification.

Not all adolescents belong to groups. Sometimes this occurs because parents press their sons and daughters to restrict their associations to a particular peer group that may not appeal to the adolescent or that may not offer membership. Another possibility is that the teenager finds no group that seems to meet his or her own personal needs, regardless of pressure from others. A third possibility is that no peer group offers friendship to a particular adolescent, causing his gradual exclusion from all existing groups in his social environment.

You can help your adolescent understand the dynamics of peer cultures. He need not face the experience unaware. Though you may never fully understand what your son sees in his friends with the blue hair, it is important for you to accept the fact that while your child appears to be diverging from your family's own customs, replacing them with the norms and expectations of his peer group, like most teenagers he holds on to the basic values learned at home. The vast majority of adolescents tend to remain true to the values formulated by years of interaction with their parents and other significant adults, even when this does not appear to be the case. For example, if education is considered important in your family, your child is likely to continue to view education as important, although he may criticize certain aspects of the school experience.

Knowing this, you should probably focus less on changes in your child that indicate a strong allegiance to his peer group and his identity within it and more on your basic compatibilities with him. Again, the quality of the parent/child relationship is very important to the adolescent's well-being. A healthy parent/child relationship can lessen the negative feelings of alienation your adolescent encounters as he strives to achieve membership in the school culture.

SCHOOL CRIME

Research shows that mental health at work is to a large extent a function of the degree to which individuals feel they work in a safe and orderly environment. The absence of feeling secure in the workplace is significantly related to the following factors: overall poor physical health, escapist drinking, depressed mood, low self-esteem, low life satisfaction, low job satisfaction, low motivation to work, intention to leave the job, and absenteeism from work.

We working adults aren't the only ones who suffer such effects. Our children are also concerned with their "working" conditions. Often, school is not the safe environment in which we would wish our children to spend significant amounts of time. Sadly, student violence escalates every year. Common incidents of such violence include verbal and physical threats, assault, injury, theft, arson, and vandalism. If a school does not promote a safe environment, it can be deleterious to the emotional and physical health of students. In the school environment, students are most distressed when they fear another student, when school activities are not well supervised, and when they hear about an incidence of violence or are themselves the victims of violence.

Students, teachers, and parents all have rights and responsibilities. School crime and disorder pose major challenges to America's schools, but they pose an even greater and more immediate challenge to parents. An effective school system must maintain a level of civil behavior sufficient to allow learning to take place.

Although many schools have taken steps to improve their climates, the bottom line is that parents, educators, and administrators must face the problem squarely: they must recognize its importance and take steps together to improve conditions in the schools—immediately.

Considerable research has indicated that the problems encountered in the schools are severe and that they should concern all of us. Recently, the National Institute of Education (NIE) conducted a national "safe school" study on the extent of criminal activity in U.S. schools. According to that study, the scope of criminal activity in America's secondary schools was as follows:

282,000 students were physically attacked.

112,000 students were robbed in situations involving weapons or threats.

2.4 million students had personal property stolen.

800,000 students stayed home from school because they were afraid to attend.

6000 teachers were robbed.

1000 teachers were assaulted seriously enough to require medical attention.

More than 125,000 teachers encountered at least one situation in which they were afraid to confront misbehaving students.

One out of every two teachers was on the receiving end of an insult or an obscene gesture.

2400 fires were set in schools.

13,000 thefts of school property occurred.

24,000 incidents of vandalism occurred.

42,000 cases of damage to school property occurred.

These figures reflect what happened during a typical *month* in U.S. schools!

In addition to the obvious deleterious stress of being a victim of a crime, all students are indirectly but seriously affected by the crime rate in schools. Research shows that students who are afraid at school receive lower grades and are more likely to rate themselves as below-average students. When a student views the school as a hostile environment, he is more likely than a nonfearful student to think that teachers are unable to maintain order and is more likely to dislike the school, teachers, and fellow students. Fear reduces the adolescent's ability to concentrate on schoolwork, creates an atmosphere of hostility and mistrust in the school, undermines morale, and teaches that the staff is not in control—that student disorder is more powerful than the adult call for order. Students who are attacked without provocation or who do not know their assailants—and the majority of assaults are of this type—experience the greatest prolonged levels of anxiety, stress, and depression. Students who have been victims of attack, robbery, or extreme verbal abuse often admit that they are afraid both on the way to or from school and while actually in school. If their uneasiness becomes intolerable, they will stay away from school altogether: Currently, more than 1 million teenagers drop out of school each year; the figure continues to increase annually.

Those students most susceptible to stress-related illnesses seem to have an impaired ability to deal effectively with fear or anger. Many students who succumb to sustained stress are unable to strike back when they find themselves the target of violence or hostility. Instead, they internalize their fear or rage. Students do not receive formal psychological training that would prepare them for the threat of violence and abuse in school, and many students are ill-equipped to confront the dangers endemic in their schools.

You can help your child feel less threatened by doing the following:

Be aware. You can help your child by being aware of his fears or anxieties about his physical safety. Don't underestimate or ignore the fears your child may be experiencing; the expectation of a stressful event can be every bit as potent as the event itself. Adolescents, like young children, need to feel that they can turn to trusted adults for help when it is needed. This, too, reduces the feelings of helplessness.

Don't hesitate to intervene. Don't let your teenager struggle in an unhealthy environment without intervening because you feel that letting him solve his own problems builds character. Adolescents who want the attention and admiration of older adolescents may become willing victims, often allowing themselves to have money or objects taken in exchange for group friendship. If this is happening to your adolescent, it may be because he lacks certain self-management skills. If so, he will need to acquire them. (Review the assertive-choice skills in chapter 2.)

Seek help. When your adolescent shares with you his experience of such problems, take them seriously. Many teens face undue harassment by another student and either cannot resolve it or are afraid to do so. Helping your adolescent acquire healthy ways of self-assertion can help him overcome victimization.

What adolescents really need is psychological training to prepare them for stressful situations. Assertiveness training, problem solving, and conflict management are all skills worth learning and can add to the adolescent's feelings of security. A local community-education program may offer workshops in skill development for teens.

Again, student support groups provide an opportunity for teenagers to share their experiences with another person or group. Such groups help improve the child's morale and also help him or her build a network for resolving problems. Many schools have a crisis-intervention team to defuse crises by implementing openforum discussions. Ask whether such a team is assigned to your school.

Learn about school security. Security procedures are necessary for every school. They can range from simple to complex, but the best ones are unobtrusive. Measures to insure physical security must focus on guaranteeing internal control of the school and external control of its perimeter. Take the time to talk to the high-school principal, groundskeeper, or security officer about what safety measures are being used on your child's school campus. Are there guards, or are teachers regularly scheduled to walk the corridors and grounds? Does a patrol car come by to check out the parking lot in instances of evening activities? The school personnel will usually be very willing to tell you about their security measures. If they are not, you might take their reluctance as a tacit admission that they recognize that the school's security measures are not as good as they should be. If you can't get any information from the school, call the police department or sheriff's office to find out whether there have been any crime reports filed from the school, and, if so, how many and of what type.

Once you have learned about school security measures, support them. If you are displeased with security measures, say so. Tell the principal or superintendent. Tell the school board. Tell the police department. If you can't get any satisfaction, tell the newspapers and television. Get your story told. When the news gets out, the community will back your efforts to make schools a safer place, but the effort may have to begin with you.

BALANCING WORK AND HOME

As parents, you and I know how difficult it is to balance our work world and family relationships and to have enough time for leisure and fitness pursuits and for socializing. Our teenagers, too, have a need for such balance, and when they don't know how to attain it, their lives become chaotic. We can help our teenagers to understand the importance of balance and how it contributes to wellness, and we can teach them by modeling a balance in our everyday lives.

It is unlikely that anyone is always "in balance." Special work projects require intense times of concentration and commitment. Keeping family unity as a priority and allowing for times of crisis require special coping skills. Striving for balance is the key.

Teenagers will still need adults who matter to them to mediate the information in their environments. Indeed, given the complexity of today's world, they need more such adult help in their lives than adolescents did in the past. Given the changed relationship between home and school—and the size of and departmentalization of schools—teachers and other adults in the schools have lost much of the power they once had to significantly influence the social and psychological development of students while they are addressing the students' intellectual development. As parents, we *can*, and we must, be there.

In the next chapter we'll be viewing feelings at closer range. In particular, we will see how negative feelings can lead to emotional despair and learn what we can do to lessen such negative feelings as alienation, loneliness, and depression in teenagers.

CHAPTER SEVEN

Alienation: Feeling Lonely, Being Alone

Have you ever attended a party where everyone seemed to fit in but you? No one paid much attention to you; no one went out of his or her way to talk to you and make you feel welcome. You decided you didn't want to be friends with these people. Why bother to smile, make small talk, or be on your best behavior? You knew you were behaving badly, but you just didn't care anymore.

Remember the overwhelming feeling of relief you had when your millionth glance at your watch showed you that the party was almost over and that you would be released soon to go home? Now, imagine how you would suffer if the evening had no end, if you had no idea when, or even whether, that awful loneliness would stop. Imagine going to bed every single night with that party to look forward to the next day. Welcome to the feelings of an alienated adolescent.

Alienation is a pervasive, lingering feeling of being unwanted. The alienated youth feels insecure and uncertain of his acceptance or status within groups that are important to him, such as family, friends, and schoolmates. Youths who are alienated believe that there is no purpose to life, that there is no reason to care, to hope, to try. Worst of all, they don't see much chance that things will improve in the future. An alienated adolescent is fatalistic in his understanding of circumstances. He is certain that his problems are caused by his parents, society, and the world in general and thus sees no hope for improvement. Sixteen-year-old

Dana said it this way: "My parents are so wrapped up in growing up themselves and working out their own problems that they don't have time for me. They are never around. I don't ever want to have kids. I would never put them through it. I don't even want to be an adult. They're so careless with people." A year older and yet much more jaded, Michelle related her personal feelings of despair to a larger social realm. "I'll never know the good life. Many of the hopes and dreams of kids my age will never be realized simply because of the numbers of us. And besides, if you do manage to find a decent job, if work stress won't kill you, nuclear war will. Why bother?"

Dramatic or not, Michelle's feelings are real, and they are echoed by many others her age. Unlike adults, who have experienced temporary feelings of estrangement, teenagers constantly feel "out of things." This unending emotional isolation and loneliness can lead to problem behavior.

Alienation can push teenagers to extremes. The following is a brief list of some of the consequences that psychologists and child behavior specialists have linked to adolescent alienation.

eating disorders, such as anorexia nervosa and bulimia, or obesity

juvenile delinquency

promiscuity

overreliance on the peer group

drug and alcohol abuse

depression

arson

BACK TO THE FAMILY

Scientists who study human behavior and development have found that the most powerful causative factor in alienation is the home environment. We tend to look at families and see parents as being either good or not so good without fully taking into account the circumstances in their lives. The circumstances surrounding the lives of today's families are different from those of a decade ago, making it less likely that significant time will be devoted exclusively to each youngster.

A parent who is physically or emotionally absent can have a significant effect on the mental and emotional health of the child. Unfortunately, the number of such parents is increasing.

There are 5 million "latchkey" children in the United States today. According to Harold Hodgkinson, a Washington-based researcher who has been studying the problem for the last several years, many of these children think of home as a "dangerous, frightening place, particularly if there are no other children in the home." They check in with parents by phone, spend many hours watching TV, and have to make decisions about knocks on the door and phone calls from strangers. While some children may in fact benefit from having family responsibilities and time alone, many others suffer greatly from this unwanted experience.

Few parents are ogres who try to segregate their children emotionally, who intentionally set out to make their children feel isolated, unwanted, alone. Parents who accidentally cause these feelings in their children may be loving, caring people who are consumed by problems of their own. Thus, alienation can be considered a temporary marker reflecting the increasing numbers of dual-career parents, single parents, and stepparents, all of whom may be experiencing any number of crises on a regular basis. How can you live through your crises without excluding your child?

The following vignettes illustrate the circumstances surrounding the lives of two adolescents. There are important differences, however, that make one home environment more prone to alienation as a potential problem than the other.

RUTH

Ruth is one of three children in a loving family. She is thirteen and in the ninth grade. She has two older sisters. One is away at college, the other a senior in high school. Like her sisters, Ruth grew up coming home from school to "table talks," mother-daughter chats at the kitchen table. Ruth and her sisters and their parents always enjoyed the closeness of these few minutes, times when the day's happenings could be shared. Everyone felt close, accepted, loved.

Things have changed now. Ruth's parents have separated, and with one child in college and another enrolling next year, Ruth's mom has had to go back to work to help pay expenses. Although she took a relatively early shift, she still gets home an hour after Ruth. Ruth is not alone at home; her high-school sister gets home a few minutes before she does. While the two of them talk, it's just not the same. The sister is interested in her boyfriend and her own friends. She's not willing to spend too much time listening to what she sees as the minor or silly problems of a "kid." Ruth is lonely, even though she is not alone. From her perspective, no one takes the time to listen or care anymore. By the time her mother gets home, Ruth is locked away in her room, sullen and withdrawn. She feels alienated and alone.

Ruth's mother realizes that her daughter is lonely, and she feels guilty about it. She also somewhat resents her daughter's behavior, thinking that Ruth should be a little more grown-up and accept the fact that her mother has to work to make money right now. Besides, she has her own phone, TV, stereo. Hasn't her working gotten Ruth a lot of nice things? The situation is one of guilt and resentment on both sides. Ruth and her mother know they are losing the closeness that they both value, but neither is certain of what to do about it.

DAVID

David, also thirteen, is an only child. He is happy, easygoing, and spunky. David's parents are divorced. He lives with his mother. Although David's mother works full-time, she has arranged her schedule so that she is home when her son returns from school. If for some reason she is unable to come home at the regular time, she arranges for a neighbor, a retired gentlemen, to look after David until she returns. David is very fond of the neighbor and considers it a treat when he is left in charge.

Even though it's just the two of them, David and his mother are fond of talking about themselves as a family. Their family evenings together have become a ritual. Homework is always done while dinner is being prepared. This also makes it easy for David's mom to assist him if he needs help. There is a family rule of no television on weekdays; instead, special TV programs are taped and become a part of the weekend fun. David and his mother have dinner in the dining room. The dinner hour is a pleasant time during which the two exchange day-to-day happenings and discuss any concerns David or his mother may be experiencing. Afterward, David helps with the dishes and completes any undone homework. While David isn't an outstanding student, he tries hard and is a favorite among his teachers.

David also helps with other household chores, and he works in the yard on weekends. Additionally, he spends three or four hours doing handy jobs for two neighbors. He is saving up for a special soccer camp he wants to attend at a local university this summer. His father said he would contribute half of the expenses. David is excited about the camp, and the goal of earning his share of the expenses is very motivating for him. Having these responsibilities has helped David understand how important it is to be dependable. This shows in his relationship with people; his friends know they can count on him.

David's favorite pastime is soccer. He not only plays for the school team but is involved in a league as well. He receives a lot of encouragement from his mother and father, who often attend to his games on the weekends. David's teachers describe him as an outgoing, well-liked, happy young man who is interested in his school and family.

How do these two scenarios differ?

Ruth's mother is sensitive, but she feels paralyzed about acting. Although both mothers work full-time, only David's parent has found a way to successfully adapt to the needs of the family. She has made an extra effort to be sensitive to the needs of her youngster and to create an environment that allows the family to function as a unit while still allowing each member to be an individual.

More and more of today's families are having to cope with the necessity of two incomes. It is common for both parents to be working outside the home. Statistics show that 69 percent of women and 87 percent of men work outside the home; 74 percent of all single female parents work outside the home. These statistics bear on child-rearing and thus become a family issue, not the "working woman's fault." The fact that so many families have both parents working has profound implications for the way families function, for better or worse. The determining factor is how well a given family can cope with pressures and demands.

As parents try to coordinate the disparate demands of family and jobs, family life can become more hectic and stressful. Tasks that were once taken for granted, such as meal preparation, shopping, and cleaning, can become major challenges. Dealing with these challenges may sometimes take precedence over the family's equally important child-bearing, educational, and nurturing roles.

The well-being of children is threatened when external havoc becomes internal, first for the parents and then for their children. The demands of a pressurized office may make the needs of a family seem secondary, though you don't have to be working away from home to make your child feel alienated. The stress and pressure that parents are under from their work often makes it very difficult for them to find extra time to be sensitive to the changes a youngster is experiencing or to deal with problems as part of a family unit. The guilt that a parent feels on recognizing that he or she is placing work before family can lead to increased stress, exacerbating an already tense situation.

When stress enters the home, it has a direct influence on the parent/child relationship. At the end of a stressful day, it is all too common for a parent to react to her adolescent in an abrasive and autocratic way ("You do as I tell you and don't hassle me!"), simply because she is too tired to take the time to solve the problem democratically. Naturally, a child who is treated in this high-handed manner will come under stress himself, thus perpetuating the cycle.

Such stress can have serious consequences. The adolescent feels inadequate, unloved, unwanted. He cannot get his needs for love and acceptance met in the family group, so he turns to his peer group for support and understanding.

A desire to belong to a peer group is natural and not in itself an indication of a problem. However, when an adolescent begins to rely on the peer group for the emotional support and nurturing he normally would get from his parents, destructive behavior can result. Research shows that overreliance on peers is a strong predictor of problem behavior in adolescents. Without constructive outlets for energy (such as family outings, play time, athletics, projects, chores, and hobbies) and in the absence of parental guidance, the youngster attempts desperately to be included in a group. This need for acceptance may cause the adolescent to do anything it takes to be "one of the gang."

THROWAWAY CHILDREN

One of the most emotionally wrenching scenes in any cartoon is the one in which the mother bird, wiping a tear from her eyes, kicks her baby birds out of the nest for their own good. Because the birds are old enough and strong enough, they can fly on their own. As parents, we have to face the same realities. We all know that our children will one day leave our nests and that their doing so is necessary and proper. Of course, most of us would never think of kicking our children out before they are able to thrive on their own. Yet that is just what many parents do, whether by alienating them or actually making their children leave home.

"Increasingly, it is the parents who toss the children out," says Nick Clark, director of Alternative House, a center for runaways in McLean, Virginia. He observes "throwaway children" whose parents drop them off at Alternative House, telling them, "I can't handle you. You're too much." While the public may have the idea that it is rebellious older teens who are kicked out by their parents, Clark notes that the average age of the children currently coming to his center is twelve. Children are being abandoned by those who are supposed to love them the most.

There are all sorts of ways of giving up on your children. According to data compiled by the House Select Committee of Children, Youth and Families, admissions of children under eighteen to inpatient psychiatric services more than doubled between 1970 and 1980. Between 1980 and 1984, adolescent admissions to private psychiatric hospitals increased by more than 350 percent. While many of those admitted were there for treatment of drug abuse and as a result of suicide attempts, others were confined for such value afflictions as "conduct disorder" and "adolescent adjustment disorder." According to committee testimony, most children were coerced into entering hospitals by their parents, who were seeking relief from uncontrollable adolescents. Hospital officials say that up to 40 percent of these hospitalizations were found to be "unnecessary."

A child who has been divorced by his parents has intense feelings of alienation, of being unwanted and unloved. As Leslie, a twelve-year-old second-time runaway and a drug user for two years, says, "I really don't care about my parents anymore. Why should I? It only hurts. Why should I go home? Why bother them when they don't need me?" Many adolescents run away from home in their attempt to overcome or overthrow the feelings produced by alienation. According to the Senate Subcommittee on Juvenile Justice, more than 1 million children run away from home every year. Unable to take care of themselves, these runaways are almost certain to encounter severe problems.

John Rabun, a manager of the Exploited Child center in Louisville, Kentucky, comments that "this is a grave social concern. Often, adolescents abused or neglected at home become easy prey for adults who exploit them through pornography and prostitution, and many of them are murdered."

Lois Lee, director of Children of the Night, a Los Angeles program that helps youths break out of prostitution, says that many children are pushed out of their homes by uncaring parents and end up sleeping in parks or abandoned buildings. "These kids develop families on the street," she says. "They'll form groups and look out for each other."

"The children themselves recognize that they need help," says Ralph Alsopp, an Atlanta psychologist. "Teenagers feel helpless, not in control of their lives. Their parental support structures are falling away. They are lonely, and they are alone."

These lonely children will reach out to whatever and whoever is available. The Runaway Hotline, established in 1973, fields nearly 300 calls a day from children who have left home.

Throwaway children are an obvious example of neglect. But what about the less obvious examples: those children who feel alone and alienated in the midst of a family? Let's look at the growing problem of alienation and suicide among adolescents.

ADOLESCENT SUICIDE: THE DARKER SIDE OF STRESS

Suicide is a topic most of us prefer to avoid. But we cannot ignore the subject when statistics indicate that the number of teenage suicides represents a national epidemic and that the numbers of suicides continue to rise each year. Every 83 minutes in the United States, a teenager commits suicide. Each year 500,000 teens attempt suicide (reported cases), and nearly 300,000 others contemplate it. Since 1965, the incidence of reported suicide among teenagers has increased over 300 percent. (Note that while car crashes are the method used most often by older youths committing suicide, such suicides are not reflected in the preceding figures.) Suicide now ranks as the third major cause of death for adolescents, ahead of deaths due to alcohol, drug abuse, and disease.

We must confront our fears and reach out to our children. It is imperative that we—and our adolescents—understand the dynamics of suicide, its causes, the complex emotions involved, and the methods of coping with suicidal feelings. Parents need information that emphasizes the importance of the impressionable years of a child's development and that teaches the many subtle ways in which teenagers can be made to feel unloved and unwanted. We must be aware of the effects that such occurrences as death, divorce, alcohol or drug abuse, suicide in the family, or repeated failure may have on a child, and we must learn how to ease the hardship these may cause. Adolescents need to learn to recognize the clues to suicide among their peers, friends, and relatives, and they must be made aware of the importance of telling others if they suspect someone they know has become suicidal.

The more we know, the better we are able to understand and therefore prevent suicide. If we can understand the causes of suicidal feelings and learn what to do in such an emergency, we may be able to help avert a tragedy. One thing is clear: most suicides are avoidable. Suicide is a scream for help, a desperate cry for needed change. Suicide is not an ordinary response to pressure. Healthy, emotionally secure children can deal with the stressors of daily frustrations and with periodic trauma. Adolescents who are thinking about killing themselves, however, are beset by seemingly insoluble problems and are trying desperately to get away from feeling unbearable emotional pain. They feel helpless to change things and unable to identify those who could help them overcome the hopelessness and despair they feel. Adolescents who feel little control over their environments may experience their families as unavailable, rejecting, or overprotective.

WHAT MAKES OUR CHILDREN SO DESPERATELY UNHAPPY?

What makes some adolescents want to end their lives when so much in our culture motivates us toward living? What leads young people who "have everything to live for" to give up everything?

Many of those in the adolescent population are dealing with various levels of alienation and depression a great deal of the time. Often, your child may have difficulty in identifying the underlying causes of his depression. He only knows that he feels bad or lonely and doesn't know what to do about it. These feelings can give rise to suicidal behaviors.

A young person may have had very negative personal experiences in reaching out to friends or adults, either in his family or in school. These experiences may account for his holding his feelings inside. In order to reach out for help, an adolescent may have to expose such family secrets as alcoholism, violence, or sexual victimization. He is often afraid of retaliation or, at least, of further rejection by other family members.

When a teenager feels little satisfaction or reward in his life, he becomes depressed. How he deals with this depression is basic to his survival. Mounting frustrations can lead to an increasing and intense sense of helplessness to change his situation. In the midst of this agonizing complexity and without the experience to understand what is happening, a young person may begin to feel there is no way out. Suicide becomes one of the options. It is not that a child wants to die but that he cannot think of any other way to stop the pain.

As sixteen-year-old Kindra, who attempted suicide by drug overdose, said, "I thought everyone would be better off if I killed myself. You think that because you're miserable, you're making everyone else miserable. You think no one would care if you killed yourself."

Not everyone reacts to painful situations in the same way. Some adolescents are more resourceful than others, and some are more sensitive than others to emotional pain. Suicidal adolescents are not weaker or somehow less capable than others; for whatever reasons, some situations are harder to cope with for some people at certain times in their lives. This is why the incidence of suicide is prevalent in families of all types.

While it is true that suicidal feelings most often develop in a person who is deeply depressed, the fact that a child is depressed does not mean he or she will become suicidal. Any person may at a particularly time find the emotional pain he is experiencing to be absolutely intolerable. In that short period he might impulsively make a suicide attempt; if the attempt is unsuccessful, the person often later regrets having made it. Taking drugs and alcohol in excess can exaggerate painful feelings, and a person who otherwise would not go that far might attempt suicide.

DISTRESS SIGNALS

All too often, even the seemingly well-adjusted child becomes a victim. The greatest danger for any parent with regard to adolescent suicide is the belief that "my child would never do that." Most parents of teenagers who have successfully or unsuccessfully attempted suicide are initially surprised that their children have moved in this direction. On closer analysis, however, parents often realize that there were warning signs that they had ignored because they were unaware of the significance of those signs. Take a moment now to familiarize yourself with the following list of danger signals so that you can recognize them and be able to give your child the help he or she might need.

Preoccupation with themes of death; expression of suicidal thoughts

Giving away prized possessions; making a will or other "final arrangements"

Changes in sleeping patterns (too much or too little)

Sudden and extreme changes in eating habits; losing or gaining weight

Changes in school performance (lowered grades, cutting classes, dropping out of activities)

Personality changes, such as nervousness, outbursts of anger, or apathy about appearance and health

Use of drugs or alcohol

Recent suicide of friend, relative, or admired public figure

Previous suicide attempt

Talk of owning guns, knives, or other weapons

Less interest in friends and peers

Verbal clues such as these: "Soon no one will have to worry about me"; "Don't worry, I won't be a bother anymore"; "I won't be around to do that anymore"; "Maybe I should just kill myself"; "My family (or you) would be better off if I just killed myself"; "You'll be sorry, just wait and see."

SHOWING YOU CARE

The period of adolescence is a time when teenagers demand independence and freedom from parental supervision yet need this supervision very badly. "The unhappiest kids in the world are those with the least parental supervision," asserts Bill Gregory, director of the Excelsior Youth Center in Denver. "What adolescents want and need most from you is to have you take them seriously and to guide them toward a better understanding of themselves."

The best way to ensure that your child is not suffering from feelings of being alone and being lonely is to assess your parent-child relationship (discussed in chapter 2), take an active interest in your teenager's friends, and keep the channels open between home and school. The following suggestions are recommended:

Take the time to appreciate your growing and changing adolescent. This is not without its rewards. Spend quality time with your child on a regular basis, even if it's only for a short time in the morning and an hour or two each evening. It's important to take an active interest. Find out what your adolescent is thinking, doing, and learning. Become a part of his life.

Have fun with your teenager. You don't have to stop playing just because your child is older. Plan family play periods. Have regular family projects and games. Read together, share what you read, and discuss points of view.

Provide love and direction. Psychologist Lea Pulkinen observed that proper guidance, which involves a combination of love and direction, is a determining factor in the development of youngsters. Offer guidance through sound advice, not through commands. For example, avoid saying, "Stop hanging out with Sue. All she does is hurt your feelings!" Instead, you might say, "Janey, it seems that you often get your feelings hurt in your friendship with Sue. What have you learned about the friendship?"

Don't compare your children's gifts and personalities. Each is unique. What is easy for one is difficult for another. Value them for what they are rather than for what you'd like them to be.

Invite your child to confide in you. Don't trivialize their problems. Offer advice when appropriate. Rather than saying, "Grow up!" ask "What plans do you have to resolve the problem? Do you need assistance on this one?"

Respect the child's friends. Criticizing your teenager's friends is not a good idea, even if you have good reason to consider a friend to be a bad influence. This doesn't mean you have to keep quiet. It does mean that you have to be very careful in how you express yourself. Remember, there is a great loyalty among friends at this age. Avoid directly attacking your teen's friends. Instead, ask his opinions. Chances are that he *knows* when a friend is a positive influence or a negative one, but he may not know how to disentangle himself from a negative relationship. Listen before you assert your feelings.

Encourage your adolescent to invite friends home when the family is at home. Provide an environment conducive to your adolescent's bringing friends home by being open-minded, friendly, and not too quick to criticize them. If you shut out your child's friends, you will also cut off an important realm of your teenager's world. Her response will be to alienate you from that part of her life. During the adolescent stage, the adolescent's home becomes an important sanctuary. Adolescents will flock to the homes where parents are open and accessible to the teenager and her friends. Does your teenager bring her friends home?

Allow for mistakes. Mistakes are important. They show us the truth about what works and what doesn't. Adolescence is a time of exploring and experimenting. It's amazing how often parents panic at the thought of all the possible trouble their teenagers can get into. You should be aware that your teenager learns a great deal about life through exploring and experimenting and that mistakes will be a part of the learning process. Give him privileges as he is able to handle them. When your teenager has been given a privilege and abuses it or "goofs," withdraw the privilege for a while and then give him another chance later. This is the best way to keep the lines of communication open between you and your teenager without alienating him.

Evaluate all aspects of requests. When your teenager comes to you with a request, evaluate it before responding. While there may be parts of that request that are unacceptable to you, do not reject the whole idea just because of the unacceptable parts. First, acknowledge that your teen's idea sounds like fun. This will let her know that you are on her side. Second, tell your teenager that there are parts of the plan that you must talk over with her. The important point is that you want your teen to know that you're considering the plan and that you're willing to negotiate something you can both live with. Then agree to disagree. The key is to establish the groundwork for channels of communication so that you will not be shutting your teenager out or creating a situation in which your child is afraid to talk to you.

Avail yourself of support groups. As noted earlier in this book, support groups can reduce the feeling of alienation among adolescents by providing a common forum in which they can share painful experiences. Support groups can also lessen the feelings of being alone and being lonely. The resource section in the back of this book provides additional information on support groups.

Strengthen home/school relations. Your child's teachers are a good source of information about his welfare. Since teachers see your child nearly every day, they are likely to be aware of problem areas or of changes in the child's behavior. Teachers can offer you advice on how you can become more involved in your youngster's educational process. It is important for you to know what's going on in the classroom and what the teacher expects of his students so that you can be supportive of the program. If you are unhappy with the method of teaching, talk to the teacher and resolve it as best you can. If need be, supplement your child's classroom experience with other activities at home. Don't create a situation of conflict with the teacher, because this will be confusing to your youngster. When children sense that their parents are not supportive of the school, they learn to not value the school. If you aren't supportive of the teacher, your youngster won't be either. The result is one less anchor in the child's life. Fostering a negative attitude will result in poor performance. Interacting in a cooperative way with teachers and school staff members will serve to strengthen the home/school connection and will serve as a support system for your child. Remember that the goal is to help your child experience support and not feel alienated.

HELPING YOUR CHILD

When a parent always hides his own pain, the child learns to hold this as an ideal of what he should be like. When he can't seem to cope with his own painful feelings, he may then feel like a failure. In contrast, when a parent admits to grief or anger and works through these painful feelings, his actions foster optimism in the teenager.

The goal is to help your adolescent realize that it is all right for both teenagers and adults to be honest about how hard it is to cope with some of life's experiences, that we *can* work through difficult feelings, and that sharing the painful feelings with others is a sign of strength and not of weakness.

As a parent, you need to encourage your adolescent to reach out for help when he is depressed, having problems, or feeling suicidal. Here's how:

Listening. Often, a child becomes accustomed to being talked at rather than listened to. Not taking your teenager's feelings seriously fosters defensiveness rather than openness. An adolescent feels with the same intensity as an adult. A teenager may be terribly upset over a friend's moving away, while that situation may seem rather trivial to an adult who has had to deal with the loss of a spouse or a job. The pain levels, however, can be equivalent. Sometimes a teenager will overreact to something even he recognizes as minor, perceiving it to be larger than life. Again, it is important to remember that an adolescent does not have the backlog of experiences we do. To him, the problem *is* threatening. Your job is to help him identify the real problem behind his pain.

Empathy. Take the young person's feelings seriously. Detecting a potentially suicidal person and assisting him requires a key element: concern. Sometimes we miss or choose to ignore warning signs from other people, or we may feel it is not our place to intervene. That attitude can be dangerous. "People don't know how to approach you," said sixteen-year-old Dan. "A lot of times people won't be honest with you. Fortunately, I had friends who had the guts to tell me I needed to seek professional help. They told me I needed more help than they could give me. A lot of times it takes someone close to you to point out your crazy behavior. The best thing about depression—if there *is* a good thing about it—is that you find out who your real friends are, because you put your friends through hell."

Family counseling. A suicide attempt, though it is a personal cry of despair, can also echo a whole family's deep need for help.

When parents are able to recognize their role in the child's diffi-culties and are motivated to reduce and eliminate the child's suicidal tendencies, they may also demonstrate an ability to work together to diminish some of their own conflicts. The ability of parents to work together for the benefit of their child cannot be overly stressed. When you and your spouse present a united front, your child feels secure and part of a family.

Adolescent support groups. Parents and educators can work to-gether to set up teen awareness groups. These groups, in which teenagers can meet in a semiformal fashion, can be held after school or in the early evenings at local schools. It is important that teenagers have a place to go to share their problems. Support groups bring adolescents together and help them realize that they are not the only ones having difficulties, and they learn that many problems do have solutions.

Support groups do work. For instance, Alcoholics Anonymous began with two members; today, AA meetings are held all over the world. Spin-off groups such as Overeaters Anonymous, Co-caine Users Anonymous, Emotional Health Anonymous, and Gamblers Anonymous, to name only a few, have also helped many people share common problems and lead happy and successful lives.

We can offer this same opportunity to our teens. If you are interested in forming such a group, visit one of the above-men-tioned self-help groups just to see how the program is structured. These groups are listed in your telephone directory, or you can call Information for the group nearest you. (The reference section at the end of this book will get you started.)

Peer support. Peer support can be a powerful tool in preventing suicide. Teach your child how to detect suicidal tendencies in peers. If your adolescent knows more about what causes suicidal feelings, how to recognize when a friend is suicidal, and how to help and get help, he will be more likely to take his own feelings seriously. As a consequence, he will be more effective as a rescuer for another.

Psychiatric hospitilization. You may be unable to make imme-diate changes that will enhance your child's well-being, such as the formation of an immediate alliance with a therapist to open pathways for productive communication. In such cases, psychiatric hospitalization for the child must be considered as the initial main intervention. Besides offering immediate protection, psychiatric hospitalization creates a defined radical change in the family system.

The responsibility for helping suicidal children does not have to rest solely on the parents. Communities can provide excellent assistance by establishing a suicide-prevention center, staffed with people who know how to spot and help troubled children. These centers can intervene during a time of crisis to ameliorate its intensity. Staff members who are receptive and who respect the principle of confidentiality can become important to a child. Dealing with the youngster's ambivalence is a most important concept in suicide intervention, and staff members can show the concern and empathy necessary to fight a child's ambivalence.

It is extremely difficult to be certain whether a troubled child will or will not commit suicide. For the time being, the best indicator of a potential suicide is a scale devised by the Los Angeles Suicide Prevention Center. To assess the probability that an adolescent might carry out a suicide threat, the center relies on the following index:

1. *Age and sex.* The probability is greater for males between the ages of thirteen and twenty-four and females between ten and sixteen.
2. *Symptoms.* The probability is greater if the child manifests such symptoms as depression, feelings of hopelessness or alienation, or a sense of powerlessness or if he uses alcohol or drugs.
3. *Stress.* The probability is greater if the child is experiencing stress from the loss of a parent (through divorce, separation, or death), from increased responsibilities as a result of serious illness, or from other major stressors.
4. *Acute versus chronic aspects.* The immediate probability of suicide is greater if there is a sudden onslaught of specific symptoms. The long-term probability is greater if there is a recurrence of specific symptoms or a recent increase in a long-standing tendency toward depression.
5. *Suicidal plan.* The probability is greater in proportion to the

lethal nature of the suicide method and the child's clarity about the plan (for instance, if the child is gathering knives, guns, pills, razor blades, or other such items).

6. *Resources.* The probability is greater if the child has no family or friends, or if family and friends are unwilling to help.

7. *Prior suicidal behavior.* The probability is greater if the child has a history of prior attempts, if he has a history of repeated suicide threats and depression, or if a close friend or sibling has been suicidal.

8. *Medical status.* The probability is greater if the child suffers from a chronic, debilitating illness or has had many unsuccessful experiences with physicians.

9. *Communication aspects.* The probability is greater if the child has no communication with family or friends or if the child rejects the efforts of family and friends to communicate with him.

10. *Reaction of important friends.* The probability is greater if family members or friends whom the teenager considers important reject him and deny that he needs help.

11. *Family interaction.* The probability is greater if there is an absence of a warm parental adult figure with whom to identify, or if active parental conflict exists, or if a parent expresses a negative attitude toward an adolescent. Also, it is greater if there is a family history of child abuse (sexual molestation or incest), emotional problems or alcoholism of a family member, or remarriage of a family member that has resulted in the child's having a sense of isolation, loss, guilt, or conflict.

TWO PROMISING PROGRAMS

You can also get in touch with your adolescent and build positive links between the home and school by supporting the kinds of learning experiences that can prevent youthful alienation. Two exemplary programs, briefly described here, incorporate recent and reliable research findings about the prevention or alleviation of feelings of alienation in adolescents. These programs are designed specifically to help get parents involved. (The resource section at the end of the book provides additional address information.)

SKILLS FOR ADOLESCENCE

Skills for Adolescence was developed by the Quest National Center in Columbus, Ohio. It focuses on early adolescence (specifically, children in grades six through eight and deals with a wide range of factors associated with youthful alienation and its prevention. One of the major goals of the program is to provide students with a forum for discussing characteristics of early adolescence in order to gain a greater understanding of the actual changes they encounter during this stage of development. This helps teenagers to see that the unpredictability and irregularity of the physiological and psychological changes they are experiencing are normal, that their concerns and anxieties are far from unique, and that they actually have a great deal in common with one another. Aimed at helping the youngster acquire skills to manage the early adolescent years in a productive and more joyous way, Skills for Adolescence uses the following topics as a springboard for discussion:

Entering the Teen Years: The Challenge Ahead

Building Self-Confidence through Better Communication

Learning about Emotions: Developing Competence in Self-Assessment and Self-Discipline

Friends: Improving Peer Relationships

Strengthening Family Relationships

Developing Critical Thinking Skills for Decision Making

Setting Goals for Healthy Living

Summing Up: Developing One's Potential

In order to help the young adolescent overcome the feelings of being alone and feeling lonely, this program also provides specific activities that encompass a wide range of factors associated with youngsters' feelings of loneliness or of being alone.

SKILLS FOR LIVING

Another effective program is Skills for Living, also developed by
the Quest National Center. This program is designed to teach
adolescents in grades eight through twelve. It addresses the problem of youth alienation by establishing links among schools, teenagers, parents, and communities. Though aimed at adolescents,
Skills for Living also addresses parents by teaching them the most
effective ways to become actively involved in the education of
their adolescents. Ten topics of interest to parents include:

> self-concept (liking and accepting oneself)
>
> feelings (dealing constructively with such emotions as loneli-
> ness or fear)
>
> attitudes (developing a more positive mental state)
>
> friends (building constructive relationships)
>
> family (appreciating and strengthening family bonds)
>
> marriage (establishing trust, loyalty, and commitment)
>
> parenting (learning the elements of effective parenting)
>
> money (understanding the principles of financial manage-
> ment)
>
> careers (goal setting and life planning)
>
> philosophy (discovering meaning in life and developing one's
> personal perspective)

If quality programs like these sound encouraging, it's because
they are. Ask the educators in your teenager's school whether
these programs or others like them are available for local students. If they are not, encourage the educators to introduce them.

Youngsters are vulnerable. The ways in which they perceive
the events in their lives, the quality of communication and support from their family, peers, and school personnel, and general
social influence all contribute to whether or not adolescents feel
lonely or alone. Adolescents who feel alienated put other youngsters at risk by impairing their immediate chances of feeling like
the happy, well-adjusted people we strive to help them become.

CHAPTER EIGHT

Substance Abuse: A "Capsule" History

The transition from childhood to adulthood in contemporary society calls for an ever-increasing ability to endure anxiety, tolerate tension, overcome doubt, resolve conflicts, reduce frustrations, and manage stress. A child who uses drugs and alcohol is less likely to succeed at these necessary challenges.

Substance and chemical abuse is so widespread in contemporary society that it crosses all age, social, and economic boundaries—affecting rock stars, homemakers, students, and executives alike. Alcohol and drug use among our adolescent children is so prevalent that no parent can afford to be complacent. Some of the most unsuspecting youngsters become dependent on alcohol and/or chemicals. When a youngster does become dependent on alcohol or drugs, most parents react with shock and disbelief that their child could have a problem of such a serious nature. Other parents feel that experimenting with drugs and alcohol is just a phase that all adolescents go through but then get over if parents don't interfere. This is particularly the case with alcohol: in comparison with drug use, drinking seems less frightening to many parents. This kind of passivity can be dangerous. The consequences of alcohol and drug abuse can be lethal.

COPING THROUGH CHEMISTRY

Many adolescents depend on a wide variety of methods to squeeze more productivity or "up-and-on" time from each day. They listen to tapes while sleeping, review lecture notes while eating, have a study date with a boyfriend or girlfriend, or simply operate on less than adequate sleep and nutrition. Some take drugs. Among the most popular drugs are those that provide a quick added edge of stamina, stimulation, energy, or creativity. Young people believe that such drugs provide a boost for confidence, mood elevation, relaxation, and overall coping with the demands of their multifaceted lifestyle. To cope with what they perceive as innumerable problems, worries, and tensions, countless adolescents reach out for "remedies"—alcohol, cigarettes, marijuana, stimulants, and megavitamins. All of these substances are all too readily available. Unfortunately, many of our young people have been led to believe that drugs and alcohol provide relief and solutions.

Many adolescents are unaware of the damage these substances do to their well-being. Drugs and alcohol not only delay the adolescent's ability to recognize that he is in distress but also work against his ability to detect the underlying cause of his problem and gain mastery over it. As Jay said, "I would do drugs to feel better about myself, but I'd end up feeling worse, so I'd do more drugs. Getting high was no longer a thing I did to feel happy and have fun. It was a part of my life. I had to get high just to feel normal and not drained and burned out."

Historically, external agents such as tranquilizing medications were used to help people overcome excessive and chronic stress responses. With the history of adults relying on prescription drugs and other relief remedies to cure everyday ailments, is it so surprising that many of our young people consider drugs as a remedy for stress?

Drugs are widespread today and do not frighten many youngsters. That's a real problem. Drugs and alcohol are not only a topic on the 6:00 news but are also seen in the advertisements of the sponsors. Ads claim that drugs will fix what ails you, and drugs and alcohol are even offered to improve the quality of daily life!

Television ads convince us not to put up with any discomfort. Feel tense? Take a tranquilizer. Feel like eating? Take an appetite suppressant. The medicine cabinet is presented as the universal answer.

Many young people have misconceptions about drugs. Part of this is our fault as parents. Young people have been led to believe that there are "soft" drugs and "hard" drugs. The notion is that soft drugs do little or no harm, do not cause dependence of any kind, and can be used with impunity. Only "hard" drugs (such as heroin) are seen as dangerous. These beliefs have created a situation in which young people associate soft drugs with soft drinks. Through their friends and families, through the magazines they read and the movies they watch, at parties, at home, and in school, teenagers have come to regard illicit drugs as commonplace. By making drugs seem "cozy," we remove the awe and fear a child should feel about them.

Today's young people are more likely to use drugs and alcohol than any age group before them and to do so at a much younger age. Even if they have never smoked marijuana, taken pills that were not prescribed for them, or used cocaine themselves, most young people know someone who has. Drug use is all around them, from the adult who takes tranquilizers to cope with daily stress to older youngsters who sell pot at school, to movie idols who glamorize drug use both on-screen and off. The result has been the increased acceptability of drug use over the last decade, making it a rite of passage for many adolescents, the difference between being part of the crowd and being an outsider. Like an adult who has a drink "just to be sociable," a child will smoke a joint with his friends. While some children do intentionally abuse drugs to escape from what they consider intolerable lives, others use them "because they're there." Haven't you ever gone to the refrigerator and had a snack even though you weren't hungry? You ate a candy bar or doughnut just because it was available. Your child, who may have no interest in drugs on his own, might one day swallow a pill or drink a beer for that same reason. It couldn't happen to your child? It is estimated that over one-third of all U.S. adolescents use alcohol and illegal drugs regularly.

As parents you cannot afford to be naive about the issue of

substance and chemical use. Just as there is no specific addictive personality and no one type of parent who makes it inevitable that a child will succumb, there is no guarantee that a particular child won't abuse alcohol or drugs. Even if you are child-centered, caring, emotionally and physically accessible, and do not drink or use drugs, your child may still encounter and abuse drugs. Every adolescent needs not only to learn the possible effects of alcohol and drug use on his personality, conduct, and overall health but also to acquire the skills that will enable him to withstand the extraordinary pressures of the teen years. Adolescents who do not do so are at risk.

THE MAKING OF AN ADDICT

How does substance abuse start? Teenagers often introduce alcohol or a drug to their friends, show them how to use it, and convince them it will enhance their ability to "feel good." This outside influence and encouragement by one's peer group gets kids started on drugs and sets the stage for a repeat experience. The period following the initial introduction to alcohol and drugs is very deceptive. The adolescent may be able to use alcohol and drugs without becoming chemically dependent or even feeling endangered—for a short while. During this period he often has the illusion that he can control his drug or alcohol intake, that the substances are not addictive.

The progression of drug use often moves through what is generally referred to as "gateway drugs"—first the legal ones, alcohol and tobacco, then on to marijuana and other more harmful drugs. Polydrug addiction is also a major trend; its common denominator is alcohol. The more adolescents drink, the greater the possibility that they will also use one or more drugs. Once drug or alcohol involvement begins, it can accelerate quickly, moving from occasional indulgence to dependence. Children are even more susceptible than adults to this snowball effect.

Do the statements "It's my body!" and "It's my life, not yours!" sound familiar? Your adolescent may pressure you, asserting that usage is a personal right symbolizing individuality, authority,

maturity, and even control over one's body. If your teenager is to
respect your stand on drug abuse and really listen to what you
have to say, you must do three things. First, agree that, yes, it
is her body, and yes, she does have a right to live her own life.
Second, point out to her that since it is her own body, she has an
obligation to herself to learn as much about it as possible. That
includes knowledge about how substance abuse can harm it. This
is the time when you can share your knowledge with your child;
just be certain that it is indeed knowledge—hard, cold, substan-
tiated facts—that you are sharing, not simply your personal opinion. Present your facts unemotionally, in a nonthreatening manner. Remember that at this point you are respecting your child's
autonomy and intelligence and merely trying to alert her to the
consequences of her actions. Third, you must provide a good role
model. Children are extremely quick to pick up on double standards. If you pop a Valium every time you have a fight with the
credit-card billing office or pour a drink every day as soon as you
get home from work, do you really think your child will listen to
what you have to say about the harmfulness of drugs?

While no one personality type is linked with drug or alcohol addiction, predisposing factors may point to youngsters at
risk. Anything that accentuates the self-doubt that kids harbor
about themselves or their abilities may lead to alcohol or
drug use. Other potent indicators that make a child vulnerable
are these:

Major stress-producing events requiring special coping skills,
such as the divorce, separation, or remarriage of parent(s);
death of a parent, sibling, or friend; home or school reloca-
tion; loss of a long-standing friendship or love relationship;
major entrance exams

Dramatic drop in self-esteem and sudden onset of a poor self-
image

Sustained family discord

Sexual or physical abuse

Continual withholding of emotional and physical affection by
parents

Long-term disharmony in the parent/child relationship

Parents who smoke, drink, use illegal drugs, or abuse prescription drugs

Long before they admit it to themselves, parents often sense that their teenagers use drugs or alcohol. They see many clues that they ignore, hoping the problem will go away. Adolescence is a time of intense feelings and wide mood swings, and distinguishing the "normal" effects of adolescence from those of drugs may not always be easy. This is another powerful reason that remaining close and accessible to your child during the adolescent years is so important. Because no one knows the intricate habits and patterns of your child quite like you do, no one can detect changes as well as you can.

Before helping your kids deal with the problems of drug and alcohol abuse, you need to understand how these substances work. By clearing up your own uncertainty about the nature of drugs and alcohol, you will be better equipped to help your teens. Your knowledge will also give you more credibility in discussing the issues. The substances most commonly abused by adolescents are alcohol, cigarettes, marijuana, diet pills, and megavitamins, with cocaine following these.

ALCOHOL ABUSE

Like an adult, a teenager drinks to forget, to relax, to socialize, and to have fun. For the adolescent, drinking is a glamorous symbol of sophistication, maturity, and independence as well as a seemingly easy way to elevate or suppress certain moods. Alcohol is readily available and relatively inexpensive. It is socially accepted; even Mom and Dad may use it. What most kids don't know is the darker side: alcohol is a very addictive drug that impairs emotional and physical functioning.

Many adolescents assume that drinking isn't all that bad for you, that most adults drink, and that as adults they, too, will drink. Thus, drinking represents rites of passage to adulthood.

Your adolescent may see liquor in his home, attend parties and functions where adults whom he admires and likes are drinking, and even witness a respected adult friend making excuses for a drunk friend or joking about a drunken state.

It is important that you as a parent take a stance on alcohol. Not all parents are opposed to their adolescent's drinking, which makes *your* no-drinking stance even tougher to uphold. An important part of the problem is that drinking is glamorized and even endorsed. Your teenager may see you drink or buy a round of drinks in celebration. He may have attended weddings or other social functions at which alcohol was available and was consumed as a toast. These experiences form your teen's opinion that drinking is not only acceptable but is also the essence of celebration and of having a good time. Your child sees adults and peers who would never think of using marijuana accepting alcohol without question.

Drinking is also a symbol of belonging to the crowd. Your adolescent wants to be part of the crowd, and he may have a hard time refusing alcohol if his friends are drinking.

Further, the media promote an attitude that not only endorses drinking but encourages it as well. Commercials portray young, energetic people drinking while biking, socializing, partying, mountain climbing, dating, and working. Drinking beer with one's buddies is what "a real man" does after a hard day's work. Or, we are shown a healthy young woman enjoying a "low-cal" wine cooler as a thirst quencher after a vigorous sports workout. These ads succeed in creating a predisposition to drinking that cultivates an attitude of acceptance toward drinking, giving the teenager a more positive inclination to drink.

Since ads are intended to sell alcohol, they portray alcohol use as enjoyable and free of adverse consequences. Statistics show the opposite of this claim. More than 15 million Americans—4 million of whom are under eighteen—have serious drinking problems. One of every two Americans will be involved in an alcohol-related accident during his lifetime. More than 50 percent of all highway fatalities are alcohol related. The costs involved in alcoholism and alcohol abuse reach $116 billion per year.

There are emotional and personal costs as well. It has long been known that alcoholism profoundly affects family stability. In families in which at least one member is an alcoholic, the rate of separation and divorce is seven times that of the general population. Suicides are also higher among alcoholics, as is the incidence of incest and child abuse.

Below are clues that may be danger signs indicating that your teenager is using alcohol. Ask yourself the following questions:

Is my liquor supply dwindling? If your child is abusing alcohol, your stock might evaporate mysteriously or turn into colored water. Unless you keep an inventory of your liquor, such practices may go undetected for months.

Has my child's personality changed noticeably? Does he have sudden mood swings, such as out-of-the-ordinary irritability, giddiness, depression, or unprovoked hostility?

Is he becoming less responsible (for example, about doing chores, getting home on time, or following instructions and household rules)?

Has my child's interest fallen off in schoolwork or extracurricular activities, including athletics? Are his grades dropping? Often, school performance will go down with alcohol abuse. In severe cases, a child may become a truant or even drop out of school entirely.

Does my teen seem to be losing old friends and spending time instead with a drinking, partying group? All social life for a young problem drinker begins to center around drinking; he has no time for nonabusing friends.

Am I missing money or salable objects? A young alcoholic has an increasingly expensive addiction to maintain.

Do I hear consistently from neighbors, friends, or others about my child's drinking or questionable behaviors? An alcoholic youngster's reputation suffers. Listen to such reports.

Is my child in trouble with the police? Even one arrest for an alcohol-related offense is a red flag that may well signal alcoholism.

Does my child spend a lot of time alone in a bedroom or recreation room, bursting forth now and then only to disappear out the door? Does he seem to resent my questions about destinations and activities? A certain amount of this mystery, aloofness, and resentment is typical of adolescent. When it is extreme, however, it can mean problems with alcohol or other drugs.

Have my child's family relationships deteriorated? When a youngster has a drinking problem, the first relationships to suffer are those within the family.

Does my youngster "turn off" to talks about alcohol and other drugs or strongly defend his right to use them?

Some parents realize their youngster is drinking but brush it off as part of growing up. Some are relieved their child drinks instead of using drugs. Still others believe that a teenager is too young to be an alcoholic. Some refuse to admit that their child drinks. Experts maintain that parents, with their natural pride in their child, will do many things to maintain their sense of their child as being okay. Denial can go on for years. For fear of provoking parents, teachers and friends are usually hesitant to point out a youngster's drinking problem. Often, parents don't get treatment for their teenager until after a crisis: he or she is arrested, expelled from school, or has a serious car accident.

To help teenagers themselves decide whether they have a drinking problem, Alcoholics Anonymous asks the following questions. If a teenager answers yes to any one of these questions, AA advises him to take a serious look at his drinking.

Do you drink because you have problems or to face stressful situations?

Do you drink when you get mad at other people (your friends or parents)?

Do you often prefer to drink alone?

Are your grades starting to slip, or are you goofing off on your job?

Do you ever try to stop drinking or drink less—and fail?

Have you begun to drink in the morning?

Do you gulp your drinks as if to satisfy a great thirst?

Do you ever have a memory loss due to your drinking?

Do you avoid leveling with others about your drinking?

Do you ever get into trouble when you are drinking?

Do you often get drunk, even when you do not mean to?

Do you think it is admirable to be able to hold your liquor?

The most effective way for parents to help a child become responsible about drinking is to strengthen the personality and character of the child and to divest alcohol of its status. While the first is an arduous and long-term process, the second is moderately easy and can be accomplished over a period of ten to sixteen months. Since secret drinking gives alcohol an air of mystery, drinking alcohol in a glass in the kitchen strips alcohol of its glamour. Likewise, a goblet of wine at the dinner table becomes associated with enjoyment of a meal and with moderation rather than with mystery, guilt, or escape. Along this line, it is interesting to note that research by the National Institute of Mental Health has led to recommendations that alcoholic beverages be served to young adults in church gatherings and be made available in college cafeterias and in other, relaxed settings conducive to demystifying alcohol. The idea is to make alcohol available for safe experimentation via moderate drinking. Actually, every adolescent needs to learn the possible effects of alcohol on his or her personality and conduct. The following suggestions have proved successful:

1. Help your adolescent learn how to assert his opinion, fearlessly and unashamedly. It takes courage for a teenager to say "no thanks" when he is with peers. Role playing can be a helpful tool here. Create a number of typical scenarios and rehearse possible dialogues with your adolescent.
2. Help your adolescent to communicate assertively. Your teenager will need to learn to say no without apology, explanation, arguments, or excuses. He will need to deal calmly with comments made about him by his peers if he is not drinking
3. Teach your teenager the skills of moderation:

- to nurse a drink for an hour or more and to sip, not gulp
- to eat prior to drinking
- to space drinks
- to fix a nonalcoholic drink that resembles a drink being served at the gathering.

4. Teach safety above all else. Tell your adolescent that if his friend or date has been drinking too much, someone else should drive him home. If no one else is available, he should call home to get a ride or take a cab. If your adolescent drove but calls home for a ride because he was drinking, focus on the goal of having him arrive home safely (discuss the incident of drinking itself at a later and more appropriate time). Reassure him that he can go back for the car in the morning.

5. Teach your teen to be in charge of his emotions. Let him know that he is never to accept a drink just because someone is intimidating him—*he* is to make the decision. Have him ask himself, "Do I really want a drink now? Do I really want to drink in this setting? Do I really want to consume the drink being served?"

The fear that their teenager will drive while under the influence of alcohol (or be a passenger in a car when the driver is under the influence of alcohol) is common among parents of adolescents. A car has unique symbolic value to teenagers. It represents freedom and power, speed and excitement, adulthood and opportunity. The following tips can help you to better ensure that your youngster understands the importance of responsible driving:

1. Assist your teenager in applying for a driver-education course. Require that he complete the course prior to being granted driving privileges.

2. Provide opportunities for practicing responsible driving. Take your child out driving.

3. Set clear limits and sensible regulations regarding use of the car (even if your teenager owns his own car). Discuss the importance of these limits with your teenager.

4. Make sure that your teenager is clearly aware of his legal and financial responsibilities, for both self and public.

5. Ensure that your teenager knows and understands traffic laws and ordinances.
6. Request that your child share with you the expenses associated with his car (payments, license, insurance, gas, and upkeep).
7. Recognize and praise your teenager for responsible behavior and driving.

THE NICOTINE CROWD

It is reported that 67 percent of all junior-high and high-school age youngsters smoke two to three cigarettes every day (25% smoke one pack or more a day).

It is estimated that more than half will become serious smokers (smoking one pack or more a day) by the time they are in the ninth grade.

Psychological and social factors have long been recognized as two major factors in cigarette smoking. New research has clearly revealed a third important link in the habit, physical dependence on nicotine, which slowly but surely develops in many smokers. When an individual first starts smoking, her body must get used to the nicotine. After smoking becomes a habit, her body may depend on getting nicotine. When she tries to quit, her body often reacts to the withdrawal of nicotine. This can result in a craving for tobacco, restlessness, irritability, anxiety, headaches, drowsiness, stomach upsets, and difficulty in concentrating.

What makes one adolescent smoke and another abstain? Teenagers who smoke typically (1) come from homes in which one or both parents or an older sibling has the habit; (2) live in single-parent homes; and (3) have close friends who are smokers. It is believed that adolescents who smoke lack a strong sense of self-identity and are less able to stand up for what they believe or to assert their rights when with peers.

Teenagers respond differently from adults to efforts to get them to stop. Because adolescents usually smoke for different reasons, efforts to "unhook" them or to discourage them from taking up the habit require different strategies. As with adults, though, if either physical or psychological addiction is entrenched, stopping is more difficult.

If you have the habit, tell your child how hard it is to give up smoking yourself. If you have tried unsuccessfully to quit, explain to your child that you want to quit and that it becomes much more difficult to do so the longer a person smokes. Avoid preaching. Remember, your child is sensing strong peer pressure, and the approval of friends is very important to him.

Know the facts about smoking before you try to discuss it with your teenager. If your adolescent informs you that "everybody does it," talk about health and well-being. Mention the responsibility each person has to care for himself. If you catch your adolescent smoking on the sly, your first impulse may be to forbid it. Chances are that this won't be very effective. There are too many opportunities for your child to smoke out of your sight, so banning smoking is not likely to be much of a deterrent.

You will be more effective with your adolescent if you operate on the theory that the desire to smoke will fade with improved self-confidence. Discuss with your adolescent the health risks of smoking, then talk about why he smokes or why he is thinking about it.

It is most important to assure your adolescent that he won't be an outcast if he says no to cigarettes. Talk about the role of peer pressure and ways to respond to it. You may wish to role play here so that your adolescent is able to rehearse the various ways in which young people offer cigarettes to each other and pressure peers into smoking to feel better about their own cigarette use. "It was really helpful when my parents showed me how to argue back," says Ken. "Last year when my friends would offer a cigarette, I accepted sometimes. I often wondered why. I guess I was afraid to say no because maybe they would think I didn't want their friendship. Through the conversation with my parents I just started saying no, and because I was so certain about it and was able to just tell friends that this was something that I didn't want to do, they accepted it. It was a lot easier than I thought. I also got a good friend to quit by sharing the negative feelings I had about myself when I would slip up and smoke."

Experts tell us that the best way to help our adolescents learn to resist the temptation to smoke is to focus on ways of helping them improve their self-esteem, relax their bodies, and develop appropriate ways to manage stress. If you feel you need professional assistance, do seek it. Because the effects of withdrawal can defeat even a strong will to quit, your adolescent's chances of quitting successfully are enhanced by a program that will allow him to concentrate on breaking the habit. Doctors at Merrell Dow, a research institute (see resource section at the end of this book), have conducted extensive research into the smoking problem. They have recently developed an alternative source of nicotine to help alleviate tobacco-withdrawal symptoms. Your doctor can provide treatment to help control nicotine-withdrawal symptoms, materials to help your adolescent overcome the psychological and social factors, and valuable counseling and follow-up care.

What seems to work best of all is but a strategy in which adolescents get the facts, a chance to discuss them, and the opportunity to draw their own conclusions. In this way you can help to "immunize" your child against the social pressure to smoke, steering clear of trying to scare with grim consequences while alerting your adolescent to his or her own best interests. Prevention begins at home. Bringing out the facts of smoking and health is something all parents must do. If you are still concerned about your adolescent after having taken these steps, find out whether his school health program deals with the problem. Query the physical education or health department. Find out whether the local school board has a policy that forbids smoking on school property or allows specified areas to be set aside where students can smoke (many schools do). If there is no policy or program, or if there is one but it is dormant, consider stimulating efforts on your own. The following are sources of help in getting started.

The local chapter of the American Lung Association may be able to help, as may the Education Development Department of the association's national headquarters (1740 Broadway, New York, NY 10019).

Periodically, teacher associations, parents, and students mount smoking-information campaigns. Leadership in such organizations changes from year to year, as do priorities, so find out what the current thinking is and be prepared to help with a project.

General information and technical assistance is available from the Center for Disease Control. Write to the Community Program Development Division, Center for Health Promotion and Education, Atlanta, GA 30333.

Local units of the American Cancer Society supply school systems with filmstrip kits and free teaching aids. A coloring book, *The Story of a Cigarette,* is designed for young adolescents. A comic book, *Taking a Chance with No Chance to Win,* is aimed at teenagers. A variety of other material is available. *Cigarette Smoking: Take It or Leave It* is a discussion guide for parents and children. Contact your local chapter or write to the American Cancer Society, Four W. 35th, New York, NY 10001.

MARIJUANA FOR YOUR MOOD

Drugs affect mind and mood. One of the drugs most commonly used by adolescents is marijuana (also called pot, weed, grass, and hemp). Marijuana is a mind- and mood-altering drug that produces feelings of euphoria, which is why adolescents using it are reported to enjoy it. Apart from being physically dangerous, marijuana use is illegal. Federal law treats marijuana as a hard narcotic like heroin. In most states possession is punishable by two to ten years for a first offense and five to twenty years for a second offense. Minimum sentences are mandatory; no parole, probation, or suspension is available, except for first offenders.

At present there are 22 million marijuana smokers in the country, according to the National Institute for Drug Abuse, and the number has stayed about the same for the last few years. In the 1950s, marijuana was known as the killer weed, the stepping-stone to heroin. A decade later, many researchers decided that the early warnings had been overblown and slightly hysterical, contending that marijuana smoking was no more harmful than the occasional cocktail. Today, the pendulum is swinging back, as recent research has turned up increasing evidence of health hazards associated with chronic marijuana smoking.

Adding to the concern is the sharply increased potency of the marijuana now in use in the United States. Some of the studies done in the past have become obsolete because the drug is so much stronger now, according to Dr. Sidney Cohen, a professor of psychiatry at the UCLA Medical School, a drug consultant for the U.S. State Department, and one of the nation's early marijuana researchers. Even some of the recent studies have been conducted with marijuana that is less potent than what is being sold today on the streets.

Research conducted for the congressional report on drug abuse cited these findings:

1. THC (the active ingredient in marijuana) causes changes in the reproductive systems of test animals, and has also been shown to impair the immune systems of test animals and decrease their resistance to infections.
2. Marijuana smoking among pregnant women can adversely affect fetal development. Doctors have recently been reporting a number of abnormalities (such as reduced central-nervous-system functioning, and mental deficiency).
3. Extensive lung damage has been documented in chronic marijuana smokers.
4. Darryl Inaba, a director at the Haight-Ashbury Drug Clinic in San Francisco, says that ever since potent marijuana became prevalent in the early 1980s he has been treating patients suffering from "acute anxiety reactions."

Many questions remain about long-term marijuana use, and the findings could have serious implications for adolescents who are still maturing. As noted, studies have indicated that THC interferes with the immune system, thus decreasing its resistance to the herpes simplex virus and inhibiting the production of lymphocytes, important in the synthesis of antibodies. Chronic marijuana smokers might also face a greater risk of developing lung cancer than cigarette smokers, said Dr. Donald Tashkin, a professor at UCLA Medical Center who has been studying the effects of marijuana smoking since 1972.

"One marijuana joint does as much damage to certain lung functions as sixteen cigarettes," said Tashkin.

Because of the recent firm evidence about the dangers of marijuana, it is important that we as parents bone up on *recent* information in order to refute the statements our teenagers may make. An adolescent may quote studies done twenty years ago in order to make the point that marijuana is harmless. In the intervening decades, study after study has shown that marijuana does considerable harm. It is now known that marijuana contains more than 400 known chemicals, 61 of which affect the central nervous system. In 1982, the U.S. Institute of Medicine of the National Academy of Sciences published an exhaustive review of the medical literature on marijuana, concluding that "the effects of marijuana on human health justify serious national concern."

STIMULANTS: DIET PILLS

The kinds of stimulants available to adolescents are numerous, from caffeine in colas, coffee, No-Doz, and diet pills to amphetamines and cocaine. Diet pills are commonly used by adolescents primarily because they do not require a prescription and can be purchased anywhere and by anyone—including children. They are relatively inexpensive and are easy to consume. Benzedrine and Dexedrine, diet pills known for their large dosage of caffeine, are very popular among adolescents. Students often rely on these and similar stimulants for increased alertness, mood elevation, quick boosts of energy, decreased appetite, and extra stamina for prolonged or physically strenuous tasks. Many teenagers believe that stimulants provide them with more alert time, allowing them to do "necessary" tasks such as staying awake longer while studying. They also are convinced that added stimulation will increase their intellectual functioning while taking tests and can significantly increase their physical capabilities during sports competition.

Unfortunately, stimulants also drastically undermine the adolescent's health. Stimulants adversely affect the body's chemistry. Caffeine is considered to be a psychoactive drug. At high concentration, caffeine stimulates the central nervous system. High doses of caffeine alone can produce symptoms indistinguishable from those of anxiety neuroses. Agitation, nervousness, irritability, headaches, and high blood pressure can occur with the forty to sixty-five milligrams of caffeine found in diet colas. With higher doses the person may experience not only headaches and high blood pressure but also paranoia, extreme aggressiveness, and hallucinations. At low concentrations, caffeine depresses the central nervous system. The immediate side effects include:

increased stimulation, followed by general fatigue

depression

extreme nervousness

irregularities of breathing

disorientation

suicidal tendencies

irritability

bizarre dreams

Overdose reactions include elevated blood pressure, vivid hallucinations, convulsions, and possible death. Long-term use of stimulants diminishes body strength, impairs intellectual functioning, and impairs judgment. Likewise, stimulants do not, as believed, enhance complex intellectual functioning. If a student takes stimulants to increase an intellectual skill he doesn't possess, he is fooling himself. The most important ingredients in good study habits are skill know-how and common sense. Staying awake all night—whether artificially or naturally—is decidedly inferior to getting a good night's sleep, and it may actually decrease an adolescent's intellectual performance.

Another danger is look-alike drugs, the newest fad around schoolyards and one that is proving to be very dangerous for young people. Look-alike drugs are purposely fashioned to resemble amphetamines, barbiturates, sedatives, and tranquilizers but actually contain only those substances found in such over-the-counter medications as decongestants and diet aids. Look-alikes are often sold by students who pretend to be selling other drugs (such as speed) so that they can charge a higher price. In 1985 the Food and Drug Administration (FDA) attributed forty-eight deaths among young people to look-alikes.

Serious health problems and even death can occur from the use of look-alikes because the stimulants in these drugs increase the heart rate and raise blood pressure. In high doses, these drugs can cause strokes. High doses of antihistamines, taken for sedative effect, can cause cardiorespiratory collapse.

A very real concern for both adolescent and parent is the tendency for an individual using stimulants to become addicted to them. Over time, many users actually increase their stimulant intake because they have built up a tolerance to the drug. When the person tries to quit, the body often reacts to the withdrawal of the chemical by producing the restlessness, irritability, anxiety, headaches, and difficulty in concentrating that are often experienced with stimulants. The effects of stimulants can defeat anyone's willpower. If your adolescent is using them, his chances of quitting may be greatest with a program consisting of adequate rest, a balanced diet, sports activities, and parental support. The section in this book on nutrition and fitness offers practical suggestions along these lines.

MEGAVITAMIN ABUSE

The word *vitamin* comes from the Latin *vita,* meaning *life.* Today vitamins have become a way of life for many of us, adults and children alike. In a society that wants a quick and easy cure for any problem, vitamins seem to be an answer. If drugs and alcohol take their toll, can vitamins repair it? The word is out: vitamins—in the form of *mega*vitamins—are wonder drugs for counterbalancing drug and alcohol abuse, poor nutrition, and inadequate rest. At least, that's the story adolescents are telling other adolescents. Teenagers are often taking a hundred times the government-recommended dosages of vitamins. Vitamin enthusiasts contend that large doses of certain vitamins will do everything from curing the common cold to preventing cancer. Medical research, however, does not bear this out.

Adolescents are so misinformed about vitamin use that parents have reason to fear the effects of megavitamin abuse, especially among high-school students. Massive amounts of vitamins are not only ineffective, they are unsafe. Substituting vitamin and mineral supplements for a balanced diet or using them to repair body damage from alcohol or drug use is not only potentially harmful but can also lead to the equivalent of drug abuse.

Scientists have long been concerned about the use and abuse of vitamin and mineral supplements. The American Dietetic Association has backed up these concerns with some startling facts about the growing number of supplement users. The $3 billion supplement industry has estimated that 50 percent of the American adult population and as much as 20 percent of those fifteen to nineteen years old take supplements daily (with the adolescent being new to the marketplace). It is estimated that of these, 15 percent take five or more pills a day. And because more and more of these supplements are being sold in dangerous doses—that is, up to ten times the Recommended Dietary Allowance (RDA)—the stage is being set for potential overdose or poisoning. Large doses of vitamins and minerals can affect the body like drugs, upsetting nutrient-absorption rates, causing nutritional deficiencies, and resulting in serious health problems.

Vitamins fall into two general categories: fat-soluble vitamins (A, D, and E) and water-soluble vitamins (C and B). Fat-soluble vitamins are easily stored in the body; an accumulation of very large doses can cause illness. An excess dosage of vitamin D, for example, can cause kidney and bone damage, extreme fatigue, and loss of appetite. Excess vitamin E can cause nausea, leg cramps, intestinal disorders, blurred vision, and a critical interference with the ability of the blood to clot normally. Vitamins A and D, because they can be stored at excessively high levels in the body, should not be taken except with a doctor's prescription.

Studies are now documenting the harmful side effects of megadoses of the water-soluble vitamins as well. In a new and alarming development, megadoses of vitamin C were found to be destructive to vitamin B-12. Dairy foods, which provide 75 percent of the calcium in the American diet, have a balance of nutrients for optimum absorption. However, large doses of calcium, such as those in supplements, can inhibit the body's use of zinc and iron. Vitamin B-6, often prescribed in megadoses for premenstrual syndrome, has shown toxic effects in doses as low as five times the RDA. Long-term intake of megadoses of B-6 has resulted in permanent nerve damage.

It is important to understand what a vitamin is and what it is not. Vitamins are substances that are essential for the maintenance of normal metabolic function but that are not synthesized by the body in adequate amounts and must be supplied by outside sources, such as diet. They function with enzymes or as antioxidants to regulate the release of energy from food and to build and maintain body tissues. There are thirteen essential vitamins; each performs one or more specific functions in the body. If any one vitamin is missing, a deficiency will develop, because the role of that vitamin cannot be fulfilled by any other substance. Extremely sensitive methods of measuring the potency or quantity of vitamins have been developed to help ensure safety. The Food and Nutrition Board of the National Academy of Sciences has established recommended dietary allowances, which are estimated safe-and-adequate daily dietary intakes for all vitamins.

Along with proteins, carbohydrates, and fats, the human body needs vitamins and minerals in proper quantities to function properly. Researchers are still unsure about how minerals and some vitamins interact and specifically contribute to health. However, there is growing emphasis on the importance of the interaction between vitamins and minerals. Because the balance among nutrients is crucial, it is necessary to be cautious about taking large amounts of any vitamin or mineral. Megavitamins are extra or superdoses exceeding the RDA. The bottom line is that few adolescents need *mega*vitamins.

The safest way for your adolescent to get the necessary nutrients is from food. The section on diet and nutrition in this book gives information on helping your adolescent get the proper nutrition for growth and development.

The potential for vitamin abuse is a real one. Adolescents observe adults consuming large doses of megavitamins and assume that doing so is beneficial, not harmful. Unless your doctor has informed you that your child is suffering from overdoses of vitamins, probably the only way you will know whether he is taking them is by asking him. If you suspect or are sure that this is happening to your adolescent, teach him the proper role of vitamins in overall health and well-being. You should help your adolescent examine what he expects the supplements will do for him. You can gain additional information on the proper uses of vitamin supplements by consulting a licensed nutritionist or your family doctor. The Vitamin Nutrition Information Service (VNIS) (listed in the reference section for this chapter) is an excellent source of facts on vitamins and on their use for each age group.

If you or your adolescent feels that he may need supplements, have him take only a multiple vitamin-mineral tablet that contains no more than 100 percent of the RDA for any one nutrient. The following guidelines can help you and your adolescent choose a safe and effective supplement:

1. Choose a balanced multivitamin rather than one or two specific nutrients. A person is rarely deficient or suboptimal in only one nutrient; usually, several are involved.
2. Choose a preparation that provides approximately 100% of the RDA for recognized nutrients, in approximately equal proportions.
3. Avoid preparations containing unrecognized nutrients or nutrients in minute amounts (these only increase the cost and are of no real value).
4. Avoid preparations that claim to be "natural," "organic," "therapeutic," or "high potency." Their extra cost is not worth any purported benefit; many disreputable firms use these claims, which may signal less effective preparations. Be careful to check the base ingredients, and go with a reputable company.
5. Choose a preparation with an expiration date on it. Certain nutrients interact with others to hasten their decomposition; as a result, vitamin preparations lose potency with time. Hot, humid environments, such as bathrooms, accelerate this process.

One more thing: if your physician asks what medications your adolescent may be taking, remember to include any vitamin supplements.

COCAINE

Cocaine is one of the most powerful, seductive, and dangerous drugs available today. It is also becoming the most abused drug. According to the National Institute on Drug Abuse, some 24 million people in this country have used cocaine. Six million of these are habitual users, and 2.9 million have a dependency. It is estimated that each day, 5,000 more people will become users. In recent years cocaine has become so widespread among young people that it is reported even at the junior-high level. A recent New York State survey revealed that almost one-third of the thirteen- and fourteen-year-olds in that state had sampled cocaine before the seventh grade. Says one senior-high student, "It's as easy to get as a can of beer." Once exorbitantly expensive, a gram of coke now costs about $70—less costly than an ounce of marijuana.

In its crystalline form, cocaine is most often inhaled through a tube directly into the nasal passages, passing quickly into the brain. Free-basing involves removing the hydrochloride and other additives by introducing a strong alkali and ether to the crystalline cocaine and heating it to its evaporation point. The cocaine base that remains is then smoked, sending the drug to the brain almost instantaneously. The effects of the cocaine last for a very short period of time—a matter of minutes (and even less when it is smoked). And the intense "high" is usually followed by an equally intense "down." For this reason, many heavy users of cocaine take repeated doses of the drug, or "run," in an effort to avoid the down.

Studies indicate that cocaine's effects on both body and psyche are far more dangerous than its users suspect. There is evidence that the changes caused in the human brain might be irreversible. Research links abuse to heart attacks, high blood pressure, respiratory ailments, lung disease, and a variety of other physical ills, some of them life-threatening. The emotional effects of cocaine range from paranoia and depression to severe psychosis, with far-reaching damage to the user's personal and professional life.

In studies done for the American Council for Drug Education, Dr. Sidney Cohen, a psychiatrist at the UCLA School of Medicine, has reported that cocaine jolts the central nervous system into believing that the body is under attack, thereby triggering the usual defense mechanisms (a sharp rise in blood pressure and a speeding up of heartbeat and respiration)—"But in fooling the brain into thinking that some important biological event has just occurred, the drug subverts and actually reprograms the body's normal survival systems so that the brain learns to identify the drug as more important than the survival drives themselves. People stop eating and sleeping and lose interest in work but literally can't see what is happening to their minds and bodies. Even a single episode of cocaine dysphoria—characterized by fatigue, depression, irritability, hallucinations, even psychosis—can lead someone to experiment with the various methods of relief, leading not only to coke addictions but to a dependency on the ancillary substances as well."

On college campuses and in high schools across the country, cocaine is fast becoming the current drug of choice. "As thousands of teens have already learned, to their families' infinite sorrow," reported the March 17, 1986, issue of *Newsweek*, "coke is IT in the 1980s market." More than any other single class of Americans, adolescents (particularly goal-oriented achievers) have bought the myth that coke is cool, sexy, and safe to use as an aid in sports performance, in studying, and so on. But here are the facts:

> Statistically, adolescents on cocaine suffer more brain seizures than adult users, have more accidents, make more suicide attempts, and get involved in more incidents of violence.
>
> Physiologically, cocaine has a stronger impact on the still developing adolescent than on an adult. The drug's potential for damaging the liver and the lungs is also greater. Drug dependency for cocaine, as for all drugs, develops at a more rapid rate in children than in adults.

According to a 1984 national survey of sixty students known to have a dependency on cocaine, a majority connected feelings of anxiety (78%), depression (68%), and poor concentration (65%) to their use of the drug. The most common physical symptoms were sleep difficulties and chronic fatigue.

Cocaine users are more apt to resort to illegal activities to support their habits: 77 percent of users said they had turned to dealing drugs and other illicit activities to get cocaine.

As noted, coke is widely available and is low in price, especially in its new and particularly destructive form, called "crack" or "rock." Crack is made by mixing cocaine with common baking soda and water and creating a paste that is at least 75 percent cocaine. After the paste hardens, it is cut into chips (thus the term *rock*). A small piece of the mixture will produce a high of approximately ten to thirty minutes in duration. Crack is smoked, not snorted, and the resulting intoxication is far more intense than that of snorted cocaine—much quicker, much more euphoric, and much more addictive. Says Arnold Washton, a psychopharmacologist at Fair Oaks Hospital in Summit, New Jersey, "Crack is the most addictive drug known to man. It is almost instantaneous addiction."

The discovery that your adolescent is using drugs is a soul-shaking experience. After your initial response of shock and outrage, you may be tempted to react with pity and indulgence, rejection, or even aggression. None of these responses will be helpful either to you or to your adolescent. Experts say that parents are still the first and best line of defense. "Parents have to take primary responsibility for their family's education about drugs and what drugs do to their kids," says Joyce Nalepka, president of the National Federation of Parents for Drug-Free Youth. It's not enough merely to tell kids to say no. Parents have to explain the dangers and give kids mental ammunition to combat the often overwhelming peer pressure.

HELP YOUR CHILD SAY NO TO
ALCOHOL AND DRUGS

Throughout this chapter, you have been given suggestions on how to help your teenager avoid drug abuse. As you have noted, there are many things you can do; you need not feel helpless in the face of what sometimes seem overwhelming odds. The following list is a review of the steps you can take to help your child say no to drugs.

Provide a healthy role model. For example, drink as you would like your teens to when they are adults—conservatively or not at all. Treat a nondrinking guest with respect.

Don't pressure anyone to "have another." Don't smoke, and do commend business establishments that enforce no-smoking rules on their premises.

Don't glamorize drinking or drug-taking.

Don't create the impression that the only way to socialize is with a drink.

Don't tolerate someone else's telling of admiring or joking stories about the friend who can "drink everyone under the table" or who uses drugs as a way to relax.

Don't intimate that alcohol or pills can be used to relax, to alleviate anxiety, or to counteract depression, melancholy, or tiredness.

Give your child increasing responsibilities to indicate maturity so he will be less likely to feel a need to use alcohol or drugs to bolster esteem and to prove he is grown up.

Set realistic goals and limits for your teenager, and enforce them consistently. Establish clear and distinct limits that your adolescent can understand.

Communicate. Teenagers *must* be given the honest facts about drugs. Scare tactics or hysterical exaggerations should not be used. In addition to pointing out what is and is not legal, share your feelings and values.

Know your teenager's friends and their parents. Provide responsible supervision at your house, and check with other parents if there is a party someplace else.

Be aware of the early signs of drug and alcohol abuse so you can get help for the family as well as for the child.

Encourage your children to get involved in activities that can give them a natural "high"—sports, recreational, religious, and volunteer activities can be real substitutes for drugs and alcohol.

Participate. Form groups with other concerned parents. Join your PTA. Invite drug counselors to meetings. Talk with school superintendents, principals, coaches, physicians, church personnel, and local politicians to make sure that others are not only aware of alcohol and drug problems but are also responsive to them and concerned with tactics of prevention as well as of intervention.

Speak with your community pharmacist, who is an expert on drugs and their effects on humans. Remember that he or she is also likely to be well aware of the drugs frequently used by adolescents in the community, including those drugs not sold over the counter (such as amphetamines).

WHAT SHOULD YOU DO IF YOUR TEENAGER IS ALCOHOL OR DRUG DEPENDENT?

Looking the other way can be lethal; if you do so, you can only expect the problem to get worse. Obviously, you should confront your child. The best time is probably the morning after an episode, not when he walks in drunk or high. A forthright dialogue the next day is absolutely essential. Try to get to the bottom of why your teenager drank, or used drugs, with whom, and what the pattern is. Make your child aware of the need to lick this habit early on.

1. The first rule is not to discuss the matter when the child is high on drugs or alcohol. Whatever you say will not get through.
2. When he gets back to normal and you can talk calmly, show your concern and ask questions. What is happening? Why?
3. Next, listen—without interrupting.
4. Examine your own attitudes about drugs and alcohol. Is it possible that you are sending conflicting messages? I can still remember the puzzled look on my daughter's face when she told me about a lecture on drinking that she and her friend Sue had received from Sue's father—who at the time was wearing a T-shirt that proclaimed, "This Bud's For You!"
5. Talk with other parents about your teens.
6. Check out the school your child attends. What kind of prevention programs does it have? How pervasive are drug and alcohol use?
7. Find out what treatment opportunities are available in your area (in schools, mental-health facilities, and drug-treatment agencies). Exactly what do they offer teenagers? How good are they?
8. Confront the problem. If you see that your adolescent has a problem, do not look the other way or pity him. At this stage, he needs your help, not your avoidance or acceptance of his weakness. Real parental love may best be demonstrated by helping a child to help himself. Teach him to develop his own strength and to find other, constructive ways of dealing with his problems and feelings.

If you find that your child's problem is too much for you to handle alone, seek help. There are many programs that you and your adolescent can attend together. One excellent one is AA, which is a strong source of support because it features one ordinary person helping another. Information about AA and about other excellent programs is given in the resource section of this book.

Honest confrontation is a must. Avoid recriminations about past lying, stealing, and breaking of trust. Focus on the present and the future. Get a grip on the problem, and, with professional help, identify its best remedy. Send the message to your adolescent that he or she cannot drink or take drugs without consequences. Make it clear that your child's home cannot and will not shield him from the consequences of his habits and actions.

Most parents find it difficult to take this stance of "tough love." The adolescent may need medical or institutional care during the initial phase of treatment. You may have to restrict your child's contacts for a few days, not permitting him to return to those places where he could associate with the same peer group. Rehabilitation is a complex and difficult process, and it is often as hard on the parent as it is on the child.

Be ready for a long haul. Alcohol and drugs provide the adolescent with gratification—instant power, pleasure, and security—without his having to work for it. Helping a youngster to kick drugs and alcohol takes time, persistent attention, and a continuing effort on the part of the parent. The path to health and maturity for the adolescent is even more difficult.

The transition from childhood to adulthood demands responsibility and maturity. It calls for an ever-increasing ability to manage the stress of life. The more we understand our adolescents and learn how to meet their legitimate needs, the better able we will be to help them choose not to abuse their bodies with chemicals. The attitudes and skills that we can help our adolescents to acquire are the best ammunition we have for guarding against the ravages of alcohol and drugs. Only by using those skills will our adolescents respectfully adhere to the limits we set and come to understand and embrace the time-honored values we want so much to give them.

CHAPTER NINE

Lasting the Distance:
Intervention and Prevention

How our children deal with stress during their adult years is determined to a great extent by what happens during their formative, impressionable years. Many scientific studies have proved the importance of early experiences in influencing later behavior. Parents should make every effort to help adolescents develop effective techniques for managing stress.

INTERVENTION

In order to last the distance, you need to have specific coping skills, techniques you can use to help your child help himself. The following sections are devoted to such skills. Go through each section carefully. Practice the techniques alone first, then with your teenager. Don't become upset if a technique doesn't seem to work for you. Think of these skills as you would clothing: "try on" each one, see how it fits and how comfortable you are, and then choose the ones you like best.

THE BENEFITS OF RELAXATION

When you relax, you become aware of the relationship between your mind and body. Stop and think about stress. Imagine what a person who is angry or tense looks like. You can see the stress in the face, the muscles, and the posture. When your muscles are tense, they reflect your state of mind. When your breathing is rapid and out of control, your emotions are also out of control. When you relax your body, you relax your state of mind. When you control your breathing, you gain control of your emotions. You calm down. Conscious relaxation produces changes in the electrical activity of the brain and in turn produces more alpha waves, which are associated with feelings of well-being. There is also a decrease in the rate of metabolism and oxygen consumption, even more than during sleep. Conscious relaxation is a simple but very effective method of eliminating tension, and it enables you to offset the damaging effects of stress. With regular practice you will feel increased benefits as you learn to release the charge of tension in your muscles and acquire more energy. You will have new vitality.

Progressive Muscle Relaxation. There you are, standing in the hall, facing the door to the Internal Revenue Service's audit division. You feel as though you have cotton in your mouth; your legs are about to melt into the carpet; your heart is threatening to explode through your ears. As you are summoning up your nerve to go in, someone passes you in the hall and says, "Oh, come on. Just relax."

While it's easy to tell someone else to relax, it can certainly be hard to learn to do so ourselves. Relaxation is a skill that everyone must possess in order to survive the stresses of daily life. As you learned earlier, your teenager may have even more stress than you do, and he desperately needs to learn how to relax. You can help him by explaining to him and practicing with him the principles of progressive relaxation.

Progressive muscle relaxation is a technique that uses physical exercise to achieve relaxation from tension. It is a proven, systematic way to control muscle tension. In addition to helping people to relax, the technique has been used for alleviating a number of disorders, including anxiety, insomnia, headaches, backaches, and hypertension. The state of physical relaxation produced is pleasant and allows one to feel rested and refreshed.

Most teenagers need more than just encouragement to relax. Having various muscles constantly tense—as you wrinkle your

forehead, squint your eyes, tap your fingers, and shift position—
is a sign that energy is being wasted. Learning and practicing
relaxation is a way to be *selectively* tense when a particular task
must be performed so you can avoid wasting energy and can
accomplish more. Baseball player Steve Garvey may get up
slowly, walk slowly to the batting mound, and become alert and
tense while waiting for a pitch. If he is unsuccessful at connecting
with the ball, he may back off from the batter's box, then approach
it again with a cautious sluggishness. A minute later, he may be
running at full speed toward first base. He does not run around
on the field while waiting for his turn at bat, nor does he jump up
and down while waiting for the next pitch. Why? He saves his
energies for those things that are purposeful to the event. This is
a worthwhile practice. People who learn to relax do not lose motivation or become sluggish, nor do they become lazy, bored, or
tired. In fact, just the opposite occurs: by using progressive relaxation, they can remain alert, avoid fatigue, and restore vitality.

This technique is called *progressive* because each muscle group
is tensed and relaxed individually, slowly progressing throughout
the body. Tensing and relaxing the muscles helps you to increase
your awareness of the body's muscular response to stress. As you
become more aware of the location and feeling of muscle tension,
the absence of tension becomes clear. You begin to recognize muscle tension and the difference between being tense and being
relaxed. The muscle groups around the head, face, neck, and
shoulders are particularly important areas of stress, and a great
deal of tension may accumulate in these muscles.

Try the following exercise. Focus on the last time you were
angry and tense. Now stand in front of the mirror and think about
that incident. Are your legs in a defensive stance? Is your jaw
tight? Do your eyes seem intense? During the next few days,
observe how you sit and stand in different places and at different
times. Notice which of your muscles seem to stay tense long after
the stressful event. Often when we are nervous, angry, afraid, or
hurried, our muscles get tense or tight.

The next exercise will teach you to feel the difference between
tense and relaxed muscles and will help you learn to condition all

of your muscles in order to achieve a state of relaxation. To prepare, first find a quiet location free of interruptions. Dim the lights. You may practice this exercise while reclining on a sofa, lying on a bed, or sitting in a comfortable chair (preferably one that reclines). It is easier to learn the exercise the first time while reclining. Later it will be beneficial to practice while sitting up or standing. Clothing should be comfortable and loose. It is best to remove shoes, eyeglasses, or contact lenses. This exercise is most effective if you follow the word-by-word script provided below. To practice, close your eyes and relax while the instructions are read to you. (Another way to do this is to have the person for whom it is intended record the script so that it is available for use at any time.)

The word-by-word script is as follows: [*for total body tension*] "First, tense every muscle in your body. Tense the muscles of your jaw, eyes, arms, hands, chest, back, stomach, legs, and feet. Feel the tension all over your body. . . . Hold the tension briefly, and then relax and let go as you breathe out. . . . Let your whole body relax. . . . Feel a wave of calm come over you as you stop tensing. Feel the relief.

"Take another deep breath. . . . Study the tension as you hold your breath. . . . Slowly breathe out and relax and let go. Feel the deepening relaxation. Allow yourself to drift more and more with this relaxation. . . . As you continue, you will exercise different parts of your body. Become aware of your body and its tension and relaxation. This will help you to become deeply relaxed on command.

[*head and face*] "Keeping the rest of your body relaxed, wrinkle up your forehead. Do you feel the tension? Your forehead is very tight. Briefly pause and be aware of it. . . . Now relax and let go. Feel the tension slipping out. Smooth out your forehead and take a deep breath. Hold it briefly. As you breathe out, relax and let go.

"Squint your eyes. Keep the rest of your body relaxed. Briefly pause and feel the tension around your eyes. Now relax and let go. Take a deep breath and hold it. Relax and let go as you exhale.

"Open your mouth as wide as you can. Feel the tension in your jaw and chin. Briefly hold the tension. Now let your mouth gently close. As you do, silently say, 'Relax and let go.' Take a deep breath. Hold it. As you breathe out, relax and let go.

"Close your mouth. Push your tongue against the roof of your mouth. Study the tension in your mouth and chin. Briefly hold the tension. . . . Relax and let go. Take a deep breath. Hold it. Now relax and let go as you breathe out. When you breathe out, let your tongue rest comfortably in your mouth, and let your lips be slightly apart.

"Keep the rest of your body relaxed but clench your jaw tightly. Feel the tension in your jaw muscles. Briefly hold the tension. . . . Now relax and let go, and take a deep breath. Hold it. Relax and let go as you breathe out.

"Think about the top of your head, your forehead, eyes, jaws, and cheeks. Make sure these muscles are relaxed. . . . Feel the relaxation replace the tension. Feel your face becoming very smooth and soft as all the tension slips away. . . . Your eyes are relaxed. . . . Your tongue is relaxed. Your jaws are loose and limp. . . . All of your neck muscles are also very, very relaxed.

"All of the muscles of your face and head are relaxing more and more. . . . Your head feels as though it could roll from side to side, and your face feels soft and smooth. Allow your face to continue becoming more and more relaxed as you now move to other areas of your body.

[*shoulders*] "Now shrug your shoulders up and try to touch your ears with your shoulders. Feel the tension in the shoulders and neck. Hold the tension. . . . Now relax and let go. As you do, feel your shoulders joining the relaxed parts of your body. Take a deep breath. Hold it. Relax and let go as you slowly breathe out.

"Notice the difference as the tension is giving way to relaxation. Shrug your right shoulder up and try to touch your right ear. Feel the tension in your right shoulder and along the right side of your neck. Hold the tension. . . . Now relax and let go. Take a deep breath. Hold it. Relax and let go as you slowly breathe out.

"Next, shrug your left shoulder up and try to touch your left ear. Feel the tension in your left shoulder and along the left side of your neck. Hold the tension. Now relax and let go. Take a deep breath. Hold it. Relax and let go as you slowly breathe out. Feel the relaxation seeping into the shoulders. As you continue, you will become as loose, limp, and relaxed as a sandbag.

[*arms and hands*] "Stretch your arms out and make your hands into fists. Feel the tension in your hands and forearms. Hold the tension. Hold, relax, and let go. Take a deep breath. Hold it. Relax and let go as you slowly breathe out.

"Push your right hand down into the surface it is resting on. Feel the tension in your arm and shoulder. Hold the tension. . . . Now relax and let go. Take a deep breath. Hold it. Relax and let go as you slowly breathe out.

"Next, push your left hand down into whatever it is resting on. Feel the tension in your arm and shoulder. Hold the tension. . . . Now relax and let go. Take a deep breath. Hold it. Relax and let go as you slowly breathe out.

"Bend your arms toward your shoulders and double them up as you would do to show off your muscles. Feel the tension. Hold the tension. . . . Now relax and let go. Take a deep breath. Hold it. Relax and let go as you slowly breathe out.

[*chest and lungs*] "Move on to the relaxation of your chest. Begin by taking a deep breath that totally fills your lungs. As you hold your breath, notice the tension. Be aware of the tension around your ribs. . . . Relax and let go as you slowly breathe out. Feel the deepening relaxation as you continue breathing easily, freely, and gently.

"Take in another deep breath. Hold it and again feel the contrast between tension and relaxation. As you do, tighten your chest muscles. Hold the tension. Relax and let go as you slowly breathe out. Feel the relief as you breathe out and continue to breathe gently, naturally, and rhythmically. Breathe as smoothly as you can. You will become more and more relaxed with every breath.

[*back*] "Keep your face, neck, arms, and chest as relaxed as possible. Arch your back up (or forward, if you are sitting). Arch it as though you had a pillow under the middle and lower parts of your back. Observe the tension along both sides of your back. Briefly hold that position. Now relax and let go. Take a deep

breath. Hold it. Relax and let go as you breathe out. Let that relaxation spread deep into your shoulders and down into your back muscles.

"Feel the slow relaxation developing and spreading all over. Feel it going deeper and deeper. Allow your entire body to relax. Face and head are relaxed . . . neck is relaxed . . . shoulders are relaxed . . . arms are relaxed . . . chest is relaxed . . . back is relaxed. . . . All these areas are relaxing more and more, becoming more deeply relaxed.

[*stomach*] "Now begin the relaxation of the stomach area. Tighten up this area. Briefly hold the tension. . . . Relax and let go. Feel the relaxation pouring into your stomach area. All the tension is being replaced with relaxation, and you feel the general well-being that comes with relaxation. Take a deep breath. Hold it. Relax and let go as you slowly breathe out.

"Now experience a different type of tension in the stomach area. Push your stomach out as far as you can. Briefly hold the tension. . . . Now relax and let go. Take a deep breath. Hold it. Relax and let go as you slowly breathe out. Now pull your stomach in. Try to pull your stomach in and touch your backbone. Hold it. . . . Now relax and let go. Take a deep breath. Hold it. Relax and let go as you slowly breathe out.

"You are becoming more and more relaxed. Each time you breathe out, feel the relaxation in your lungs and in your body.

[*hips, legs, and feet*] "Now begin the relaxation of your hips and legs. Tighten your hips and legs by pressing down the heels of your feet into the surface they are resting on. Tighten these muscles. Keep the rest of your body as relaxed as you can and press your heels down. . . . Now hold the tension. . . . Relax and let go. Your legs feel as if they could float up. Take a deep breath. Hold it. Relax and let go as you slowly breathe out. Feel the relaxation pouring in.

"Next, tighten your lower leg muscles. Feel the tension. Briefly hold the tension. . . . Now relax and let go. Take a deep breath. Hold it. Relax and let go as you slowly breathe out.

"Now curl your toes downward. Curl them down and try to touch the bottom of your feet with your toes. Hold them and feel the tension. . . . Relax and let go. Wiggle your toes gently as you let go of the tension. Let the tension be replaced with relaxation. Take a deep breath. Hold it. Relax and let go as you slowly breathe out.

"Now bend your toes back the other way. Bend your toes right up toward your knees. Feel the tension. Try to touch your knees with your toes. Feel the tension. Hold the tension. . . . Relax and let go. Feel all the tension vanish. Take a deep breath. Hold it. Relax and let go as you slowly breathe out. Feel the tension leaving your body and the relaxation seeping in.

[body review] "You have progressed through all the major muscles of your body. Now let them become more and more relaxed. Continue to feel yourself becoming more and more relaxed each time you slowly breathe out. Each time you breathe out, think about a muscle and silently say, "Relax and let go." . . . Face, relax and let go . . . shoulders, relax . . . arms, relax . . . hands . . . chest . . . back . . . stomach . . . hips . . . legs . . . feet. . . . Your whole body is becoming more and more relaxed with each breath.

"Spend a few more minutes relaxing if you like. If you find yourself getting upset about something during the day, remember the relaxation you have just experienced. Before getting upset, take a deep breath, hold it, and as you slowly breathe out silently say, 'Relax and let go.' With practice, you will be able to use this technique to relax whenever you begin to feel the stress."

It is important to include a termination process at the end of each relaxation exercise. This process consists of flexing the arms, taking a deep breath, and slowly opening the eyes. This helps the system adjust gradually to the higher state of arousal needed for getting up and walking around. You might say in the script, "Now flex your arms. Take a deep breath and release it slowly. I'm now going to count from four to one. When I reach one, your eyes will open and you will be awake, feeling calm and comfortable. Four . . . three . . . two . . . one. Open your eyes, feeling calm and comfortable." The count is done slowly, allowing the relaxation period to be ended easily and quietly. Since the relaxation state is similar to a sleep state, the final steps allow a better transition to the alert phase.

Use relaxation techniques at least three times each week with your child, more often if possible. A good time to do so is when your teenager might typically need to relax. For instance, he might need it to unwind after a long, tense day at school or to calm down before going to bed on an evening when he is feeling particularly excited or keyed up. Make a point of allowing your child to observe you taking time out to relax, talking yourself through it and describing how you feel afterward: "That feels much better. Now I feel calm." During the first two weeks of practicing this skill, check for signs that your body is giving you indicating you are tense. To look for cues that your body is tensing up, ask yourself these questions: Is my forehead wrinkled? Are my jaw muscles tight? Is my stomach knotted up? Are my fists clenched? Allow the relaxation to replace tension. Tensing and relaxing muscles help you to increase your awareness of your body's muscular response to stress. As you become more aware of the location and feeling of muscle tension, the absence of tension becomes clearer.

Autohypnosis. You can also counteract tension with autohypnosis. This exercise temporarily lets your body know that it's time to relax. The simple steps are as follows:

1. Sit comfortably in a chair facing a wall about eight feet away. Pick a spot or an object on the wall that is about one foot above eye level when you are seated. This is your focal point.
2. Look at your focal point and begin counting backward from 100, with one number for each breath you exhale.
3. As you count and continue to concentrate on your focal point, imagine yourself floating down through the chair, very relaxed.
4. As you stare at your focal point you will find that your eyelids feel heavier and that you begin to blink. When this happens, let your eyes slowly close.
5. While your eyes are closed, continue to count backward one number for each time you exhale. As you count, imagine how it would feel to be as limp as a sandbag, totally relaxed and floating in a safe, comfortable space. This is your space.
6. As that safe, comfortable feeling flows over you, stop counting, relax, and just float in your space.

7. If any disturbing thought enters your space, just let it flow out again; continue to feel safe and relaxed.

8. When you are ready to come out of autohypnosis, either let yourself drift off to sleep or count from one to three and exhale, using the following steps: at one, let yourself get ready; at two, take a deep breath and hold it for a few seconds; and at three, exhale and open your eyes slowly. As you open your eyes, continue to hold on to that relaxed, comfortable feeling.

Diaphragmatic Breathing. Many people do not know how to breathe properly. If you observe yourself and others, you may notice that breathing is often done with the chest, in short shallow breaths. This type of breathing (thoracic breathing) is thought to be indicative of unrecognized tension. It may also be detrimental to health, as it causes stale and unused air to be retained in the lungs. The healthy way to breathe is through diaphragmatic, or belly, breathing. This is the way that babies and animals breathe. It is also the proper way to breathe for achieving body relaxation. Notice your actions throughout the day. Occasionally you may sit back, stretch, and sigh deeply. In doing so, you fill the lungs and the diaphragm completely with air and then let it all out slowly. This is your body's natural way of breathing.

As you inhale air, the bloodstream is oxygenated and purified. In addition, breathing has a major impact on the functioning of the heart. If you breathe slowly and regularly while sitting upright, your heart rate will slow down. At the same time that you are breathing deeply, you are automatically slowing down the rate of respiration. With practice the respiration rate can be decreased to five or six breaths per minute from fifteen or twenty. Here are the basic principles involved:

1. *Inhale* deeply, first filling the diaphragm area with air (stomach goes out). Continue inhaling as the lower part of the chest expands. Finish inhaling as the upper ribs are expanded and the top of the lungs fill with air.

2. *Exhale* slowly. The air flows out smoothly from the top of the chest, down through the middle, and completely out as the stomach draws in.

3. *Rest*. Allow yourself to experience the physical sensations that accompany breathing in this relaxing manner. Begin the process again by inhaling deeply.

The following exercise is designed to help you teach adolescents how to relax through proper breathing techniques. This technique can be used almost anytime or anywhere. Follow these steps:

To prepare, find a quiet, peaceful place where there are no distractions. Lie down. Get as comfortable as possible. Loosen any tight-fitting clothing. If your shoes feel tight, take them off.

The breathing technique: First, place your hands very lightly on your abdomen just below the navel, with your fingertips touching. As you inhale through your nose, your abdomen should swell out. This may feel a bit awkward at first if you are used to shallower chest breathing. You may have to make a conscious effort to "push" your stomach. (An alternative method for checking to see whether you are using your diaphragm appropriately is to make a "bridge" by placing a book or an 11″ board on yourself from chest to abdomen. When you inhale, you should see the lower end of the bridge tilting higher.) After inhaling deeply, begin to exhale through the nose. Exhale slowly and draw in the stomach so that your fingertips come together again. If necessary, make a conscious effort to pull in the stomach slightly. When you have finished exhaling all of your air (without forcing the air out), rest for a moment until you feel it necessary to inhale again.

In order to give your youngster adequate practice in using this breathing pattern for relaxation, take a three- to five-minute "time-out" session twice a day, preferably at a set time each day, perhaps at noon or right after school or work hours. The technique is very useful for your adolescent when she wants to become more at ease before undertaking a difficult task, such as a test. This would be an excellent opportunity for her to practice the technique and to experience its positive results. By minimizing the tension-producing effects of test taking, she will gain confidence in using the technique on her own in other settings where she might need it. Say to her, "When you are seated at your desk begin breathing slowly and deeply. Concentrate on inhaling and exhaling for a minute. Just keep in mind that you are to breathe in deeply, exhale smoothly and slowly, and rest. If your thoughts slip away from concentrating on your breathing pattern, don't worry. Just redirect your thoughts and bring them back to your normal breathing. Focus on the air from the moment it enters your mouth until it enters the most distant reaches of your lungs. Picture the air making a return trip."

The breathing technique can be used alone or in combination with other relaxation exercises, such as progressive muscle relaxation or visual imagery. Some adolescents find it helpful to imagine all of their tension "flowing" out as they exhale. As the breathing exercise is practiced in combination with muscle tension and relaxation, it may become possible to breathe in deeply, breathe out slowly, and automatically relax all of the muscles. It can thus serve as a quick and convenient way to relax and can be integrated into a busy and stressful day as many times as may be needed.

Visual Imagery: Achieving Mental Relaxation. The previous two relaxation techniques dealt with physically letting go, with muscle relaxation. It is possible to relax our minds as well as our bodies, and it is just as important.

Visual imagery—sometimes called guided imagery or visualization—is a powerful tool in relaxation. The goals of imagery are to reduce and control mental anxiety. Visual imagery is a technique to produce positive, relaxing images and thoughts. These images and thoughts can be used to block out intruding and upsetting thoughts. For example, you may be physically tired and yet be unable to sleep because of upsetting thoughts. By using pleasant visual images, you can control upsetting thoughts and enjoy a deep state of relaxation. Learning to control your thoughts involves knowing what you need to think about, practicing those thoughts, and then using them when you want to relax.

Mental imagery is a little like a daydream. You may want to start by trying to visualize a pleasant scene, perhaps one you have seen many times. Try to reexperience the scene in every way you can, including the use of images from senses such as smell (for example, the scent of flowers), touch (the feel of grass beneath your feet), sound (the sound of birds singing in the trees), and taste (the salt air at the beach). Soothing music can also be used to achieve a calm state. Prerecorded music on tape can be very helpful (a list of musical selections is given in the resource section at the end of the book). When you practice visual imagery without a prerecorded tape, you may want to add your favorite soothing music.

To become proficient at visual imagery, it is helpful to begin with exercises proceeding from simple to more complex images. The steps are outlined below. Each step is a plateau in the learning of imagery. Once your adolescent is able to visualize freely, encourage him to begin to create his own images. Only he can experience and know what images are relaxing to him.

Be patient with yourself as you begin to learn mental relaxation. Complete concentration, even on pleasant images, requires a great deal of practice. Do not get upset if unwanted thoughts come to mind; simply redirect your thoughts.

To prepare:

Find a quiet place without distractions. Sit or lie down.

Loosen any tight-fitting clothing.

Close your eyes. Take a deep breath. Imagine breathing in the clean air. As you breathe out, feel the relaxation spread over your body. As you take another breath, feel yourself floating down.

Tense and relax your muscles.

Continue relaxing for a few minutes, picturing yourself in a relaxing scene.

When you are finished, stretch your arms, take a deep breath, and open your eyes.

Here are some ideas for guiding visual imagery:

1. You are lying on the beach, warm under the sun. The sand feels nice and soft underneath you. You're very calm and

relaxed, almost falling asleep. The ocean breeze feels good against your skin. You can taste the salt air on your lips. You can hear the waves rolling in gently. You feel very comfortable, relaxed, peaceful, and calm.

2. You are walking slowly through a beautiful green forest. The only sounds you can hear are the sounds of the birds in the distance and of water flowing over the waterfall in the distance. It is very peaceful, and you continue to walk slowly and quietly, enjoying the calmness and peacefulness. It is a warm day, but the forest is very comfortable. You have the forest all to yourself, with nothing to disturb you.

3. It is a lazy Saturday morning. Everyone else is still asleep. A cool rain is falling outside, making gentle sounds that can be heard against your window. You are still sleepy. The fluffy covers on your bed are warm and soft. You bask in the thought of not having to get up, and you turn over and begin to daydream about something you like.

It's wise to practice the visualization exercise and then to create some ideas of your own. Look at the following questions. Using your imagination, create your own relaxing picture. Practice relaxing using your own script.

1. Name a place that makes you feel relaxed.
2. Put yourself in a beautiful and serene setting. What are you doing?
3. What's the weather like there?
4. How do you feel when you are there?
5. Why would you like to return?

While learning this technique, practice it two or three times each week. Make a point of allowing your child to observe you taking time out for visual imagery relaxation, and describe how you feel afterward: "That is a soothing feeling. I really feel mentally calm now."

Visual imagery can be used for tasks other than relaxing. As children are taught to visualize themselves in problem situations or situations of conflict and to imagine themselves dealing successfully with those situations, they learn to be in control of their behavior.

PREVENTION

The purpose of this section is to inform you of the importance of diet, nutrition, and exercise as these contribute to good health, of the role these factors play in alleviating stress, and of the ways in which you can help your adolescent to develop habits that will contribute to his or her physical and mental well-being.

THE CASE FOR GOOD NUTRITION

To a great extent, as health experts say, "we are what we eat." Good health depends on a balanced diet. A deficiency of certain vitamins, minerals, and nutrients can upset body chemistry. Any diet that emphasizes one type of food (proteins, vegetables, carbohydrates) to the exclusion of other foods may be very harmful to the body. Stress, illness, and injury may be superimposed upon preexisting marginal health status. In short, when the body is deprived of basic nourishment, resulting in a deficiency of essential nutrients, it is even less capable of withstanding the ravages of stress and even more susceptible to major health breakdowns.

Can you sit down right now and list what your teenager had to eat today? What did she have for dinner yesterday? When was the last time she had proteins, carbohydrates, and a full complement of vitamins and minerals all in one meal? You probably are not completely aware of your child's eating habits (only of the fact that whatever you bring home from the store disappears with alarming speed), but you should be. Diet and nutrition play vital roles in your teenager's life.

Good nutrition starts in the early years, but making sure that it carries over into the teenage years is especially important. All children need regularly scheduled meals, with an emphasis on dark-green and yellow vegetables, whole-grain or enriched cereals and breads, and milk. Active children and those engaged in strenuous physical activities also need snacks rich in protein, minerals, and vitamins. Adolescent girls need about 2500–2700 calories a day; adolescent boys need about 2800–3000 calories.

The U.S. Senate committee on Nutrition and Human Needs has established the following dietary goals for balanced nutrition and suggests the following guidelines for food selection and preparation:

1. Increase consumption of fruits, vegetables, and whole grains.
2. Decrease consumption of refined and other processed sugars and foods high in such sugars.
3. Decrease consumption of foods high in total fat, and partially replace saturated fats, whether obtained from animal or vegetable sources, with polyunsaturated fats.
4. Decrease consumption of animal fat and choose meats, poultry, and fish that will reduce saturated-fat intake.
5. Except for young children, substitute low-fat and nonfat milk for whole milk and low-fat dairy products for high-fat dairy products.
6. Decrease consumption of butterfat, eggs, and other high-cholesterol foods.
7. Decrease consumption of salt and of foods with a high salt content.

In all, the body needs about forty-seven different nutritional substances to sustain its internal chemistry. Nutritionists agree that eating a balanced diet is the best way to get the proper mix of nutrients, but vitamin supplementation is frequently needed to replace the supply of nutrients robbed by the effects of chemical and other pollutants and to help maintain the body's natural defense against stress. Vitamins can help improve general resistance to illness. For example, vitamin B complex, magnesium, potassium, and calcium folate provide relief from the fatigue and depression of which many adolescents are victims. The best advice when it comes to vitamin supplementation is this: a balanced diet should provide all the essential nutrients, but taking a one-a-day vitamin tablet that contains all the essential vitamins and nutrients is also a good idea. All other doses and megadoses of single vitamins and nutrients should be taken only on the advice of a physician. The section on megavitamins in chapter 8 provides additional information on vitamin supplements.

When a teenager's body lacks essential nutrients, it cannot function properly. School performance is affected. Research has found the omission of breakfast to be a factor in a youngster's inability to function in school. Adolescents who eat breakfast and lunch show greater hemoglobin concentrations, resulting in better school performance overall in tasks demanding attentiveness and alertness. The USDA Nationwide Food Consumption Survey shows that skipping breakfast is most prevalent among adolescents. It is estimated that nearly 70 percent of teenagers skip breakfast and that, of those, more than 30 percent also skip lunch.

Fortunately, we can help our children improve their nutrition. Here's how you can encourage better dietary habits in your teenager:

Breakfast is a must. Breakfast must not be missed (by either adults or children). It should consist of fruits and grains, which will steadily release glucose during the day, providing the brain with fuel. All too often breakfast is an "every man for himself" affair. Teenagers, if they get any breakfast at all, tend to rush off to school with breakfast in hand.

Planning the night before can help to make breakfast time a little easier. If the breakfast table is set with all the plates, bowls, glasses, and silverware so that your youngster has only to pour juice into a glass and pop the bread in the toaster, he will be more likely to eat something nutritious. If the entire family can rise early enough to eat together, even better! If breakfast is on the table, most likely the adolescent will eat. It does take some planning on the part of the parent and teen to get everything ready the evening before. It also takes cooperation from the entire family.

Eating and stress should not occur together. It's difficult for the body to digest food when the mind is in turmoil. By carrying on pleasant conversations, the family can make mealtime a part of the day to which each member looks forward. Mealtime is conducive to sharing events that have happened during the day and to exchange feelings of goodwill. Do not allow heated discussions to be carried out during mealtime—make this a ground rule.

Family dinners can be a cooperative effort. Good nutrition needn't be only your responsibility. Your adolescent can takes turns being responsible for the dinner one or two nights per week. Or, meal preparation can be a cooperative effort. Menu planning can be done on the weekend so that all the needed food items will be on hand for each dinner that week. You can even go so far as to write a weekly menu, allowing each parent and child to plan their favorite meals. Alternatively, one adult and one child can jointly share the responsibility and plan special meals. However your family chooses to carry out meal planning and preparation, every family member should be involved in the nutritional regime for healthy eating.

Beware of your teen's "special diets." If your teenager is involved in bodybuilding or is on a team, he may try to convince you that he needs steak and eggs (in other words, a lot of protein) in his diet to the exclusion of other foods. If he is on the wrestling team, he will likely be trying to drop weight (to compete in a lower-weight class). Either way, he may go on a binge-and-purge diet. Wrestlers, for example, eat little or nothing for three or four days before a match, going on a food binge immediately after the match to make up for days of near starvation. Do get expert medical advice before permitting your teenager to go on any diet that is not completely balanced in all areas. Calling in medical experts to give advice can often help you persuade your athlete to do sensible nutritional planning.

Dieting among teenage girls may involve approaches similar to those of athletes, but such diets generally focus on losing weight for reasons of appearance. Always aware of their growing and changing bodies, many teenage girls are very self-conscious about the problem of being overweight. Ranging from fad diets to the extremes of binge-and-purge diets, the incidence of such eating disorders as anorexia and bulimia is highest among adolescent girls, as is the use of diet pills.

It is important that your teenager's health should be assessed prior to any diet. Ask your family physician to assess your child's state of health and to evaluate particular strategies for maintaining health and nutritional control. Just as dieting can be harmful if it is not done carefully, being overweight poses problems, too. *If your child has a weight problem, take stock.* Are you contributing to poor eating habits and to weight problems in your adolescent? Are foods, especially sweets, being used as a reward? Does your teenager turn to food for self-gratification, or does he or she eat as an outlet for depression? Look for patterns in food consumption. When does your adolescent snack? What are her favorite fattening foods? Does she overeat when she is feeling blue or bored or when watching television? This can help identify eating triggers and high-risk situations that can then be avoided. Consult a physician, school nurse, or nutritionist for more information.

FITNESS AND EXERCISE

We live in a time when physical fitness is often on our minds. The past fifteen years have seen a physical-fitness revolution; a good many adults have taken another look at the importance of being physically fit. But by and large, adolescents in contemporary society lead a sedentary life. A recent federal study of 8800 elementary and high-school students showed that both boys and girls are significantly more overweight than those examined in the 1960s. According to a report issued by the U.S. Department of Health and Human Services, 80 to 90 percent of Americans fail to get enough exercise. With the movement away from neighborhood schools to large integrated and centrally located schools, busing has replaced bicycling and walking. Coupled with unfamiliar neighborhoods and with the incidence of danger lurking in the streets, children now ride to school and leisure activities. The physical fitness of youth in this country is far below that in countries where physical exercise is still a necessary part of daily activity. Worse, our young people tend to spend more hours watching TV or playing video games than they do in aerobic activity.

As parents we often assume that our children get sufficient physical activity, while in reality this may not be true. With the recent trend in education of going back to "the three R's," emphasis on physical education has diminished. In some schools, for example, physical-education classes—which used to be mandatory throughout high school—can now be met by taking a textbook-education health course. Compulsory physical-education programs are instituted in school for fifty minutes each week. Too often this fifty minutes is scheduled into one period, once a week. Usually it is the last period of the day so that the school does not have to contend with arrangements for the taking of showers.

The inescapable conclusion, warns Ash Hayes, executive director of the President's Council on Physical Fitness and Sports, is that "millions of Americans in every age group are unfit. One important solution to this shocking national problem is for parents to accept responsibility for their own physical fitness and for that of their children. Working together in family activities in a spirit of fun and cooperation is one of the very best hopes we have of getting ourselves in shape."

Following is a summary of some of the benefits of exercise:

1. increased circulation
2. assistance to heart
3. added oxygen to the body
4. improved digestion
5. relaxed nerves, balanced emotions
6. increased resistance to disease
7. reduced fatigue
8. strengthened muscles, bones, and ligaments
9. improved figure and complexion
10. sharpened mental powers

But don't just marshal your statistics—you can take an *active* role in getting your child up and about.

Set an example. As parents, we need to provide positive role models for our youngsters. If you smoke a pack of cigarettes a day and sit in front of the TV eating potato chips when you return from work, your child will most certainly not learn how to become physically fit. If you really want to have credibility with your teenager, you must first and foremost get involved in some type of fitness program yourself. If you aren't fit, work toward it. If you are fit, stay fit. You want your teenager to see the importance of fitness to overall health. Your teen is setting patterns that he will take with him into adult life, and you can provide the model.

Encourage individual activities. Provide activities that channel your teenager's need for risk, adventure, and challenge in a productive and positive way. Don't depend on the school to do this, and don't assume that it is the school's responsibility (or anyone else's) to keep your adolescent fit.

If your teen has had it with calisthenics in gym class—which do not necessarily do much for the cardiovascular system anyway—an alternative is a new fitness program called Challenge Exercise (CE). CE adds a new dimension to the concept of physical fitness with the element of challenge. This challenge adds the bonus of mental well-being to the well-known euphoric experience of exercise, with a degree of well-being rarely experienced after a non-challenge exercise. It is believed that it is this experience rather than the fact that exercise is good for the body that makes people return to CE sports.

In essence, this response is a sensation that envelops the challenge taker after the activity. The sensation varies in intensity and duration according to the individual and the degree of risk. This point is noteworthy, because CE differs from the adrenalin high some risk takers say they have experienced. Whereas adrenalin is simply a fight-or-flight secretion that speeds up the body or gives it more energy, the CE response goes further, taking on both strong sensory and cerebral dimensions.

Examples of CE sports are swimming, skiing, surfing, horseback riding, bicycling, mountain climbing, scuba diving, and other activities that combine a high degree of physical and mental coordination. (Non-CE sports are those such as calisthenics, jogging, walking, or golf.) Because of its benefits to both mind and body, CE provides an excellent means of reducing stress. If your teenager is not already involved in a CE activity, you might gently encourage him to do so, perhaps by example.

Encourage team sports. Some parents think that team sports don't provide as much opportunity to stay fit as individual fitness regimes. This is a misconception. Have you ever watched your child during swim-team practice? Undoubtedly, he gets as much exercise horsing around with his friends as he does from the formal practice. The same is true of softball practices, soccer games, and other team-sport activities. While you and I would probably be annoyed if our friends intentionally threw the ball over our heads to make us run for it, to kids, that's part of the fun! Additionally, interacting with others allows a teenager to do a lot of shouting and screaming, releasing some of his aggression, lessening stress. Doing this during team practice is encouraged and is a great way to blow off steam.

Develop family fitness. When your children were little, you probably loved going on family outings, taking walks on summer evenings, bicycling to the park, or swimming at the lake. As your children became teenagers, they probably pulled away from such family activities, preferring to spend more time on their own. If you feel that your child needs to work on his fitness, perhaps it's time for you to start up the family sports again. Saturdays and Sundays are a good time for family outings. Going to the beach, camping, hiking, and bicycling are some of the activities that can be enjoyed by all. With a little planning, they can be a regular part of your family's time together. Working together in the spirit of fun and cooperation is one way to make fitness a total part of our health routine. *Reader's Digest Special Report on Family Fitness* suggests four specific ways to get your family involved in physical fitness. They are:

- *Sign contracts.* Have each family member write down one fitness goal for the month. For example, "I want to be able to run one mile nonstop." Sign and date the contract and have it co-signed by a family member.
- *Exercise as a family.* Agree to exercise before watching TV or before dinner. If schedules are too complicated during the week, set a time on Saturday and Sunday. Then everyone can exercise on his own during the week.
- *Record scores.* Post a chart on the refrigerator for the scores of each family member. Update the chart each time you retake the test and record each workout.
- *Reward achievements.* When you reach a goal, give yourself

a prize (for example, fitness clothing or sports equipment—
not food). When all family members reach certain goals, reward everyone with an activity you all enjoy as a family. For
example, you might take a fitness vacation (such as backpack-
ing) together.

Be careful not to impose your own likes and dislikes of certain
physical activities on your teenager. What you really want is for
your child to become involved in physical activity, to enjoy it, and
to benefit from it. The type of activity he becomes involved in is
his own choice. The concept of suitability is an individual one.
What you consider suitable exercise (perhaps ballroom dancing)
might drive a child to despair. What a teenager considers suitable
exercise, such as dancing and cavorting around your house, using
every table and wall as a drum, might not be your first choice,
either. But the key is to recognize that different isn't necessarily
wrong.

Build fitness slowly and regularly. The essential component of
any effective health program is that it be aerobic in nature (one
in which you must exert a good deal of effort but that doesn't
consume oxygen faster than your heart and lungs can supply it).
Experts recommend three sessions of vigorous activity weekly,
with each session lasting from twenty to thirty minutes. These
can include walking, swimming, bicycling, aerobics, jazzercise,
and so on. Remember, however, to start off slowly if you are not
in shape (this applies to teens and adults alike). Pick up your pace
and raise your expectations as your body adjusts to your exercise
regimen. Consult your physician if you are overweight, afflicted
with any health problems, or in doubt about the status of your
health.

GETTING HELP

I grew up in a farm community where it was not uncommon to
see neighbors join forces to help someone in need. When a man
was ill, or even behind schedule in the fields, neighboring men and
their sons where there to assist; in canning season, if a woman was
ill or home with a new infant, neighboring women gathered to

prepare food and help out with other children. Neighbors worked together and supported one another in times of need. I marveled at the camaraderie that allowed diverse people to work together so well. With help from friends, a family was able to get something done that would have been impossible or very difficult to do on their own.

In the recent movie *Witness,* there is a scene in which the members of an Amish community all join forces to build a barn. For about five minutes, the viewer sees people working together, helping one another. The movie producer shot the scene with almost no conversation, only music. By the end of the scene, the barn has been built. Friends who saw the movie with me were amazed that so many families were willing to help one another. A barn raising is a good example of a support group in action. When you have an emotional crisis, such as being under too much stress to handle on your own, you could use a support group.

Unfortunately, too many people think a support group is somehow shameful, that one should be able to make it on one's own. Nonsense. If your home were destroyed in a fire or earthquake and others offered assistance, would you be too ashamed to accept it? Of course not. Why should you then be ashamed or reluctant to accept help when your emotional stability is destroyed by stress?

Support groups, whether they be parents helping parents, teens helping teens, or parents helping teens, can be an excellent way of learning more about the stress of being a parent or an adolescent. Getting together with friends who will listen and share things with you can be therapeutic. A candid exchange can effectively lower the collective stress level.

Those adolescents who have developed a source of social support—that is, those who have strong family ties and warm relationships with friends and peers—generally deal more effectively with stressful events than those who do not. Other people are an essential part of our lives. Those people whom you care for and who also care for you can provide support, advice, comfort, and protection during troubled times. With them, you can share your innermost thoughts, feelings, and opinions.

There are many ways in which you can expand your social

network. Join a social organization, sports club, or church group. Broaden your range of interests and activities and invite others to join you. Look up old friends and keep in contact with your family. By demonstrating your interest in others—in their ideas, activities, and feelings—you will provide the basis for mutually fortifying relationships. You can teach your teen this facet of good health, too.

PROFESSIONAL ASSISTANCE

There are times when another sympathetic individual is not able to give you all the help you need. Extreme cases, such as severe depression, overwhelming family or emotional problems, or drug or alcohol use, should be dealt with under the guidance of a professional.

Although many stress-related symptoms clear up when the stressor is removed or the emotional difficulty subsides, chronic problems may require the attention of a specialist. Counseling may help you to plan a lower-stress lifestyle and better, more health-enhancing habits.

A counselor will not tell you how to live your life, but he or she can provide guidelines for you to follow. Therapy can help you gain perspective. Having a professional to talk to about your particular difficulties in getting and staying well is conducive to achieving these goals. Developing a stress-coping strategy that conforms with your particular temperament and lifestyle will help you to maintain a sense of well-being and confidence.

Through tests and questionnaires administered by a skilled professional in the area of stress, you can learn what health hazards loom large in your life and, through counseling, you can learn how best to reduce those hazards. In selecting a stress specialist, look at her basic professional credentials. She should be a psychiatrist, a well-informed internist, or a behavioral or clinical psychologist. All of these must have special training and experience in the field of stress and disease. Parenthetically, we need to decide who is going to determine the appropriateness of the credentials. A good source is the American Institute of Stress (see the resource section).

Many people who go to a psychiatrist or psychologist have been stigmatized as weak, unable to solve their own problems, or mentally ill. Fortunately, such stereotypes are being displaced. There are several reasons for obtaining counseling or other forms of therapy. It permits us to

ventilate feelings from the distant or recent past

learn to adjust to a demanding situation

gain insight into feelings or actions

learn new ways of experiencing self

make major life decisions wisely

Different kinds of help are available from various professionals: the psychiatrist, the psychologist, the marriage and family counselor, the social worker, and the minister, priest, or rabbi. Each of these therapists or counselors has a particular background and training as well as an individual style. The therapist or counselor may follow one of a wide range of theoretical and practical approaches.

Events and conditions that cause change are often very stressful and demand adjustment. A qualified counselor with whom you feel comfortable can draw from his or her wealth of experience and may be the best person to help you achieve the relief from stress and the quality of life you desire.

RESOURCES

CHAPTER 1

McCullough, C., and Mann, B. *Managing Your Anxiety*. Los Angeles: Tarcher, St. Martin's Press, 1985.

Cousins, N. *Anatomy of an Illness*. New York: Norton, 1979.

Pelletier, K. *Mind as Healer, Mind as Slayer*. New York: Delacorte, 1977.

Selye, H. *Stress Without Distress*. New York: Lippincott, 1974.

Selye, H. *The Stress of Life*. New York: McGraw-Hill, 1976.

TAPES
Understanding Anxiety, Psychology Today Tapes, P.O. Box 770, Pratt Station, NY 11205.

MAGAZINES
Children and Teens Today, 2315 Broadway, New York, NY 10024.

ORGANIZATION
The American Institute of Stress, 124 Park Avenue, Yonkers, NY 10703, (914) 963–1200.

CHAPTER 2

Canter, L., and Carter, M. *Assertive Discipline*. Los Angeles: Canter & Associates, 1976.

Dinkmyer, D., and McKay, G. D. *Raising a Responsible Child*. New York: Simon & Schuster, 1973.

Dreikurs, R., and Grey, L. *A Parent's Guide to Child Discipline*. New York: Hawthorne Books, 1970.

Krantzler, M. *Creative Marriage.* New York: McGraw-Hill, 1981.

Winship, C. E. *Reaching Your Teenager.* New York: Houghton-Mifflin Co., 1973.

FOR ADOLESCENTS

Allan, M. *The View Beyond My Father.* New York: Dodd, 1977.

"Helping a Teenager Grow Up Gradually." *Boston Globe,* July 8, 1983.

FOR PARENTS AND ADOLESCENTS

Bingham, E., Edmondson, J., and Stryker, S. *CHOICES: A Teen Woman's Journal for Self-Awareness and Personal Planning;* and *CHOICES: A Teen Man's Journal for Self-Awareness and Personal Planning.* Mission Publication, P.O. Box 25, El Toro, CA 92630.

Dyer, W. *What Do You Really Want for Your Children?* New York: William Morrow and Company, 1985.

Youngs, B. *Stress in Children: How to Recognize, Avoid and Overcome It.* New York: Arbor House, 1985.

PARENTS' NEWSLETTERS

Newsletter to Increase the Joys of Effective Parenting, 7052 West Lane, Eden, NY 14057. This eight-page newsletter is issued five times a year; an annual subscription costs $12.95. Parents of preschoolers through teens are targeted in such features as "How to Talk with Your Children about Nuclear War," "Together Time," and "Selecting TV Programs."

TAPES

Parent Effectiveness Training—An Update. Thomas Gordon. This interview with Thomas Gordon updates his P.E.T. methods of facilitating parent/child relationships. *Psychology Today* Tapes, P.O. Box 770, Pratt Station, NY 11205.

PARENT SELF-HELP GROUPS

Community Service Foundation, P.O. Box 70, Sellersville, PA 18960.

Parental Stress, Inc., 654 Beacon St., Boston, MA 02215, (800) 632-8188 (in Massachusetts only), (617) 437-0110 (elsewhere).

CHAPTER 3

Elkind, D. *All Grown Up and No Place to Go.* Reading, Mass.: Addison-Wesley, 1984.

Katchadourian, H. *The Biology of Adolescence.* San Francisco: Freeman & Sons, 1977.

Norman, J., and Harris, M. *The Private Life of the American Teenager.* New York: Rawson-Wade, 1981.

ADOLESCENTS

Betancourt, J. *Am I Normal?* New York: Avon, 1983.

Blume, J. *Are You There, God? It's Me, Margaret.* New York: Dell, 1970.

Byars, B. *The Summer of the Swans.* New York: Viking, 1970.

Csikszent, M., and Larson, R. *Being Adolescent: Conflict and Growth in the Teenager.* New York: Basic Books, 1984.

Danziger, P. *The Cat Ate My Gymsuit.* New York: Dell, 1973.

Friedenberg, E. *The Vanishing Adolescent.* New York: Dell, 1959.

Green, H. *I Never Promised You a Rose Garden.* New York: Holt, 1964.

Heide, F. *Growing Anyway Up.* Philadelphia: Lippincott, 1976.

Neufeld, J. *Lisa, Bright and Dark.* New York: S. G. Phillips, 1969.

Postman, N. *The Disappearance of Childhood.* New York: Delacorte Press, 1982.

Storr, C. *Thursday.* New York: Harper, 1972.

Whitney, P. *Nobody Likes Trina.* Philadelphia: Westminster, 1972.

TAPES

Leefeldt, C., and Callenbach, E. *How to Make and Maintain Friendships*

Albert Ellis. *Effective Self-Assertion. Psychology Today* Tapes, P.O. Box 770, Pratt Station, NY 11205.

CHAPTER 4

FOR PARENTS

Bayard, R., and Bayard, J. *How to Deal with Your Acting-Up Teenager —Practical Self-Help for Desperate Parents.* San Jose: The Accord Press, 1981.

Berman, C. *Making It as a Stepparent: New Roles/New Rules.* New York: Doubleday, 1980.

Helfer, R., and Kempe, C., eds. *Child Abuse and Neglect: The Family and the Community.* Cambridge, Mass.: Ballinger, 1976.

Lewis, H. *All About Families—The Second Time Around.* Atlanta: Peachtree Publishing, 1980.

Ricci, I. *Mom's House, Dad's House: Making Shared Custody Work.* New York: Macmillan Co., 1980.

Roosevelt, R., and Lofas, J. *Living in Step.* New York: Stein & Day, 1976.

Wallerstein, J., and Kelly, J. *Surviving the Breakup.* New York: Basic Books, 1980.

BOOKS FOR ADOLESCENTS

Bradley, B. *Where Do I Belong? A Kid's Guide to Stepfamilies.* Reading, Mass.: Addison-Wesley, 1982.

Byars, B. *The Animal, the Vegetable and John D. Jones.* New York: Delacorte Press, 1982.

Corcoran, B. *A Dance to Still Music.* New York: Atheneum, 1974.

Gardner, R. *The Boys' and Girls' Book about Stepfamilies.* New York: Bantam Books, 1982.

Haar, J. *The World of Ben Lighthart.* New York: Delacorte Press, 1977.

Hoff, S. *Irving and Me.* New York: Harper, 1967.

Jackson, M. and Jackson, J. *Your Father's Not Coming Home Anymore.* New York: Ace Books, 1981.

LeShan, E. *What's Going to Happen to Me? When Parents Separate or Divorce.* New York: Four Winds Press, 1978.

Wood, A. "Stepparents: How to Deal with Them." *Seventeen* Magazine, February 1983.

TAPES

Sandra Scarr, "Discovering Yourself." *Psychology Today* Tapes, P.O. Box 770, Pratt Station, NY 11205.

FAMILY SEVICE AGENCIES

Check the telephone directory or contact the United Way organization in your area for the Family Services Agency nearest you. These organizations offer a variety of counseling services to families, including treatment for alcoholism.

ASSOCIATIONS

Stepfamily Association of America, 28 Allegheny Ave., Ste. 1037, Baltimore, MD 21204, (301) 823-7570.

The national Stepfamily Association provides information about local chapters and issues a newsletter; local chapters offer classes, workshops, and support groups for blended families. Membership in the association provides an excellent way for these families to find each other and form support networks for dealing with the problems and feelings unique to their situation. Some have membership fees, but many classes, workshops, and services are free.

Parents United, P.O. Box 952, San Jose, CA 95108.

Daughters United (same address as above).

Sons United (same address as above).

Parents United is a support group for couples in which one partner has been the aggressor in an incestuous involvement. Daughters United and Sons United are support groups for those who have been victims of sexual advances by parents or other trusted adults or family members. Child Protective Services or the department of social services in your area may have the number if none is listed in your directory. Your local agency that deals with child abuse should have information regarding these groups. By writing to the above address you can obtain a listing of the areas in which Parents United, Daughters United, and Sons United meetings are held. Information is free.

CHAPTER 5

FOR PARENTS

Berzon, B. *Positively Gay*. Mediamix Associates, 1984.

Borhek, M. *Coming Out to Parents,* Pilgrims Press, 1983.

Brown, H. *Familiar Faces, Hidden Lives*. San Diego: Harcourt, Brace, Jovanovich, 1979.

Coles, R., and Stokes G. *Sex and the American Teenager.* New York: Harper Colophon Books, 1985.

Goodman, E. "The Turmoil of Teenage Sexuality." *MS.,* July 1983, pp. 37–41.

O'Brien, S. *Child Abuse and Neglect: Everyone's Problems.* The booklet costs $5.40 per copy, plus 54 cents postage and handling, and may be ordered from the Association for Childhood Education International, 11141 Georgia Ave., Ste. 200, Wheaton, MD 20902, (301) 942–2443.

Steel, B. "Abusive Fathers," in *Father and Child,* ed. S. Gath, A. Gurvitch, and J. Ross. Boston: Little, Brown & Co., 1981.

Tietze, C. "Teenage Pregnancy: Looking Ahead to 1984." *Family Planning Perspectives,* 1978, pp. 205–207.

Weinberg, G. *Society and the Healthy Homosexual.* New York: St. Martin's Press, 1972.

FOR ADOLESCENTS

Blume, J. *Then Again, Maybe I Won't.* New York: Dell, 1971.

Burkhart, K. *Growing into Love: Teenagers Talk About Sex in the 1980s.* New York: Putnam, 1981.

Ephron, D. *Teenage Romance.* New York: Ballantine, 1981.

Hanckel, F., and Cunningham, J. *A Way of Love, A Way of Life: A Young Person's Introduction to What It Means to Be Gay.* New York: Lothrop, Lee & Shepard, 1979.

LIBRARY FILMS

Who Do You Tell? produced by M.T.I., 3710 Commercial Ave., Northbrook, IL 60062, (800) 323–5343.

Child Abuse and Neglect, N.E.A. Multimedia Training Program with booklets for parents and children. Also included are booklets on detecting and reporting child abuse. N.E.A. Professional Library, P.O. Box 509, West Haven, CT 06516.

Child Sexual Abuse: What Your Children Should Know. The series of five programs includes a program for parents and teachers and separate programs for grades K–3 and 7–12. A fifth program focuses specifically on students in high school. Audio-Visual Center, Student Services Building, Room 008, Indiana University, Bloomington, IN 47405, (812) 332–0212.

ORGANIZATIONS

Parents and Friends of Gays: P.O. Box 24528, Los Angeles, CA 90024.

Parents FLAG (Friends of Lesbians and Gays): P.O. Box 24565, Los Angeles, CA 90024.

Tapes from the above address: *Facts and Misconceptions about Homosexuality; Current Status of Social Research on Homosexuality; Lesbian Adolescents*.

CHAPTER 6

Combs, A. "Humanistic Education: Too Tender for a Tough World?" *Kappan.* 62(6) (1981), pp. 446–449.

cummings, e.e. "A Poet's Advice to Students," in *Glad to Be Me,* ed. D. P. Elkins. Englewood Cliffs, N.J.: Prentice-Hall, 1976, p. 48.

Phillips, B. *School Stress and Anxiety.* New York: Human Science Press, 1978.

Samples, B., Charles, C., and Barnhart, D. *The Wholeschool Book.* Reading, Mass: Addison-Wesley, 1977.

Schultz, E., and Heuchert, C. *Child Stress and the School Experience.* New York: Human Science Press, 1984.

Wolfgang, C., and Glickman, C. *Solving Discipline Problems.* Boston: Allyn & Bacon, 1980.

ORGANIZATIONS

National Education Association, 1101 16th St. N.W., Washington, DC 20036, (202) 833–4000.

National Institute of Education, 1200 19th St. N.W., Washington, DC 20208, (202) 254–5750.

Children's Defense Fund, 1520 New Hampshire Ave. N.W., Washington, DC 20036, (202) 483–1470.

Center for Law & Education, Inc., Gutman Library, 6 Appian Way, Cambridge, MA 02138, (617) 495–4666.

National Center for Law & the Handicapped, Inc., 211 W. Washington St., Ste. 1900, South Bend, IN 46601, (219) 288–4751.

CHAPTER 7

Beckwith, L. *The Spuddy.* New York: Delacorte Press, 1976.

Bensman, J., and Lilienfield, R. "Friendship and Alienation." *Psychology Today,* October 1979.

"Shelters and Streets Draw Throwaway Kids," *New York Times,* June 3, 1983.

Zelnick, M., and Kantner, J. "Sexuality, Contraception and Pregnancy Among Young Unwed Females." *U.S. Research Reports,* Commission on Population Growth and the American Future, vol. 1, Washington, D.C.: Government Printing Office, 1980.

ORGANIZATIONS

Skills for Living: A Program for Adolescents and *Skills for Adolescence: A Program for Young Adolescents*, Quest National Center, 6655 Sharon Woods Blvd., Columbus, OH 43229, (614) 882–6400.

National Runaway Switchboard, (800) 621–4000 (a toll-free service offering crisis help and referrals nationwide).

Child Find, Inc., 7 Innis Ave., New Paltz, NY 12561, (212) 245–6200 or (914) 255–1848.

Crisis Centers, National Youth Work Alliance, 1346 Connecticut Ave. N.W., Washington, DC 20036 (provides the name of a runaway or teen-crisis shelter in your area).

CHAPTER 8

RESOURCES

Vitamin Facts: Basic Reference for All Thirteen Vitamins, Vitamin Nutrition Information Service (VNIS), Hoffman-LaRoche, Inc., 340 Kingsland St., Nutley, NJ 07110, (201) 235–5000.

Parents who want information on what types of programs can be developed to aid in the fight against drug abuse can call or write: PRIDE, Robert W. Woodruff Building, 100 Edgewood Ave., Ste. 1216, Atlanta, GA 30303, (800) 241–7946.

Fair Oaks Hospital, 19 Prospect St., Summit, NJ 07901, (800) CO-CAINE.

National Federation of Parents for Drug-Free Youth, 8730 Georgia Ave., Ste. 200, Silver Spring, MD 20910, (800) 554–KIDS.

American Council for Drug Education, 6193 Executive Blvd., Rockville, MD 20852, (301) 984–5700.

You will also find drug- and alcohol-abuse organizations in your area that are most anxious to work with parents and adolescents on strategies to stop drug and alcohol abuse.

In association with ACTION and PADA (Pharmacists against Drug Abuse), your community pharmacist has agreed to help parents learn about the kinds of drugs that youngsters may use and what you as a parent can do to help prevent drug abuse.

RARE (Rehabilitation of Addicts by Relatives and Employers). AWARE (Addiction Workers Related to Rehabilitation Education). These organizations work toward changing the social conditions that contribute to addiction.

ASA (Addiction Service Agency) directs its programs at many fronts: relatives of addicts, concerned citizens, organizations, and susceptible or at-risk youngsters. Consult the telephone directory for the one located nearest to your city.

Alcoholics Anonymous, General Service Board, New York, NY 10016.
Alcoholics Anonymous (AA) was founded in 1935. Today, there are more than a million members in more than 30,000 local groups. AA is an international fellowship of men and women who share the common problem of alcoholism. Members share their recovery with others seeking sobriety. The groups follow the twelve suggested steps of AA. As with a number of other self-help groups, AA has a strong belief system. Family members of alcoholics can receive help through groups associated with AA, such as Al-Anon and Al-Ateen.

Al-Anon Family Group Headquarters, P.O. Box 182, New York, NY 10159–0182. Local groups are listed in your telephone directory under "Al-Anon Family Groups."

Al-Ateen, Al-Anon Family Group Headquarters, P.O. Box 182, New York, NY 10159–0182. Local Al-Ateen chapters are listed in some telephone directories, or you can contact a local Al-Anon group for more information.

National Council on Alcoholism, Inc., 12 West 21st St., 7th Floor, New York, NY 10010.

National Clearinghouse for Drug Abuse Information, P.O. Box 416, Kensington, MD 20795. Information about alcoholism and about available treatment programs is free to the public.

National Association of State Alcohol and Drug Abuse Directors, 444 N. Capitol St. N.W., Ste. 530, Washington, DC 20001. Every state has a department of drug and alcoholism services that can provide you with information about treatment resources available in your state. Write to the above agency, or look in your telephone directory under the state government listings.

Family Service Agencies: Check the telephone directory, or contact the United Way organization in your area for the Family Services Agency nearest you. These organizations offer a variety of counseling services to families, including treatment for drugs and alcoholism.

National Institute on Drug Abuse, P.O. Box 2305, Rockville, MD 20852.

Straight Talk, c/o Drug Fair, Inc., 6295 Edsall Rd., Alexandria, VA 22314.

PARENT SELF-HELP GROUPS

Toughlove, Community Service Foundation, P.O. Box 70, Sellersville, PA 18960.

Parents Anonymous, 22330 Hawthorne Blvd., S208, Torrance, CA 90505.

Hotline (crisis counseling and information available twenty-four hours a day, seven days a week), (800) 352–0386 (in California), (800) 421–6353 elsewhere.

BOOKS FOR PARENTS AND TEENAGERS

Cross, W., *Kids and Booze.* New York: E. P. Dutton, 1979.

Jackson, M. and Jackson, B. *Doing Drugs.* New York: Martins/Marek, 1983.

York and Hochte. *Toughlove.* Garden City, N.Y.: Doubleday, 1982.

CHAPTER 9

FOR PARENTS

Anderson, J., and Cohen, M. *The West Point Fitness and Diet Book.* New York: Rawson Associates, 1977.

Fauher, E. *Surviving.* New York: Scholastic, 1985.

Gernsdbacher, L. *The Suicide Syndrome.* New York: Human Science Press, 1985.

Giovacchini, P. *The Urge to Die: Why Young People Commit Suicide.* New York: Macmillan Co., 1981.

Klagburn, F. *Too Young to Die.* New York: Pocket Books, 1981.

Lupin, M. *Peace, Harmony, Awareness. A Relaxation Program for Children.* Austin, Tex.: Learning Concepts, 1977.

Mack, J., and Hickler, H. *Viviene: The Life and Suicide of an Adolescent Girl.* Boston: Little, Brown, & Co., 1981.

Matthews, D. *You Can Do It! Kids' Diet.* New York: Holt, Rinehart and Winston, 1985.

McCoy, K. *Coping with Teenage Depression.* New York: New American Library, 1982.

The Planetree Health Resource Center publishes an excellent catalog of self-care books, products, and cassette tapes. Copies may be obtained from the center at 2040 Webster St., San Francisco, CA 94115.

Seff, M. "Anatomy of a Suicide Attempt." *Boston Globe,* November 20, 1981.

Shealy, C. N. *Ninety Days to Self-Health.* New York: Dial, 1977. Dr. Shealy provides many excellent relaxation exercises in his systematic self-care program.

Silberstein, W. *Helping Your Child Grow Slim.* New York: Simon & Schuster, 1982.

Toolan, J. "Depression in Children and Adolescents." *American Journal of Orthopsychiatry,* 32 (1962):415.

FOR ADOLESCENTS

Bergstrom, C. *Losing Your Best Friend: Losing Friendship.* New York: Human Science Press, 1984.

FILMS

Teenage Suicide: But Jack Was a Good Driver, 16-mm (Code 106666–7), CRM McGraw-Hill Films, 110 Fifteenth St., Del Mar, CA 92014.

Urgent Message, 16-mm, Laser Educational Media Society, Crisis Intervention & Suicide Prevention Centre, 1946 West Broadway, Vancouver, BC, Canada.

ASSOCIATIONS

American Association of Suicidology, Denver, Colorado.

Emotional Health Anonymous (consult your directory for the one nearest you).

PUBLIC SERVICES

Suicide Prevention: Almost every state now has one or more suicide hotlines and suicide prevention centers. Your local telephone operator can give you the number for the hotline in your area.

CONTACT—Churches sponsor crisis intervention centers in cities throughout the country. These centers are listed under the name CONTACT in local telephone books. For a list of all CONTACT centers, write to: CONTACT Teleministries USA, Inc., 900 South Arlington Ave., Room 125, Harrisburg, PA 17109.

RESOURCE CENTER

Brownell, K. *Lifestyle, Exercise, Attitudes, Relationships and Nutrition.* Filled with familiar cartoon figures such as Garfield and Cathy, this 215-page booklet can help parents and adolescent dieters with everything from keeping a food diary to learning the basic food groups. For more information, write Dr. K. Brownell, Dept. of Psychiatry, University of Pennsylvania, 133 South 36th St., Philadelphia, PA 19104.

BIBLIOGRAPHY

See the list of suggested readings for other books cited in the text.

Alcohol in Perspective. Mt. Vernon, New York: Consumers' Union of the United States, Inc., 1983.

Berman, C. *Making It as a Stepparent: New Roles/New Rules.* New York: Doubleday, 1980.

Bingham, E., Edmondson, J. and Struker, S., *Choices: A Teen Woman's (A Teen Man's) Journal for Self-Awareness and Personal Planning.* Mission Publications, P.O. Box 25, El Toro, CA.

"Bugalusa Heart Study." *Journal of the American Medical Association,* July 1985.

Charell, R. *How to Get the Upper Hand: Simple Techniques You Can Use to Win the Battles of Everyday Life.* New York: Stein and Day, 1978.

"Children Having Children: Teen Pregnancy in America." *Time,* December 9, 1985, pp. 78–90.

Coles, R., and Stokes, G. *Sex and the American Teenager.* New York: Harper Colophon Books, 1985.

Deal, T., and Kennedy, A. *Corporate Cultures: The Rites and Rituals of Corporate Life.* Reading, Mass.: Addison-Wesley, 1982.

Deci, E. "The Well-Tempered Classroom." *Psychology Today,* March 1985.

Diet, Nutrition and Cancer. Committee on Diet, Nutrition and Cancer, Assembly of Life Sciences, National Research Council, National Academy Press, Washington, D.C., 1982.

Dietary Intake Source Data: United States 1976–80. Data from the National Health Survey, Series 11, No. 231, DHHS Publication No. (PHS) 83–1681, March 1983.

DiPrete, T., Muller, C., and Shaeffer, Nora. *Discipline and Order in American High Schools.* Washington, D.C.: National Center for Education Statistics, 1981.

"Do You Know What Your Children Are Listening To?" *U.S. News & World Report,* October 28, 1985.

Dyer, W. *What Do You Really Want for Your Children?* New York: William Morrow and Company, 1985.

Elkind, D. *All Grown Up and No Place to Go.* Reading, Mass.: Addison-Wesley, 1984.

"Family Fitness: A Complete Exercise Program for Ages Six to Sixty-Plus." *Reader's Digest* (Special Report), 1986, pp. 2–12.

Gernsbacher, L. *The Suicide Syndrome.* New York: Human Science Press, 1985.

"Has Rock Gone Too Far?" *People* Magazine, September 16, 1985, pp. 47–53.

"Implications of Recent Brain Research." *Educational Leadership,* October 1981, pp. 6–16.

"Kids and Cocaine: An Epidemic Strikes Middle America." *Newsweek,* March 17, 1986, pp. 58–63.

Klagsbrun, Francine. *Too Young to Die.* New York: Houghton Mifflin Co., 1981.

Krantzler, M. *Creative Marriage.* New York: McGraw-Hill, 1981.

"Latchkey Children: The Fastest Growing Special-Interest Groups in the Schools." *Phi Delta Kappa* (Special Research), March 1986.

Lester, David. *Why People Kill Themselves.* Springfield, Ill.: Charles C Thomas, 1983, chapters 1, 4, and 5.

Levinson, Daniel J. *Seasons of a Man's Life.* New York: Alfred A. Knopf, 1978.

Mack, John, and Hickler, H. *Vivienne: The Life and Suicide of an Adolescent Girl.* Boston: Little, Brown & Co., 1981.

Magnuson, E. "Private Violence." *Time,* September 5, 1983, pp. 18–22.

Maris, R. "The Adolescent Suicide Problem." *Suicide and Life-Threatening Behavior,* 15:2 (1985), pp. 91–109.

McCubbin, H. and Figley, C. *Stress and the Family.* New York: Brunner/Mazel Publishers, 1983.

National Institute of Education. *Violent Schools, Safe Schools: The Safe School Study Report to the Congress,* vol. 1. Washington, D.C.: NIE, 1978.

Nutrient Levels in Food Used by Households in the United States, Spring 1977. Nationwide Food Consumption Survey 1977078. Preliminary Report

No. 3. Washington, D.C.: U.S. Department of Agriculture, Science and Education Administration, January 1981.

Pelletier, K. *Mind as Healer, Mind as Slayer.* New York: Delacorte Press, 1977.

Pfeffer, C. "Intervention for Suicidal Children and Their Parents." *Suicide and Life-Threatening Behavior,* 12:4 (1982), pp. 240–248.

Postman, Neil. *The Disappearance of Childhood.* New York: Delacorte Press, 1982.

Rolling Stone. Dear Mom and Dad: Teenage Suicide in America. New York: Behavioral Publications, 1972.

Rosenthal, Sol Roy. "Challenge Exercise: An Extra Bonus." *Adventure Education,* February 1985.

Rutter, Michael, et al. *Fifteen Thousand Hours: Secondary Schools and Their Effects on Children.* Cambridge, Mass.: Harvard University Press, 1979.

Seyle, Hans. *Stress Without Distress.* New York: Lippincott, 1974.

Seyle, Hans. *The Stress of Life.* New York: McGraw-Hill, 1976.

Sheinkin, David. *Food, Mind and Mood.* New York: Warner Books, 1980.

"Shelters and Streets Draw Throwaway Kids." *New York Times,* June 3, 1983.

Shneidman, Edwin. *Death and the College Student.* New York: Behavioral Publications, 1972.

Silberstein, W. *Helping Your Child Grow Slim.* New York: Simon & Schuster, 1982.

Skills for Adolescence and *Skills for Living.* Columbus, Oh.: Quest National Center, 1985.

Smith, Jack L., Jefferson, L. Sulzer, and Goldsmith, Grace A. "Prevention of Vitamin and Mineral Deficiencies Associated with Protein-Calorie Malnutrition," in *Protein-Calorie Malnutrition,* ed. Robert E. Olsen. San Diego, Calif.: Academic Press, 1975.

Sorosky, Arthur. "Adolescent Suicide," in *Adolescent Psychiatry, Volume IX,* ed. Feinstein et al. Chicago: University of Chicago Press, 1981.

Statistical Abstracts of the United States. U.S. Department of Commerce, Bureau of the Census, Washington, D.C., 1980.

Straus, M., Gelles, R., and Steinmetz, S. *Behind Closed Doors: Violence in the American Family.* New York: Anchor-Doubleday, 1981.

Syed, Husain, and Vandiver, T. *Suicide in Children and Adolescents.* New York: Spectrum Publications, 1984.

"Teenage Fathers." *Psychology Today,* December 1985, pp. 66–70.

Tietze, C. "Teenage Pregnancy: Looking Ahead to 1984," *Family Planning Perspectives,* 1978, pp. 205–207.

"Treating Troubled Teens." *Newsweek,* January 20, 1986, pp. 52–54.

"Young Arsonists: Stamping Out Fires." *American Health,* April 1986.

Young Unwed Families. U.S. Research Reports, Commission on Population Growth and the American Future, Vol. 1. Washington, D.C.: Government Printing Office, 1980.

Youngs, B. *Stress in Children: How to Recognize, Avoid and Overcome It.* New York: Arbor House, 1985.

Index

305.235
Y811

LINCOLN CHRISTIAN COLLEGE AND SEMINARY

115881

3 4711 00187 3662